PRAISE FOR

PASSION AND POWER: A LIFE IN THREE WORLDS

"With elegance and grit, Harriet Newman Cohen traces her trailblazing personal and professional journey through the evolving landscape of modern relationships and the law. *Passion and Power* is as much about the reshaping of American cultural norms as it is about one remarkable woman's outsized role at the forefront of legal and social transformation. A wise and riveting memoir."

—**CARL BERNSTEIN,** *Pulitzer Prize-Winning Author and American Journalist*

"From the first page, *Passion and Power* grabs you by the collar and doesn't let go. This book reads like a legal thriller, except every word is true. Harriet Newman Cohen—sharp, fearless, and endlessly compelling—takes us inside the courtrooms, boardrooms, and backrooms where the rules of love, money, and power in America were rewritten. At times heartbreaking, at others deeply inspiring, this is an emotional journey through the triumphs, losses, and hard-won wisdom of a legal pioneer who's seen it all. A truly wonderful book."

—**BEN MEZRICH,** *New York Times Bestselling Author of The Accidental Billionaires, Bringing Down the House, and Dumb Money*

"A page-turner from beginning to end, *Passion and Power* is the story of one remarkable life and an idiosyncratic, witty, and absorbing tour through recent USA history. Harriet Newman Cohen is a funny and edifying guide—precise, curious, warm. Entirely unsentimental. Marriage and its many paths to dissolution is rich territory and this book is filled with the strange, glamorous, desperate, and sadistic characters you hope to meet in the very best novels. I can't wait to read it again."

—**GILLIAN LINDEN,** *Author of Negative Space*

"In Harriet Newman Cohen's *Passion and Power*, loss and suffering are among life's guarantees. So are love and success—if you can find the patience and determination within yourself to open doors everyone but you sees as closed. With each door Harriet opened, what wild dreams came true."

—**BEOWULF SHEEHAN,** *American Photographer Known for Portraits of Authors, Artists, and Celebrities*

"A captivating book packed with intriguing vignettes about the famous and not-so-famous who've overcome life's troubles with the help of a whip-smart lawyer just as lively and engaging as the book itself."

—**AMY GAJDA,** *Journalist, Author of Seek and Hide, Lawyer, and Professor of Brooklyn Law School*

"A terrific story! Not only the deeply personal memoir of an extraordinary woman and attorney, but a fascinating exploration of the way we live now and the way we lived then. Harriet Cohen was in the ring for the major battles over divorce law and the rights of women, sure, but she also surrounds these stories with rare insight into how America has fared and why. There are major moments and bold-faced names. There's also plenty of dead-on, no-nonsense observation and advice. Read this book…even if you're planning to stay married."

—**ROSS KLAVAN**, *Screenwriter of Tigerland, Author of Schmuck*

PASSION AND POWER

PASSION AND POWER

A Life in Three Worlds

Harriet Newman Cohen with David Feinberg

BLOOMSBURY ACADEMIC
NEW YORK • LONDON • OXFORD • NEW DELHI • SYDNEY

BLOOMSBURY ACADEMIC
Bloomsbury Publishing Inc, 1385 Broadway, New York, NY 10018, USA
Bloomsbury Publishing Plc, 50 Bedford Square, London, WC1B 3DP, UK
Bloomsbury Publishing Ireland, 29 Earlsfort Terrace, Dublin 2, D02 AY28, Ireland

BLOOMSBURY, BLOOMSBURY ACADEMIC and the Diana logo are trademarks of Bloomsbury Publishing Plc

First published in the United States of America 2026

Cover design: Amy Z. Cohen
Cover image: © Photographer Beowulf Sheehan

Library of Congress Cataloging-in-Publication Data

Names: Cohen, Harriet Newman, author, with David Feinberg.
Title: Passion and Power: A Life in Three Worlds / Harriet Newman Cohen.
Description: New York : Bloomsbury Publishing Inc., 2026. | Includes bibliographical references. | Summary: "Through a vivid retelling of some of her most interesting and provocative cases braided together with her personal experiences in and out of the courtroom, Harriet Newman Cohen offers a candid view of the divorce process and what it's like to be a woman in a male-dominated industry"-- provided by publisher.
Identifiers: LCCN 2025023636 (print) | LCCN 2025023637 (ebook) | ISBN 9798765164679 (hardback) | ISBN 9798765164686 (epub) | ISBN 9798765164693 (pdf)
Subjects: LCSH: Cohen, Harriet Newman. | Women lawyers--United States--Biography. | Lawyers--United States--Biography. | Divorce--Law and Legislation--United States.
Classification: LCC KF373.C61735 A3 2026 (print) | LCC KF373.C61735 (ebook) | DDC 340.092 [B]--dc23/eng/20250521
LC record available at https://lccn.loc.gov/2025023636
LC ebook record available at https://lccn.loc.gov/2025023637

ISBN: HB: 979-8-7651-6467-9
ePDF: 979-8-7651-6469-3
eBook: 979-8-7651-6468-6

Typeset by Deanta Global Publishing Services, Chennai, India

For product safety related questions contact productsafety@bloomsbury.com.

To find out more about our authors and books visit www.bloomsbury.com and sign up for our newsletters.

This book is dedicated to
My four precious girls
And their children
And their grandchildren

CONTENTS

INTRODUCTION

In early July 2024 I was interviewed by a journalist for the Associated Press who was working on an article about older Americans in the workforce and their reaction to the Trump-Biden debate of June 27. The article was headlined:

Too old to work? Some Americans on the job late in life bristle at calls for Biden to step aside.[1]

I was one of those *not* bristling. It was disheartening to watch the president shamble onstage, and uncomfortable to see his awkward gestures and inability to articulate his ideas. It seemed clear to me that whatever else was going on he would not be able, physically or mentally, to prosecute—or endure—a vigorous campaign for re-election.

"I've been so lucky," I told the AP. "But the president hasn't been."

The article was published nationwide on Friday, July 19. It was fifty years since I had graduated from Brooklyn Law School, and I was in my law office, at Cohen Stine Kapoor, working with one of two new clients who had come to me that week.

Two days later Joe Biden withdrew from the race.

* * *

I've been so lucky . . .

As I told the Associated Press, age has brought me "more acuity, more keenness, more energy," and that is, to some extent, unearned. The luck of genes. The luck of biology. My husband Arthur's mind was as keen as ever; he hadn't lost a step mentally, but his body gave out. One of his good friends, a brilliant, older fellow physician, suffered from early-onset dementia. His body—what Arthur called "the machine"—functioned beautifully for another decade and a half, long after he had been lost to himself. I've been blessed with a fitness of mind and body and that's what I call "luck"—though it is, in fact, something more. I am far from the biggest sports fan in the world, but I was told a beautiful story about Tommy Henrich, the great New York Yankee outfielder, who was asked how he could justify making a living playing a child's game.

He answered that:

Catching a fly ball is a pleasure, but knowing what to do with it after you catch it is a business.[2]

And it is the same way with "luck"—having it is a blessing but knowing what to do with it—how to make it the linchpin of a life and a career, how to center it within your profession so that it is meaningful not only to you but to the people you represent, your clients, and to your co-workers, is something else. I make no allowances for my age because I don't want anyone else making allowances either and I approach my work with the same determination, the same energy, critics might say the same single-mindedness- or cussedness, as I did ten years ago or twenty or forty. I prepare a certain way, I dress a certain way, I carry myself a certain way. I meet the world in a certain way. I demand a level of professionalism from myself and from others—my co-workers, my adversaries, and the court—and, in terms of age or experience, I don't expect any quarter. And I don't give any.

Which is not to say that age and experience don't have their benefits. I've been doing this for a while now and I understand, in deep and dimensional ways, the geography of my profession, its contours and its guardrails. Within that broad understanding the knowledge I have acquired over the years, the abilities I have sharpened are able to be exercised, to the extent of my talents, along lines of excellence: at this point the work, as it were, offers many challenges but no mysteries. I know what I'm doing, and I know why.

And I also know what I'm *not* doing because that, too, is part of the knowledge and confidence that age and experience can bring. Not long ago I received a telephone call from a woman I'll call Elaine, who'd been recommended to me by a former classmate at Brooklyn Law School. Elaine was worried about her 35-year-old daughter who had just signed a very restrictive prenup, *a terrible prenup*, Elaine called it, adding that her daughter hadn't told her about it because she was afraid that she'd interfere. When I asked what that meant, Elaine said that her daughter had had several failed relationships over the years, including one broken engagement for which she blamed her mother. Elaine said she feared for the financial future of her daughter and asked that I take a look at the prenup and then advise her about a path forward. I told her to email the document, that I'd read it and then we'd go over it together on Zoom.

I read the prenup, and it *was* restrictive—but only because that's the nature of prenups. In fact, when I represent the *have* as opposed to the *have not*, that's the kind of prenup I myself write. And Elaine's daughter was definitely the *have not*: her fiancé ran a very successful family business and was worth several million dollars. In any event—if the marriage failed the daughter would receive spousal support and other reasonable, though certainly not overly generous, benefits.

I went over my analysis of the prenup point by point with Elaine, but she kept insisting on its unsuitability and asked if there was anything I could do to lessen its severity. I knew I could work along the edges of the agreement—and perhaps, as a younger lawyer, that is something I might have done—but to what end? The terms of the prenup hadn't bothered Elaine's daughter, who had signed it and was looking forward to marriage and starting a family. That was how she defined her happiness. Her mother? Not so much.

It wasn't the prenup that was unsuitable; it was the idea of her daughter marrying that so upset Elaine. There was something poignant about the way she spoke to me about her hopes for her daughter, something poignant and chilling as well, as she sought to justify her actions and her feelings—to me and, I suspected, to herself. It put me in mind of *Washington Square* by Henry James and *The Glass Menagerie* by Tennessee Williams and the kind of parental love that turns into something else—something like love but warped and destructive. Elaine's daughter was a grown woman, and I felt strongly that she should have the right to define and to choose the type of future she desired.

Elaine and I spoke for close to two hours. It seemed to me, I told her, that what her daughter wanted was to be a wife and a mother, not to secure a great prenup. If the marriage remained intact, they'd be living off her husband's money and she'd have plenty of opportunities, over the years, to suggest ameliorations to the document. They probably wouldn't live under the terms of the prenup anyway, but if they did . . . Your daughter, I said, had already achieved her goal, which was to be married.

I kept thinking about *Washington Square*—and all the years that are left to us, if we so choose, to be alone and unhappy. I told Elaine that she should accept the prenup as it was. Leave your daughter alone, I said. Buy her a beautiful wedding dress and try to celebrate her happiness. And your own.

That was how we left it. I didn't charge her for the consultation. I had a multitude of feelings within me, and I couldn't figure out how to do it. I told my Brooklyn Law School classmate that I'd spoken to Elaine as a professional courtesy.

Several weeks later Elaine wrote me a letter, thanking me for my advice, saying that I had calmed her agitated nerves and brought peace to her home. You've never met my daughter, she told me, but you know her.

I've always remembered that Arthur said that many of the patients who came to him would, within a short while, recover on their own, that time would, often enough, work its own healing magic. It doesn't happen quite that often in my profession, but knowing when *not* to operate, when not to interfere, is often a matter of the confidence that only time and experience can bring, coupled with the knowledge gained not only within the profession but in the wider world, in a lifetime's journey.

They don't teach Henry James in law school. They probably should.

* * *

This book grew out of a series of conversations I had several years ago with a historian and subsequently with a journalist. I wanted to tell my family's story *to* my family—my children, grandchildren, great grandchildren, nieces, and nephews. Those were the readers I originally envisioned.

But as I continued to write, what started out as an intensely personal story began to broaden out to embrace political and cultural elements as well. I had no desire to write a treatise, much less a textbook, but I found it impossible to disentangle the people and events I was describing from a wider social context. When I wrote about my mother and father immigrating to the United States in 1920, I noted that had they waited just a bit longer they'd have been denied entry—under terms of a restrictive immigration act passed in 1921. My father and mother would have remained in Europe—Morris in what he called "*the* Ukraine" and Marion in Poland, in a small town just west of Warsaw. They would have remained unknown to each other and, with other members of their families, likely have been murdered in the Holocaust.

My mother and father were proud to call themselves Americans and because they arrived just before the doors slammed shut, they were able to do so. And as I wrote their story I was simultaneously following the current ongoing debate over who gets to come here and who gets to become a citizen—and I felt I could not write honestly about one reality without acknowledging the other. Similarly, and in more depth, I felt compelled to deal with other issues: abortion, contraception, women's health, women's political rights, gay and transgender rights, the power inequality—legal and social—between men and women. All the old issues confronted once again, all the old battles refought—because, as it turns out, they are not really old issues or old battles at all. Even the battle over vaccinations, which had seemingly been decided, forever, by Edward Jenner in 1796.

And always I was determined to tell this story through the lives and experiences of people—my family, myself, my clients—from the bottom up, as it were, rather than from the top down.

When I first went into court as a practicing lawyer, I was many times the only woman there, often mistaken for the client, rather than the lawyer. Now when I go to court, it's not unusual that the judge is a woman, the clerk is a woman, opposing counsel is a woman, and there's no man present *except* for the client. Though it can seem like a dream, this breathtaking journey exists in my personal memory, in my personal sphere, but also, it seems to me, in a wider social and professional sphere. And making sense of it all seems a worthwhile project, not only for the understanding of myself and my family but also for the reader. At least that is my hope.

I know that the world I knew as a child, the world I knew as a young woman and a fresh out of law school attorney seems, for many if not most readers, even to the brilliant young attorneys I mentor at my firm, as far away in time and meaning as the shtetls where my mother and father were born, on another continent, in another century; like a stone ax, a silent film and a rotary phone, all part of the same undifferentiated past. But I believed that through my eyes, and through the eyes and experiences of my loved ones, the colors of the past, the reality of the past, with all its uncertainties and ambiguities, might come alive once more and that a personal story, linked to a wider consciousness of history and memory, might seem valuable and worthy of preservation.

PART I

A MAN'S WORLD

It was a man's world. When I graduated from Barnard, I don't think two of us went to medical school or two of us went to law school. We were educated to get husbands. Latin, Greek and music. What was I going to do with that? Men had all the power. And that's where I wanted to be. That's where I felt I belonged.

1 YOU'LL FIND OUT

A Masquerade

I was born in Providence, Rhode Island, on December 8, 1932. And even as I put a period on that sentence, I'm shaking my head. 1932. It doesn't seem real, a date out of fiction, or maybe science fiction, and from where we are now—2026—so far away. Yet the memories those numbers evoke, the images before my eyes, seem so immediate and near. If you start in 1932 and add ninety-three years, we end up *here*, at this moment, with you reading the words I have written. Of course, if you start in 1932 and *subtract* ninety-three, we end up in 1839—and that is unsettling; to realize that when I was born, there were people walking the streets who voted for Abraham Lincoln.

My mother faced the world, and understood the world, in terms of an unsentimental seriousness. She bequeathed that attitude to me, and I don't think it is sentiment that provokes these feelings; rather the difference, the disquieting difference, between the way we think about time, the way we measure it, and the way we *experience* it. It has always seemed to me that only an unserious person looks at the world and says: *This is the way it is. This is the story, the only story.* That's not true in court, and it's not true in life. A shadowy sense of "doubleness" seems to infuse the world, a haunting, acknowledged even by Buttercup in Gilbert and Sullivan's *H.M.S. Pinafore*, a stanza that has always had particular meaning to me:[1]

Things are seldom what they seem,
Skim milk masquerades as cream;
Highlows pass as patent leathers;
Jackdaws strut in peacock's feathers.

A Wedding

My parents were married in Brooklyn on January 2, 1932, at the Half Moon Hotel in Coney Island. They never became famous, but the hotel did: in November 1941 Abe Reles, aka Kid Twist, the most feared contract killer for Murder Incorporated, fell out of a sixth-floor window at the Half Moon Hotel.[2] He was under police guard at the time, about a dozen city detectives and patrolmen, and was scheduled to testify that same day before a grand jury about corruption in the New York City Police Department. It was clear Reles had been "helped" out the window by some of those guarding him, but no one was ever charged. Said one detective: "He sang like a canary, but he couldn't fly."[3]

Marion Seidman was twenty years old at the time of her marriage. Morris Newman was twenty-six. Jan Peerce, "Toscanini's favorite tenor," sang and played violin at their wedding, only he wasn't Jan Peerce yet. He was still Jacob Pincus Perelmuth, picking up some pocket money as the Half Moon's wedding singer. Later that year he would become John Pierce, and still later Jan Peerce. As with many of us, it took some time before he found out who he really was.

Marion and Morris

My mother was born in 1911, in Zyrardow, Poland, which was then part of the Russian Empire. My father was born six years earlier in what was then called *the* Ukraine. If you look at a map of the world from that year, 1905, it bears no more resemblance to the world as it is today than a map of Middle-Earth or a map of Atlantis. Vanished kingdoms. Vanished countries. Vanished worlds. For Morris, the world of his youth couldn't vanish fast enough. As a child he had survived a pogrom and witnessed the murder of his grandfather and the rape of his sister. All his life he held great bitterness for the Ukraine. "I curse them," he'd say. "I'd burn in hell before I'd go back."

Marion expressed no especial bitterness toward Zyrardow, a small textile and lace manufacturing town 28 miles west of Warsaw.[4] She was the youngest of thirteen children, a twin; her father, a scholar, made a living reading and writing for his illiterate brethren; her mother worked in a store. The family was part of a Jewish community that numbered 2,500, roughly 12 percent of the total population. There had been Jews in Zyrardow since the town's founding around 1840 and 100 years later, in 1940, the community numbered about 3,000, including members of my mother's family. That's when the Germans rounded them up and sent them to Warsaw. From Warsaw they were sent to Treblinka and exterminated, all but a handful, maybe seventy or eighty. None of the survivors ever returned to Zyrardow. That story was over.

Years later my husband and I visited Zyrardow. I walked the streets my mother had walked as a girl, saw where the Jewish quarter of town had once been, where my grandmother sold dry goods. It was largely abandoned: derelict buildings and broken windows. When you walked into an entrance hallway, you heard things scurrying and there was a bad smell. There were no ghosts; there was nothing romantic about it. This was just the most sordid section of a rundown town. We walked through the Jewish cemetery and then to the town hall, past the shuttered red brick factory building and the empty housing for workers scattered about it, like barracks for an army that would never mobilize.

At the small Registry Office, we were shown photographs, maps, and census documents. These documents were all in Russian, but a woman translated for us, and I saw the papers of my mother's family, the names of the few who had emigrated, and the names of the many who had stayed. It was like wartime, looking over a list of casualties. Later, with night coming on, we walked to the car for the drive back to Warsaw. We passed the train station, brilliantly lit in the gathering dusk. It had recently been renovated.

My mother used to tell me that her earliest memory, the first thing she could ever recall, was lying beside her twin sister in a crib in the kitchen of the family flat in Zyrardow. Since her sister died of diphtheria before her first birthday, I used to think, even as a girl: Can this be true? Now I think, in all the most important ways except the purely factual, it probably is.

Immigrants

Both my mother and father emigrated in 1920, part of the last great wave of Jewish immigration to pass through Ellis Island. The Emergency Quota Act of 1921 and the National Origins Act of 1924 just about shut down emigration from Eastern Europe and from Asia, so they became Americans just under the wire. Morris, fifteen years old, was sponsored by an uncle who had a factory in Pawtucket, Rhode Island, that made ear wires and ear backs for earrings, and that's where he headed. He was clumsy on the factory floor, once cutting off the tip of a finger, but he had a great eye and a great head for business. And he was honest. Once a month or so he would travel down to New York to oversee the company's business office near Herald Square, and his uncle sent him to Japan, twice, to locate new sources of special wire and artisan findings for earrings and jewelry. I'm holding a photograph, yellow with age, of my father in Osaka in 1926 or 1927. There are a group of men and women, maybe thirty or so, all facing the camera. Some of the men are in traditional Japanese clothing, but others are in business wear and off to the side is the only westerner: Morris Newman. The picture appears to have been taken at a banquet, perhaps in his honor. He had come a long way from dodging Cossack boots and the slaps of impatient teachers at the *gymnasium* in Kiev. He too is wearing business wear: high collar, white shirt, dark tie, black suit, and is staring straight into the camera; a small, dapper man who looks exactly like what he is—the heir apparent.

My mother Marion, *her* mother Molka (Mollie), and an older sister and brother entered the United States on July 26, 1920. They were brought over by two older brothers, Max and Julius, who had emigrated earlier and now owned a women's clothing factory in the garment center in New York City. The family had traveled by rail from Zyrardow to Warsaw and then from Warsaw to Cologne, where they were able to obtain their immigration visas at the American Consulate. From Cologne they traveled by rail to Paris and from Paris to Le Havre, where they boarded the *SS Lafayette*, a workhorse of the Compagnie Generale Transatlantique, or French Line, which could accommodate close to 450 passengers. The *Lafayette* sailed from Le Havre to New York via Plymouth.

Each step of the Seidman family voyage from Zyrardow required visas and documents and transit papers, tickets and vouchers and signatures and passports and, almost certainly, bribes. Max and Julius had worked through Jewish agencies and other middlemen to make sure everything was in order all along the route. They had paid a small fortune to bring the family out of Poland, which was, at the time, at war with Bolshevik Russia, and in Le Havre they paid a bit more: the family boarded the *Lafayette* as second-class passengers. It was a six-day voyage, the weather fine, the seas calm, and Marion, nine years old, had the run of the ship. She always remembered how nice the crew had been to her, how she loved skipping along the deck in the afternoon and at night watching the moonlight across the water. She would describe this voyage to me with delight, and it was a source of great pride that she and her family did not arrive in the United States in steerage.

The Jimjams

A year or two later Julius's wife, Gussie, gave birth to her second child. Afterward she was listless. She was sad all the time and wasn't all that interested in her children—Harold or the baby Yetta. Gussie had the blues; or the baby blues; the jitters or the willies or the jimjams. Maybe she was emotional or selfish, lazy or even wicked. It was hard to know. There were a lot of names for what Gussie had, all but the right name: postpartum depression. In any case, this wasn't something for doctors or psychologists. Marion was living with her mother on the Lower East Side, going to school and working, and earning some money to help support the family. Julius asked if she might come to the Bronx, to live with his family and help raise his children until Gussie got better. Marion was a child herself, but that's what she did. That was her life then. Eventually Gussie *did* get better, and Marion went back to the Lower East Side. She went back to school.

Harold grew up and became a Colonel in the US Army. All his life, he was devoted to Marion. He loved her like a mother.

Chasing the Inch

Marion prized education above all else, and she worked hard to get herself educated. It wasn't easy. She had to work, she had to take care of Molka, who never learned English, and she had other family responsibilities. She finally got her diploma in 1928 from East Side Evening High School in Manhattan and then began taking night classes at City College. She wanted that degree.

She was a beautiful young woman: slim, with blonde wavy hair and blue eyes, clear skin, and exquisite features. She was small but resolute—four feet eleven: "If I'd been five feet," she used to say, "I'd have been unstoppable." She used to joke with me that she chased that inch for years but never quite caught up to it. It was the same way with the college degree. She chased it for years—not only at City College but, later, at Brooklyn College as well, but it always eluded her. It was one of the great disappointments of her life.

My mother went to work at "Clover Bead" near Herald Square, the business office for the factory in Pawtucket, and it was here that she met the boss's nephew. Morris fell in love immediately and soon produced an engagement ring, but Marion turned him down. She still hoped to return to college and resume her studies. Morris told her he would keep the ring until she changed her mind. He wrote her a very un-Morris-like love letter, ardent and emotional, and promised that when they married, her mother could live with them. As always, he was as good as his word, and the day following the wedding at the Half Moon Hotel, the three of them, Marion, Morris, and Molka, took the train to Providence.

I think of a certain moment in my mother's life: a pretty young woman working at "Clover Bead," turning down my father's marriage proposals, determined to return to school. She played the violin and the piano, and she wanted to resume her studies. *That* moment. But the Boom was over, and the Depression had brought the economy near rock bottom. There were no more trips to Japan for Morris, and the dream of a college degree must have seemed to Marion just that: a dream. Or a dream within a dream. She needed to wake up. When Morris proposed again, she said "Yes."

Strategy

The apartment my father found was on the east side of Providence near Brown University, on a tree-lined street with plenty of sunlight. Near the end of the block was a park. The apartment itself was full of light, and there was more than enough room for the three of them, but they lived there a little more than a year. I was born in December, and by early March we had moved to 70 Davis Street. The new apartment was a railroad flat, a second-floor walkup, the first floor occupied by a hairdresser.

Davis Street was a short block directly behind the state capital; when the kids on the block wanted to play on grass, we'd run over to the statehouse lawn because there was nothing green about Davis Street—one or two scraggly trees and that was it. Across the street from us was the imposing wooden façade of a bible school.

It was my mother's idea to move. She was the family strategist and had learned that every child who lived on Davis Street was guaranteed admission and free tuition at the Henry Barnard School, an elite and expensive private school between one and two miles away from our home. It was where the Governor's kids were educated. Marion had learned that a flat had become available on the block and insisted on the move. You know how parents today try to game the admissions process by making contributions to a school when their child is born? This was the ancestor of that, only *better:* it was guaranteed and didn't cost a cent.

Why this was so, what deal had been struck, what secret legislative tradeoff agreed to, no one was sure. Lord Palmerston said the Schleswig-Holstein question was so complicated that only three people in Europe understood it: one was dead, one went mad, and the third forgot about it. This was just like that, an American version, only with sewer contracts and construction grants thrown in. In any case, it was real.

So, there we were: Marion, Morris, Molka, and me, three months old, sitting in a railroad flat above a hairdresser's on an ugly street in 1930s Providence, Rhode Island. We were waiting for me to be old enough to go to school.

My Dog Pal

Yes, and while we waited, my father worked six days a week at his factory in downtown Providence, and my mother continued to strategize. In those days newspapers published poetry, and about this time the *Providence Journal* printed a poem entitled *It Couldn't Be Done* by Edgar Guest. Here's how it began:[5]

Somebody said that it couldn't be done,
But he with a chuckle replied
That "maybe it couldn't," but he would be one
Who wouldn't say so till he'd tried.
So he buckled right in with the trace of a grin
On his face. If he worried he hid it.
And he started to sing as he tackled the thing
That couldn't be done, and he did it.

Marion loved this poem. She clipped it out of the paper and referred to it often because it expressed much of what she believed, much of what she taught us: "If you can't go through, go around. If you can't go around, go over and if you can't go over, go under. But somehow, in some way, always reach your goal." She particularly liked the idea of singing while you accomplished your goal because music was very important to her. We had an upright piano in the apartment, and when she wasn't playing herself, music was always coming from the radio, which was kept on all the time. She liked "Don McNeil's Breakfast Club," and one of my earliest memories is marching around the table with her when McNeil issued his "Call to Breakfast."

She had me take elocution lessons, which were common then for the children of immigrants. Our parents didn't want us talking like mockies or greenhorns. They wanted us to speak like Americans, like Yankees. We did recitals, which I enjoyed, and I remember on one occasion bringing the audience to tears with a heartbreaker called "My Dog Pal." They were crying, and I was thinking: *I don't even have a dog!* It was an early, tentative understanding of the power of performance and of words and stories.

My mother wanted me to take piano lessons, and the teacher she found was Rita Bicho, a young woman who still lived with her mother on Governor Street and who studied music at Rhode Island College.[6] Bicho was a phenomenon, and she molded and encouraged the talent I had and sponsored me for the Chopin Juvenile Club, which met and performed twice a month in downtown Providence. Rita carried a big brown leather purse, and at the end of each lesson she would open it with a CLICK! and pull out a box of gold stars, which she'd award me if I'd done well. I can still hear that CLICK! and I still have a notebook page full of stars. Neighbors would hear the music coming from our apartment and ask Marion, "Who is that teacher? She sure is doing a good job." And Marion would say: "You're mistaken. She's not good at all. Not reliable. Forget about her. She's not for you." She was afraid someone else would hire Rita and she wouldn't be available when I needed her.

Somehow Marion had found the best piano teacher in Providence. Rita Bicho went on to train hundreds of pianists and to have a thirty-year teaching career at Rhode Island College: "A beautiful lifetime's work," she called it when she retired in 1979. There is a memorial scholarship in her name at the College—so something from that long ago time lives on. Not much does. Even 70 Davis Street is gone, vanished in some urban renewal project in the 1960s.

Davis Street. You might hunt it on a map, but it is not there.

My Harriet

The Great New England Hurricane made landfall on Wednesday, September 21, 1938.[7] It caused historic damage up and down the coast, but the most serious impact was on Rhode Island. The storm surge brought flooding almost 14 feet high, and in downtown Providence people drowned in their cars. Over 600 people died in what was considered, for a time, the Storm of the Century.

I don't remember the storm itself, but the aftermath remains vivid. I was five years old and had started kindergarten at the Henry Barnard School earlier in the month. On Monday, September 26, my mother woke me up and told me that school had reopened, but when we opened the door onto Davis Street, trees were obliterating the street. She said, "It's up to you. Do you want to go to school, or do you want to stay home?" I said I wanted to go. Usually, I took the trolley car down Smith Street Hill, but there was no trolley or electric bus service. We had to walk. The streets were filled with fallen trees and abandoned cars. There were empty buses, deserted mid route, and downed power lines, and the street itself was filled with mud or silt and all kinds of debris and trash. We went around it all.

It took us a long time to reach the school, and when we did, the building appeared deserted. The first-floor corridor was dark and quiet, but there was a faint light coming from the kindergarten classroom, and when we walked in Miss McGuinness was at her desk. She saw us and smiled. The classroom was empty; I was the only child to show up for kindergarten that day, and I had Miss McGuinness all to myself. It was probably the best day of school of my life.

I was the type of student who loved her teachers and wanted them to love me. I remember all their names: Miss McGuinness, Miss Bernstein, Miss Fish, Miss Kelly . . . And I remember the names of my classmates as well; one in particular, Anthony Migliaccio. He was dark and handsome and very smart, and we became very close until my family left for New York City in 1945. I never forgot him. Anthony stayed in Providence, became a physician, married, and had children. I know this because years and years later I was talking to my husband about him and became curious. I thought I would give him a call. There were a surprising number of Anthony Migliaccio's in the Providence directory, but I finally tracked him down. When he came on the line, I said, "Anthony, this is Harriet Newman." We hadn't spoken for half a century.

He said: "My Harriet?"

You'll Find Out

I was close to all my teachers, but I was especially close to Kathleen Kelly, who taught third grade. She was pretty and young, and I adored her. She sent me a Christmas card that year: *hair of blond and eyes of blue, you are a lovely child and I love you.* I *did* have blue eyes and blonde hair, which I wore in banana curls. Everybody knew I was her favorite.

My fourth-grade teacher, Miss Campbell, had a round face and a square body. She had close-cropped hair that she wore straight back, sometimes combed up like a man's pompadour. She never wore any make-up and used to tell the girls in her class, nine- and ten-year-olds, that *we* should never wear make-up either because it was manufactured with poison and would kill us. Miss Campbell seemed to take personal offense at the fact Miss Kelly was so close to me. I could feel that anger and her intense dislike from the moment I walked into her classroom.

Within the first week she pulled me aside. She knelt down so we were on the same level, and she could look into my face.

"You'll find out what life is like," she told me. "You'll learn that not everybody loves you."

Sometimes I try to believe that her motives were positive, that she was trying to toughen me up, wake a girly girl from her dreamy dreams so she might better face the world as it is. But I think there were other motives, and what she said to me was cruel, bordering on the abusive. But it *was* a lesson. When I told my mother what had happened, she told me to stay calm, avoid angering Miss Campbell, study hard, and do the best I could. That was a lesson, as well, I guess.

There was no end to lessons for a young girl, but they often seemed to be the same lesson. Several times a week in the afternoon I would go to Yiddish School. Mr. Siegel was the teacher, and he used to come with a driver and pick up the children in a station wagon; one of those old, wooden-sided station wagons with room for 7–8 children; all girls, because the boys went to Hebrew School. And he would pile on the kids but always hold me back to sit with him, sit on his lap on the front seat. I didn't like it and knew there was something wrong. I told my mother, and she said, tell him you don't want to ride in the front seat. You want to sit with the others. So that's what I did, and from then on, he'd sit alone on the front seat with the driver. I knew what I was saying. I was young, but I'd been told to be very careful with men. It was all done quietly, and there was no thought of telling anyone, someone in authority, an outsider. Something similar happened in the beauty parlor at Shepard's Department Store in downtown Providence: a hairdresser "helping" me by running his hands over me, over my nothing breasts; and my mother saying later, when she found out: Well, we won't go back. And we didn't. And that hairdresser kept his job and "helped" how many young girls?

This was just the way it was. You kept quiet and handled it yourself and didn't make trouble. *Your* shame. *Your* vulnerability. There was no one to go to. This was the way the world operated, the world of which Miss Campbell was a part. She never let up on me the whole year. I couldn't do anything right, and I never entered her classroom without feeling anxious and fearful. Yet she was, in ways, a good teacher; even I could see that. There was a boy in our class, Robert Reynolds; today he'd be called dysfunctional; then he was just a troublemaker. He became her project. She was determined to turn him into a good student and a "good boy," and by the end of the year, she had succeeded. She completely turned him around. She saved him.

Mary Tucker Thorpe

At the Henry Barnard School, the principal's office, the other administrative offices, and the kindergarten were on the first floor. All the other classes were on the upper floors. So when I began school, I often saw the principal. She would walk down the hallway, sometimes oblivious, but sometimes seeing us kindergartners and smiling or patting a head or two. We were in awe of her. When she came to our classroom to watch Miss McGuinness teach, or to talk to us herself—telling us to work hard, listen to teacher, and be good—it was like a visit from a princess. There really was something regal about her. She was tall, with an angular face and high cheekbones, olive skin, and dark hair which she wore braided in a long ponytail down her back. I thought she was beautiful, but beautiful in an unusual way I had not seen before. Her name was Mary Tucker Thorpe.[8]

Except it wasn't. She'd been born Mary Dahood in Beirut, then part of Syria, in 1899 and had been brought to this country in 1904. Shortly afterward her father died, and her mother, unable to care for her, placed her in the Rock Nook Home for Children in Norwich, Connecticut. A wealthy Rhode Island couple, Job and Florence Thorpe, found her there and became her guardians. She grew up in their home in Westerly, with their three other children, one of whom, Elliott, became a Brigadier General in the United States Army. He was General Douglas MacArthur's chief of counter-intelligence during the Second World War. You can't get more American than that.[9] In 1917, Mary's mother, Hadla, after unsuccessfully trying to annul the Thorpe guardianship, tried to kidnap her daughter. She wanted to bring her back to Brooklyn, New York, to work in a boarding house. The police were called and Hadla was arrested. The Thorpes then took measures to protect Mary, formally adopting her in 1920. That's when she took the name Mary Tucker Thorpe.

In writing a memoir, it can sometimes seem that everything that happened *had* to happen, as if each story has a neat beginning, middle, and end. But that wasn't true for Mary Tucker Thorpe, it wasn't true for Molka or Marion or Julius or me. Writing it down tends to take the messiness out of life, but I think it is worth the effort to try and put the messiness, the *arbitrariness*, back in. At any event, that is what I am trying to do. Mary Tucker Thorpe's life could have gone in many directions. There was nothing preordained about it. She might have remained Mary Dahood, a little girl in Beirut, or the Thorpes might have found another child to rescue. Hadla might have been successful, and Mary might have ended her days with her mother, running a boarding house in Brooklyn. Instead, she became a distinguished educator. A professorship is named in her honor at Rhode Island College. A Residence Hall, as well.

I don't think anyone at the Henry Barnard School knew any of this. In those pre-internet days, you were, more or less, who you said you were, and finding out someone's actual background took time and money. Why bother? I think of her walking down the first-floor hallway of the school, pretending to be who she actually was: Mary Tucker Thorpe. And me? I was, in James Agee's beautiful phrase, "disguised to myself as a child."[10]

She's walking down the hallway and catches my eye. She smiles at me. We recognize each other.

2 THIS WORLD AND ANOTHER

Notes from the Century Before

Morris and his younger brother Nathan decided to go into business for themselves in New York City, and we moved in February 1945. Molka had died three years earlier, so there were five of us: Marion and Morris, my brother Alvin, six years old, my sister Molli, eleven months, and me; another sister, Sandee, was born in 1946. I hated to leave Providence, a city I always think of as child-scaled, where I could ride the trolley by myself and wander about downtown on a weekend afternoon with no one looking after me or worrying about me. For years afterward I had a recurring dream about the Henry Barnard School, but it wasn't one of those anxious dreams where you're late for class or forget about a test. I was just sitting in a classroom with the friends I had made and the teachers I loved. At my new school, P.S. 222 in Brooklyn, I would cheerfully tell the teacher during math class, "That's not how we did it in Providence." And she would reply, increasingly less cheerful, "If I hear you say that one more time . . ."

This World and Another

The war in Europe ended that May and the full scope of the German extermination of the Jews became known. There were articles and horrific photographs in newspapers and magazines, nightmarish images in the newsreels—bulldozers moving hundreds of bodies into mass graves. You lived with the knowledge that this could actually happen. My mother and father had not been particularly religious or observant, but their reaction to it all was to intensify their identification as Jews. As a consequence, while I remained in public school, my brother and sisters were educated in Yeshiva—orthodox Jewish primary and secondary school. It was as if I was their guide, their emissary to this world, and my siblings their emissaries to another.

I was old for my age, a little mother, taking care of my brother and sisters, criticizing my own mother if I didn't like the way she was raising them. I was impatient of her fears: of deep water, of dogs. We'd walk down the street, and I'd have to keep my eyes open for imagined threats. *Too* old for my age really, but both my parents encouraged it. At school, my Providence education overmatched that of my classmates, my hand always up, answering every question. I skipped grades, moving through PS 222 and then James Madison High School, entering college in the fall of 1949. I was sixteen.

That's My Kid

Morris and Nathan bought a building in the Bedford-Stuyvesant section of Brooklyn, the old Borden milk company factory, "the home of contented cows." The building was cavernous, dark, and gloomy, and there was a constant vibration, the low thrum of large freight elevators. On Saturdays, my father would sometimes take me with him to work, where he'd sit me at a desk and go about his business while I went through the mail or typed up the bills or stuffed envelopes. I'd hear him showing a customer around, their voices low, and when they'd pass the office where I was working, he'd say, "That's my kid."

I knew my father loved me, but he sometimes had difficulty expressing his feelings. He was clumsy, not only on the factory floor (that missing fingertip) but at home, leaning down to kiss my cheek but always missing it and kissing my ear instead—something I hated. "Daddy, stop," I'd say. But even now I can hear him, the timbre of his Russian-accented voice as he walked through his factory, talking to strangers.

That's my kid.

The Wild Frontier

The Newman brothers made plastic toys in their Brooklyn factory, under the company name Premier Products, basically knockoffs of more successful or well-known brands like Matchbox or Tonka. They made a good living, skittering along the border of Copyright and Patent, sometimes just this side of the line, sometimes the other. They were sued twice, once over a toy pistol and once over "Bubble Hen," a yellow plastic hen, ludicrously popular, that lay pellets of bubble gum when you pressed down on its wings. The cases were in the Federal Court, and they won both times. You might think a federal judge had better things to do than hear testimony about the firing mechanism of a cap gun, but you might also think that a multi-million-dollar divorce wouldn't be delayed for years over who gets a blanket in a chest of drawers. Yet it happens all the time.

Then in 1958 Premier Products entered an agreement granting them manufacturing rights to a new item, a hoop made of plastic tubing. This was like cornering the market on coonskin the week before *Davy Crockett, King of the Wild Frontier* was broadcast. Twenty-five million Hula Hoops were sold in four months: more than one hundred million over two years. If you opened *Life Magazine* or *The Saturday Evening Post* or *Look* there were photographs of people, whole families, celebrities, even nuns, Hula Hooping away; the same if you turned on Steve Allen or Dave Garroway. *Time* and *Newsweek, The Saturday Review* had articles about what it all meant.[1] What difference did it make? Premier Products just kept turning them out. Morris made his fortune.

Carthage on the Boardwalk

We spent the first summer after we moved to New York at Asbury Park on the Jersey shore. Morris would take the train to the city each morning to work at his factory and then take the train again to join us each evening. My mother and father never spent a night apart. Marion would shake her head at those women who spent the summer in the Catskills, leaving their husbands back in the city, subject to all manner of temptation, primarily sexual. There were women who had husbands and other women who wanted those husbands. Marion believed that men, as the weaker sex, were peculiarly susceptible to sexual and emotional snares, and that a woman's sexuality was both more powerful and more pernicious—capable of doing greater damage, not only to a marriage but, by extension, to society at large. This wasn't a quaint or folk belief—the culture echoed it and the law, for generations, codified it. It would be foolish to believe anything else.

I knew all this because I was my mother's confidant, her liaison, fully at home in this new world as Marion, who dreamed and thought in Yiddish, her mother tongue, was not. I seemed to dominate the household in ways that were not particularly healthy either for her or for myself: the little mother, given tremendous freedom and responsibility. In the summer mornings, I would leave Marion with my infant sister, Molli, and, taking six-year-old Alvin in hand, would wander out into the day, usually ending up on the Boardwalk, which was over 10 miles long and featured endless shops and restaurants, food stands, exhibits and amusements, even a miniature golf course, and a Ferris wheel and carousel. The south side of the Boardwalk was dominated by the Casino, a huge building with a long pier that stretched out into the ocean and an accompanying Arcade and Amusement Hall. It was cool inside, and we often spent time there.

On this day there was a new display: an edifice, like a long hut, had been built on one side of the Casino and for a nickel you could walk inside and see what was described as an amazing example of modern science at work for the benefit of mankind. A poster proclaimed that all monies collected went to Sister Kenny—someone I had never heard of. The hut itself seemed to vibrate, and there was a sound from inside, partly a wheeze, like a breathless giant or a tuneless accordion, partly the whirr of powerful machinery—altogether intriguing. I paid the two nickels, and Alvin and I went in.

On either side of the narrow interior were iron lungs, yellow and blue, each with a child inside, polio victims, only their heads visible, protruding from the end of the machines toward the center of the room. Some of the children appeared asleep, others stared up at the ceiling, unblinking; still others tried to turn their heads to catch a glimpse of their visitors and engage them in conversation. The noise of all those iron lungs in operation was hellish, and, to a child who knew nothing of Sister Kenny and her revolutionary treatments, it was impossible to tell if the children were being helped or tortured by the machines in which they were encased. It was as if a veil had been torn away, giving us a glimpse of another world, an invisible world that coexisted with and seemed to mock the verities of the one we knew. Or perhaps it was a glimpse of the far future; or the dim and distant past, the pre-Christian past, Carthage, perhaps, or Assyria, whose depredations and sins against the righteous were chronicled in the Bible.

Or maybe it was just the world, our world, the one Adam glimpsed when he first tasted the apple.

Alvin began to cry, and we quickly left. At home we told Marion what we had seen, and she explained to us who Sister Kenny was and how her treatments benefited the stricken children. But the image remained, that glimpse into *elsewhere*, and in my mind it was linked, in ways hard to understand, with absent husbands and vigilant wives. For weeks afterward Alvin would suffer from nightmares, his cries and shouts waking us all. Marion would comfort him and look at me with disappointment. She'd say: "What were you thinking?"

Keep Her in Line

Morris didn't drive, so every morning a Yellow Cab would show up at our home on Quentin Road and take him to work in Bed-Stuy. The driver was always the same: an enormous man, morbidly obese, who was called, naturally enough, Tiny. That joke never got old. And if you looked again at all those photographs of Hula Hoopers in *Life* or *The Saturday Evening Post* or *Look* you'd notice there was usually one picture of a very chubby kid or an overweight man struggling to get the thing twirling. The newsreels would do something similar, only they could do it in slow motion: the strained face and the rolls of flesh moving up and down in strenuous and comic effort. Fat people were very entertaining. They were always good for a laugh.

Black people were good for a laugh, as well. *Amos and Andy* was ubiquitous. You could follow the slow southern ways of Lightnin' and the mock clever machinations of Kingfish on both radio *and* TV. What a pair! Jews were funny, too, with their big noses and sly ways. And immigrants, like the Italians and Chinese, all mangled English and exaggerated gestures.

This was part of the life we lived, all these assumptions, unexamined and cruel, for while everyone could be an object of humor, there were some groups that could be made fun of, that could be ridiculed, and it wasn't the same. You couldn't explain it. You just *knew*. You breathed it in.

But funnier than anyone else, even funnier than fat people, were women. What made them funny was that, so often, they didn't get the joke. A comedian might wave his fist under a woman's nose and threaten—POW!—to send her right to the moon; or an actor might mush a grapefruit in her face.[2] It was all in good fun. Why couldn't they see that? The frazzled wife misunderstanding a husband's attention toward a glamorous secretary; the career woman marooned by success until meeting a handsome male rival; the pretty society girl hoping to catch the butler's eye. The movies we saw, the stories we read, the plots so familiar as to seem dreamlike, all ended happily. It was almost perverse that so many women persisted in being *unhappy*.

Morris, who never raised a hand in anger and treated his wife and children with love and respect, was talking with a group of relatives about a woman we all knew. She was somewhat wild and tempestuous. Sensual. She had a mouth on her and an attitude and was, in the terminology of the time, thought of as "difficult." And whose fault was that? Morris didn't blame her. He blamed her husband. She was, he felt, the kind of woman who needed a smack, maybe one good smack. He never quite came out and said it, but that was what he implied. It was a man's world—the man had to be the master of his household or he was unworthy of respect. He was nothing.

"He needs to keep her in line," said Morris.

An Educated Woman

The woman who had to be kept in line was Audrey Black. I met her at James Madison High School, and we became lifelong friends. We went to Barnard College together, riding up there in her blue convertible every day. In our senior year we were asked to debate the role of the college-educated woman on WNYC-Radio. Audrey argued about the need to find a meaningful career, to do something important in the public sphere—anything else would be a waste of our education.

I argued that we were in college to meet extraordinary, wonderful men and to marry and have children and be the best mothers. My education wasn't wasted, I said, because women were the most important cog in the marriage wheel and the next generation, the one that we would raise, was going to be educated by these amazing women. What could be more fulfilling than that?

I don't know who won the debate on the radio, but in life it was no contest. We graduated from college on Thursday, June 5, 1952, and ten days later, on Sunday, June 15th, so many of my friends and classmates were getting married that we couldn't attend each other's weddings. I was one of them, marrying my high school crush and college sweetheart, Philip M. Cohen. Marion warned me not to.

"He doesn't like people," she said.
"He likes me," I told her.
"You'll be next," she said.

An educated woman.

3 EVERY UNHAPPY FAMILY

The Only Thing You Have to Do

Phil was the most beautiful boy I had ever seen. We met at a party during my sophomore year in high school—I was fourteen and he was seventeen. We dated through college and, following our marriage, moved to Wilmington, Delaware, where he'd been offered a job with DuPont. At various times over the course of our 22-year marriage, Phil was a scientist, a chemist, a salesman, and a businessman. But in his heart he was really none of those things. He was an artist, a musician. He was extraordinarily talented, a virtuoso and soloist on the piano, and played several brass instruments as well. In addition, he had a wide and engaging knowledge of music—classical and modern. This tension, between how he was seen in the world, how he was forced to present himself, and how he actually saw himself, was a source of great frustration, bitterness, and anger, and it wasn't until long after our marriage was over that he achieved some kind of resolution and a measure of contentment. But while we were married, almost from the very beginning, that anger and tension was always there, and it was exacerbated by other factors. The world saw him as a faithful husband, a good provider, and a loving father. And he was, to a greater or lesser extent, none of those things.

There was a moment . . . this was years later, when we had left Wilmington and moved back to New York City. We lived in a lovely home in a residential neighborhood, just one long block from the ocean. We were having dinner; I was at one end of the table, Phil at the other. And between us were our daughters—Martha (Marti) the oldest was seventeen, then Amy, Sue, and Patti, the youngest, who was seven years old. I think Sue had some friends over because it was one of those evenings when the room was filled with chatter and gentle teasing, junior high school gossip, and laughter. And Phil was taking it all in with absolutely no expression, a grim and brooding presence. It was clear he resented having to be in this room with these people. With me. By this time his responsibility to the family was diminishing in ways that were impossible to ignore: bills weren't being paid, he was staying out longer and coming home later. In the years to come he would disappear for days at a time, none of us knowing where he was. But at that moment none of it mattered—not the bills or the absences or the atmosphere we lived in of stress and anger and a kind of dreary longing. What *did* matter, what seemed important to me right then, was that there be some acknowledgement of *this* moment, some appreciation of the great gift we'd been given: our four beautiful daughters.

I was looking at Phil and thinking: *the only thing you have to do is be happy.*

The World as It Is: I

In 1953 the US Labor Department published a report entitled "The Status of Women in the United States," based on material—statistics, interviews, surveys—gathered the previous year.[1] In essence it was a snapshot of the world into which I graduated, the world I knew as a young married woman and mother.

The report notes that while women are participating in civic affairs at increasing numbers "the idea that a woman might run for election to the presidency is not considered seriously." Women on average were paid a bit more than 40 percent of what men received for "the same or comparable work," and though "the principle of equal pay for equal work is generally accepted in theory" it was nowhere accepted in practice because "legal loopholes exist which make it difficult to enforce."

In 1952 no-fault divorce did not exist in the United States, and then, as now, states were free to pass their own legislation regarding a wide range of all matrimonial matters. While there were numerous differences—some states criminalized inter-racial marriage, for instance—there was one great similarity: divorce, because it involved behavioral transgression, was seen as a moral issue: one party acted in such a way as to break the marriage vow, the promise made to the other party—through adultery perhaps, or cruelty or desertion—and this had caused the marriage to fail. Of course, terms such as "desertion" or "cruelty" meant different things in different states and these laws were never static; for instance, "cruelty"—which involved physical injury, actual or menaced—evolved over time into "mental cruelty"—a non-physical injury so intense as to warrant the dissolution of the marriage. But the subtext remained the same: if a marriage failed, one of the parties had done something wrong.

Similarly, the idea of "fault-based" itself underwent changes, as several states competed for the lucrative "migratory" divorce business, Nevada taking the lion's share by lowering its residency requirement, in 1931, from one year to six weeks—adding a wink and a nod to the divorce process. That's why in all those screwball comedies of the 1930s, the wives are always rushing off to Reno, where they meet Ralph Bellamy or George Brent and hi-jinks ensue. Nonetheless, Nevada was an outlier and divorce remained a chancy, difficult and expensive proposition in the vast majority of the other forty-seven states—which explains why, in the pulp and mystery fiction of the period—*The Postman Always Rings Twice, Double Indemnity,*

Strangers on a Train—the surest and quickest route to marriage dissolution was . . . murder. Not the least of the accomplishments of the "divorce revolution" of the 1970s and 1980s was that it saved lives. Fictional ones, of course, but real ones as well. Including mine.

Business

We moved from Wilmington back to New York because Morris had offered Phil an unusual and lucrative opportunity. The genesis of that offer went back about a year, to 1953, when the "Matchbox" brand, a line of die-cast cars and trucks, was introduced into the United States. These miniature toys had revolutionized the market: the first, a reproduction of Queen Elizabeth's coronation coach, sold a million copies. Morris believed Premier Products might earn a healthy profit, drafting to the slipstream created by Matchbox, and he and his brother Nathan decided they would manufacture their own miniature toys at the Brooklyn factory. But while Matchbox miniatures were made entirely from metal, Premier Products used plastic—durable and much cheaper to manufacture. However, there was a problem: the fenders and bumpers of the toy cars, front and rear, had to be shiny and metallic, and simply painting the plastic wouldn't do. They had to use a process which applied a thin metallic luminate to a porous plastic surface and getting it to adhere required special machinery, Vacuum Metallizers, that could not be installed in the Brooklyn factory. So they bought their own machinery and built a new factory in Maspeth, Queens. And that was the offer to Phil: become a full partner with Morris and Nathan and take complete charge of the new factory. All he had to do was move back home.

And yet he hesitated. Phil enjoyed his work at DuPont and was loath to leave, but I wanted to move and, emphasizing the financial and social advantages on offer, convinced him to change his mind. We made the move in January 1954, and almost immediately he went to work at the new factory, overseeing the hiring process and the installation of machinery. When I first knew Phil, he had wanted to be a doctor. He took pre-med courses in college but could never master physics and eventually gave it up and began studying chemistry, earning a master's degree at the University of Michigan the year before we married. So he had left New York a scientist and now was returning to New York as a Jewish businessman, in partnership with two other Jewish businessmen, older men, neither of whom he liked and neither of whom he respected. The decision to go into partnership with my father, a decision I strongly encouraged, proved catastrophic and marked the beginning of the long death of our marriage.

Partners

Part of the problem was cultural. My father was a short man, physically unprepossessing and clumsy. He never learned how to drive a car, and all his life he spoke with a thick Russian accent. He was very smart and learned but had no great interest in the wider American culture or in any ostentatious display. To Phil, he seemed old-fashioned in his ways and old country in his manner. My husband spoke beautifully, was extremely handsome, and physically adept. A skier. A tennis player. Graceful. He was interested in and appreciated the higher culture around him and had a sense, perhaps too highly developed, of the finer things in life.

But there were other problems as well. The factory in Brooklyn was a blue-collar affair. Morris was the boss, made all the key decisions, but there was no sense of hierarchy. People were free to wander in and out of the small, unadorned offices, and he was often on the factory floor, lending a hand to the best of his limited ability—I often saw him helping to tie up packages with heavy rope, preparatory to shipment. It was different at the factory in Queens. It had been thought that Phil's background in chemistry would be helpful, and it was to some degree, but by and large the machinery, the Vacuum Metallizers, did the work and the machinists Phil hired kept an eye on them. Phil was free to be a boss. He did this by building a large office, wood paneled, with a big desk and a full carpet. It was like something out of *Executive Suite*. Morris and Nathan rarely went out to Queens, but when they did, and when they saw the carpet, they were appalled. It seemed to symbolize everything *wrong* about the way Phil went about his business. Their business. Behind his back they sneered at him and his pretensions. The big *macher* with his green carpet.[2]

And there was one final difference. My father was a success, with a keen business sense. He liked his life, looked out for his family, paid his bills, and made a lot of money. Phil didn't like being a businessman, was basically uninterested in it all, though he liked the perks a successful business brought him, the toys he could play with. There was always a fancy car in the driveway, a Mark V four-door Lincoln Continental convertible, and we took long and expensive vacations. And meanwhile, the butcher wasn't being paid, and I'd wonder if they'd turn off the electricity. Phil had begun running his factory at the cusp of the greatest and most sustained economic boom the nation had ever known. They called that time "The Go-Go years." And by 1967, he was bankrupt.

Every Unhappy Family

There was always something wrong, something that irritated him, something I did and couldn't fix.[3] Something unfixable. One night he'd come home from work and the mail hadn't been sorted correctly. The next night I made sure it *was*

sorted correctly, but he told me I'd left it in the wrong place, on the wrong table. Something. The worsening financial situation was part of it, of course, a tension, an apprehension that never fully disappeared even during the better moments. And there were better moments: family outings, concerts, visits with friends and family. We'd have people over for an evening of music, Phil and I, sitting close to each other, playing four-handed piano in our living room. He played so beautifully. But those moments became fewer and, over time, even the memory of them seemed unreal. As for the rest: it was like an undertow, always there, you felt the pull and the power even if you weren't conscious of it. The house just felt different when he was inside it, the atmosphere, the *weather*, all of us felt it, an ominous flutter, my daughters and myself tiptoeing around in a futile effort not to upset him. I used to think to myself: he has malaise, something dark and untreatable within him: he can't help himself. There was a coat I'd bought, a plaid coat with a high fur collar. This was around the time of *Doctor Zhivago*, the movie, and I thought of it as a Zhivago-type coat, something Lara might wear in the snow. I loved it and thought I looked beautiful in it. It transformed me, in my own head. And Phil would tell me, with venom in his voice, how ugly it looked. How much he hated it. And he said this so often, with such intensity, that I finally said to him: You know Phil, it's not the coat you don't like. It's me. And we just looked at each other. I knew that he didn't love me and that I could never make him love me. I also knew that I would never be the one to end the marriage.

He used to tease the kids. He'd hurt them, but it was always—*I was only kidding*. He was particularly hard on Marti. She'd been born in August 1953, when we still lived in Wilmington, and she was a colicky baby, always fussing, always crying. We'd been so happy when I became pregnant, but Phil just couldn't handle her, her crying, he shut right down, shut himself completely off. He threw a shadow over their relationship that existed until the end of his life. And the way he acted, his emotional withdrawal from his firstborn, made me think, even there in Wilmington, that I'd made a mistake, that Phil and I should never have been married. That was one of the reasons I so wanted to move back to New York, to family.

There was a maliciousness to his teasing, a kind of gleeful malevolence. Our daughter Sue was a sensitive child, prone to worrying about plans and details. It's not uncommon, and children grow out of it, but when she was young, it was something we had to be aware of, something we always had to deal with. And one time we were going on a family trip and the girls were all piled into the car. We were still in the driveway, Phil hadn't even turned the ignition, and he said, "Sue, we're lost." And she became upset, and Phil said, "Oh Sue, we haven't left home yet and we're already lost." And I was begging him to stop and Sue was crying but Phil just kept on.

We're lost. We're lost.

The Dreaming Suburb

I didn't tell my friends, not even my closest friends, that we were bankrupt. I told them we had suffered financial reverses and I was going to get a job to help out until things righted themselves. It was both true and untrue, which just about sums up our lives back then. We lived in a nice house in a suburb of nice houses; had a big car in a neighborhood of big cars; sent our kids to good schools, as did our friends and neighbors; presented a public face of domestic happiness, or at least contentment, just as they did. And we had no money and worried about car payments and couldn't afford those good schools our kids attended, and my marriage was in slow-motion collapse. Were we the only husband and wife with financial or marital problems? Hard to believe, but impossible to know, as no one spoke of anything important; no one confided. In those dark short stories of suburban angst, Cheever perhaps, or Updike, the couples always seemed to be chatting away about gin and adultery but, although there was plenty of both to go around, what I remember about that time is the silence, this great silence about anything that mattered. We might have been sleeping, and life happening around us, while we dreamt. And what did we talk about? Crabgrass. That's how my husband, Arthur, described it. He was raising his family in a suburban community similar to mine during this period. "We talked about crabgrass," he said.

Looking back it is easy to see this was a liminal moment. Epochal change was approaching, political, of course, but also social and legal changes that would forever alter the way men and women understood their relation to one another, their obligations to each other, even the nature of their emotional feelings—their love for one another. But living through it, moment to moment, it just felt like . . . life. The life we were living, the life that would go on forever. This home. These streets. There was nothing dramatic about it, and change, if it was recognized at all, did not seem all that important; like heat lightning on the horizon—faraway and of no great consequence, no threat to the way we lived now. I deal with that type of feeling in my practice all the time. It is impossible to understand a marriage or a relationship from the outside looking in, and there are scores of marriages that go on for ten, twenty, thirty years—a lifetime—with no intimacy, no connection between the couple, sometimes without even a distant kind of friendship. They go on *because* they go on, and nobody but those two people know the truth—and often even they try to ignore the implications of that knowledge. It might seem unlikely, but I've seen it and, to some extent, I lived it. I imagine people in Pompei stopped paying attention to the rumblings after a bit and talked about more important matters. The price of bread, the quality of fish oil . . .

There was a movie that came out about that time called *The Servant*. It's about an upper-class man who hires a manservant, and that manservant, through psychological and sexual gamesmanship, gradually takes over the household.

The two men exchange positions. The weak becomes strong. The strong becomes weak and dependent. The theme song, sung by Cleo Laine, is a jazzy little number entitled "*All Gone*."[4] The film works on several levels: politically, it is about the fecklessness of the powerful, who assume they will always be giving orders; psychologically, and more hauntingly, it is about the porousness of personality, the permeability of all that seems most substantial about us, about our circumstances. I've seen something similar happen, at times, in court, during the divorce process, where the party assumed to be in in a more powerful, unassailable position, the party in control, is undone either by the pressure of circumstance, or emotion, or feelings of regret, and turns out to be the weaker, more vulnerable party.

There was a girl in my high school, Marilyn—I've never forgotten her name—a fellow student, extremely smart, who became pregnant. She was in class one day and gone the next. She never came back. Nothing was ever said publicly, but we all knew why and spoke about it among ourselves. Her vanishing was a caution but also a warning: you could be made to disappear. The same thing happened to a young woman named Honor, in my class at Barnard. For the generations of women born after the Pill, it may be hard to understand just how the fear of pregnancy haunted our inner lives, shaped our dreams and our nightmares, determined and twisted our behavior—both before we were married and, often, after. Another example of our lives being governed not by what was said, what was told to us, but what was left unsaid. The Pill would change all that, just as the upheaval in divorce law would change many of the assumptions we made about marriage—all the folkloric, received wisdom we imbibed that shaped how we lived our lives, how we *understood* our lives. None of these changes guaranteed a happier or even a more fulfilling life. But they did seem to promise that even if we failed, that failure would be according to our own standards, and not the standards imposed upon us.

I think of all the women I knew those years ago in the dreaming suburb—friends, acquaintances, even the strangers I passed while shopping or just out on the street, and the life we lived that seemed so permanent, so impervious to change.

All gone.

The Women Men Don't See

I graduated from Barnard *cum laude*, with a BA in Latin and Greek and a Music minor. When we lived in Wilmington, I commuted to Bryn Mawr College, heavily pregnant with Marti, taking classes with all those sweet young girls, who looked at me as if I might be a messenger bringing ambivalent tidings from the future; as indeed, for so many of them, I probably was. I earned a Master's in Latin from Bryn Mawr; my thesis was on Seneca's role in the Pisonian Conspiracy against Nero (spoiler alert: guilty as charged). My interests were Latin and Greek and music, and I knew a lot about treason in Roman times. Now I had to find a job. What had my education prepared me for? It had prepared me to find a husband and live in suburban New York with four daughters and a failing marriage. Was anyone hiring or were all *those* positions filled?

There was a grim kind of humor about it. My father compared me to my cousin Eleanor, who went to Brooklyn College, came out with a teacher's degree, and now was making a comfortable living, with every summer off, teaching grade school. *But you*, he'd shake his head, *we spent all that money to send you to those fancy colleges and get those fancy degrees and you're unemployable.* I knew he was teasing (more or less), but it stung—partially because there was some truth to it, but mainly because I knew that, based on the uncertainties he'd experienced in his own life, Morris believed that everyone, women as well as men, should be able to earn a living.

I'd always felt that, sometime in an ill-defined future, I might teach Latin at the college level, but by the time I needed to get a paid job, I lacked the necessary qualifications. What I was qualified for, after passing a certification exam, was a position as a "permanent substitute" in the New York City public schools. And that was what I did for the next four years: taught math, five days a week, to seventh, eighth, and ninth graders. It was a bad time for me, my marriage had entered its death spiral, and a bad time for the public school system—with strikes, virulent arguments about parental control, and a lack of funding. I didn't do myself any good, and I know I didn't do many of my pupils any good. The job was both exhausting and unfulfilling—the cherry on top was that it didn't pay very well, either. But we needed every penny, and there wasn't anything else I could do. I just didn't see any way out. Both physically and emotionally, it was as close as I'd ever been to rock bottom.

But if life teaches us anything, it is that it is always possible to fall further. One evening Phil and I went to a cocktail party, and I was having a conversation with a man who asked me what I did. When I told him I was a junior high school teacher, I watched his eyes slide off me and search the room for someone interesting, someone who might have something intelligent to say. I'd have caused the same reaction if I'd said I was a housewife. This man, many men, didn't care what housewives or teachers—or, often enough, their wives or daughters—thought or did. They didn't pay attention to anything about them. A few weeks before, at a League of Women Voters meeting, I had been called "contented." I knew what was meant: I was blonde and blue-eyed, an aging co-ed, seemingly complacent, anxious to please, anxious that everyone get along. This sweet mother. I didn't say anything, but I'd felt insulted, as if I was being called a cow. A contented cow. A coward. I thought: I have to matter *more* than this. And now I was finding out that, in fact, I mattered *less*. I was invisible. I had nothing to offer, nothing to conceal. I'd always thought of myself as attractive. I was well educated, well read and well spoken. And now, without quite knowing how, I had become part of that vast involuntary cohort: The Women Men Don't See.[5]

There has been a good deal of feminist literature and theory published in the last decades, much of it focusing on the intersection of gender with social, legal, and cultural issues: the subtle, pervasive, often unplanned bias that permeates our institutions and benefits even those who are most enlightened and seemingly free of any *personal* bias. (*Keep her in line.*) We didn't have any sophisticated theories or books to help us understand our place in the scheme of things, and the only text we read was our own lives, our lived experience. Concepts such as "the male gaze" didn't yet exist. There was a more prosaic, though no less encompassing, way of putting it: It was a man's world. Men had all the power. They made the rules and, more importantly, they enforced the rules. And when that man, at that suburban cocktail party all those years ago, let his gaze shift from me and search the room for somebody, anybody else to speak with, that is when I made my decision.

A man's world. That's where I wanted to be. That's where I felt I belonged.

Cold Comfort

The decision I made was this: I was going to go to law school. I was going to become a lawyer. It seemed to me that lawyers were respected. People listened to what they had to say. They had gravitas. I wanted to be respected and to have my voice heard. I didn't want to be invisible. And the law seemed to provide the quickest and surest route to that end.

In addition, I knew lawyers. I was around them all the time: some were friends, others were neighbors or acquaintances. There was nothing intimidating about them. I thought, with the proper training, I could do what they did. I thought I could succeed.

But it was *a decision*. This was 1971, and women who wanted careers—not a job but a career—had to weigh the pros and cons, the pluses and minuses, and make a choice. Men had careers by assumption—that's what they did. It wasn't that simple for women then, and, even with all the changes brought about by the women's movement—all the changes we have experienced in law and custom—I know, from my family law practice, that it's not that simple now. Women remain the chief caregivers of the family, and it's often assumed—by the court and by the parties themselves—that the woman will fulfill that duty. I can't count the number of times a man has been lionized in court as a great father because he picks his kids up from school . . . once a week. What a shining exemplar! The wife, who does it the other four days, and then takes the kids to weekend activities and to the doctor and to the dentist and does the shopping—not so much. Because it is expected of her. By her husband, by the legal system, by her children, and, most often, by herself, as well.

When I told Phil *my* decision, he said, "Over my dead body." He meant he wasn't going to pay for it, which, given the state of our finances, his refusal to change his spendthrift ways, was probably true whether he wished to or not. But he wasn't warning me only about money. He knew that my decision to go to law school was a threat to our marriage—in a way that his spending, his absence, his anger and emotional parsimony was not. And it was a threat to *him*, to how he thought of himself in relation not only to me and our family, but to others. To himself. We both valued education, and now I was planning to become more educated, more accomplished, while he remained the uninterested businessman, with his shiny toys and desultory flirtations, eking out a living just this side of outright failure.

So I went to my parents and asked them to advance me whatever money they were planning to leave me as my inheritance. My mother said, "If you go to law school, your husband will leave you. Your marriage will be over."

"Well," I said, "If he's going to leave me don't you think I should prepare for it, prepare to make a living and take care of myself and my daughters?"

A pretty good answer, one I'd thought about and carefully considered. But I didn't have an answer to the next thing she said.

"This is not your time," she told me. "This is the time for the children."

I didn't have an answer because there is none. There is only will and determination. It *was* the children's time. I knew that just as I knew there would be consequences *for me*, stemming from the decision I was making. I was prepared to pay those consequences. That was my choice. But there would also be consequences—serious consequences—damaging consequences—for the people I loved most in the world—my daughters, aged eight to 18—and I was making that decision for them. They had no choice, but they would pay for it just the same—and continue paying for it, in one way or another, for the rest of their lives.

This is a problem, in my experience—both personal and professional—unique to women; a burden only we bear. I told myself then, and I believe now, that I made the right decision—that going to law school, which precipitated the end of my marriage, was ultimately the best choice for *all* of us. But believing you are right—even being right—can be very cold comfort as when I brought Patti to class with me even though she was sick with a cold and fever. I had to—there was no one at home to take care of her. Or when I forced my daughter Susie to go to a local college rather than the one she had chosen. I sacrificed her dream for her, but I couldn't let her go. I needed her at home to help me. By this time Phil had walked out and there was no one else. We were all alone.

The Shakes

One of the lawyers I knew was I. Leo Glasser, a distinguished professor of law at Brooklyn Law School. He and his wife, Grace, were very close friends, and Leo spoke to the Dean about the possibility of my being admitted. Without his help, I don't know if it would have happened. There was much I had to overcome, many obstacles I faced, but I also benefited from great good fortune: in race, in class, in friends, in simply having good and generous parents. And there was one other factor, a surprising one, that played to my advantage. In 1971, the modern feminist movement was beginning to make its presence felt in politics, in culture, and in society at large. And many institutions and businesses were actively looking to recruit women—token or otherwise. Including Brooklyn Law School.

I was the right gender, at the right place, at the right time, and was admitted to law school in the spring of 1971. I had no doubt I could do the work and was anxious for September and the beginning of classes. So that spring I visited Brooklyn Law School, just to see what it looked like. And except for the librarian, Lucy Jurow, I didn't see a single woman. All the deans were men. All the teachers, all the professors were men. There wasn't a single woman on the faculty. I found a place to sit in the classroom, and every student I saw was a man. A very young man. Forget about doing the work, I didn't think I'd even know how to buy the required textbooks. It was a warm spring day, and I was exactly where I wanted to be, but all my confidence vanished. I started shaking. Literally shaking.

4 CHATTERING YOUNG MEN

Returnees

I was thirty-eight years old, the second oldest member of my class. The oldest, at forty-three, was a woman named Joan Koven, and we became good friends. Two other women, one in her thirties and the other in her twenties, Helen Neuborne and Gail Alpern (Schneider), also became friends, and together we formed a study group. It was unusual, at that time, for women of our age to be back in school, and we three older women became known as "The Returnees." I don't remember who named us, but it stuck, and that was how the school first knew us; even our professors referred to us that way. We had taken different paths to Brooklyn Law School, but it was more than circumstance that united us. We had all seen enough of life to understand the great opportunity that lay before us, and we were all determined to make the most of it. And we did. Each of the Returnees made the Law Review at the end of that first year. We were members throughout our entire time in school.

In 2020, Brooklyn Law School named me "Alumna of the Year," and feted me at the annual luncheon that was attended by my family, friends, co-workers from my law firm, deans and faculty from the school, and members of the class of 1974, some of whom had first met me half a century ago, an apprehensive and financially desperate woman trying to navigate a new and unexpected world.[1] It was an honor to be Alumna of the Year, but the enduring honor is simply to be known as an alumna. Everything I am, everything I was able to become and to achieve, has its roots in that school.

Joan Koven clerked for a federal judge and was, for a time, an associate at a prestigious New York City law firm. Ten years after graduating, she returned to Brooklyn Law School where, for the next twenty years, until her retirement, she taught Family Law and served as Associate Dean for Alumni Affairs. It might be said that she came to Brooklyn Law and never left. In a sense, an abiding emotional sense, neither did I.

Revelations

I was a student at Barnard College sixteen, seventeen years old, when it came to me with the force and clarity of a revelation, that my mother and father were ignorant. They were captive to old-world habits and mores, hamstrung by old-world fear and superstition, ill-equipped by nature and ill-prepared by choice to navigate the world in which they found themselves. This feeling is common in adolescents and even stronger in the children of immigrants, where language itself often becomes the focus of confusion and conflict. It's all there in a play like *Golden Boy* by Clifford Odets or in the novels of Henry Roth (*Call it Sleep*) or Daniel Fuchs (*Summer in Williamsburg*). I had always been, was *expected* to be, more capable than my parents, and now I felt smarter, as well. I was ashamed of them then, as I am ashamed of myself now for ever having believed that this was true.

Brooklyn Law School afforded me a second revelation, less transient and more humbling: I didn't know anything; or, more accurately, I didn't know why I knew what I knew. I didn't know how to think. The law appeared to offer an intellectual precision that mirrored the precision I had found and embraced in my study of music and of Latin and Greek, but the scope was more encompassing: rather than etymology and linguistic discipline, or the construction and progression of a series of chords, I believed that I was being shown a new, more rigorous way of understanding the world, and of evaluating my own experience within that world. I couldn't help thinking back to those interminable cocktail parties in the dreaming suburb—the men, and they were mostly men, endlessly pontificating to a group of nodding and silent women. It was this experience that had propelled me into law school, but it now seemed to me that those men had no idea what they were talking about, were offering opinions and prejudices masquerading as fact, and their belligerent self-assurance and apparent authority were part of that masquerade. As were, in many cases—as I had reason to know—their marriages.

I can still feel the exhilaration of those days, the sense of wonder and fulfillment, as if the pulse of my new life was beating beneath the skin of this unhappy and increasingly artificial life that I was living. I embraced it with the enthusiasm of a convert—and a convert's blind fervor, as well. While the law that I was taught in the classroom and the law that I practice in the courtroom and in negotiations have more than a nodding acquaintance with each other, they are not the same. The precision I sought and found at Brooklyn Law School, the precision I still treasure, that clarity of purpose, has often proven, over the years, as illusory as the belief in my parents' ignorance. Each client, each case, every negotiation is different. Think of a musical note, which, when written down, has an absolute value in pitch and duration but which sounds different when played by an amateur or when played by a master. And it also sounds different to the *listener* based on habit, knowledge, and preconception. Which is why the same piece of music exists simultaneously as the fourth movement of the overture to Rossini's opera *William Tell* and as the theme to *The Lone Ranger.* The law is similar, offering a kind of "transactional" precision, shaped and tempered by time and experience, that varies from case to case and from client to client, always different but, at the same time, always true, always valid.

Brooklyn Law School provided that essential bedrock, though it took some time for me to understand that my education, which I thought was complete, was really only just beginning. The confidence the school provided enabled me not only to better understand the past, and the choices I had made, but to envision—and to begin to create, however slowly, however fumblingly—a different future both for myself and for my four daughters. That confidence is with me still. It never changed, although just about everything else did.

The World as It Is: II

In the spring of 2002, Ruth Bader Ginsburg, associate justice of the Supreme Court of the United States, gave a lecture at the Wilson Center in Washington, D.C., entitled *Litigating for Gender Equality in the 1970s.* During that time, Ginsburg had been director of the Women's Rights Project at the ACLU, spearheading a nationwide effort to break down legal discrimination against women. The balance of her talk focused on the first three or four years of the decade, presenting a detailed picture of the world I had known as a student at Brooklyn Law School, the world I graduated into in 1974. The Associate Justice had been one year behind me at James Madison High School in Brooklyn, and when I first knew her she wasn't Ruth Bader Ginsburg or even Ruth Bader. She was Kiki Bader, a cheerleader, proudly wearing the school colors of black and gold, shaking her pom poms on the sidelines of the football field and shouting:

> *James Madison High*
> *For two cents I would spit in your eye.*

Decades later I was a sponsor of one of her last public appearances in 2020, the year she died, so, as they say, I knew her before the beginning and just about after the end.

"What was the mission in the 1970s?" Ginsburg began her speech in 2002.[2]

The grand aim was to place women's rights permanently on the human rights agenda. . . . We worked on three fronts: We sought to advance, simultaneously, public understanding, legislative change, and change in judicial doctrine. In one sense, our mission was easy: the targets were well defined. There was nothing subtle about the way things were.

She then proceeded to give examples of this "target-rich" environment by citing a number of state and federal laws, including Idaho's version of the so-called "domicile rule" that prevailed in many states:

The husband is the head of the family. He may choose any reasonable mode or place of living, and the wife must confirm thereto.

California's Penal Code made it a misdemeanor to use "indecent language within the presence or hearing of women or children."

Florida placed no women on the jury rolls . . . out of patriarchal concern for women's place at "the center *of home and family life.*"

There were many other instances. In municipalities all across the country, for example, in virtually every state, it was illegal for a married woman to use what was then called her "maiden" name or birth name. She couldn't get a loan, buy insurance, take out a mortgage, or be employed, unless she used her husband's last name. In one case in Wisconsin, in 1971—a case so egregious that the Women's Rights Project at the ACLU filed an amicus curiae brief, written by Ginsburg—a county circuit judge ruled that *"it is well settled by immemorial custom that a woman upon marriage abandons her maiden name and assumes her husband's surname"* and that if she refused to do so *"it would be better for them, any children they might have and society in general that they do not enter into the marriage relationship."*[3]

The judge may have been wrong about the case and confused about the law, but he well understood the stakes in play: *society in general.* As did Justice Ginsburg, looking back in 2002, at the revolution she had helped to instigate:

> *Our mission was to educate, along with the public, decision makers in the nation's legislatures and courts. We tried to convey to them that something was wrong with their perception of the world.*[4]

One of the more difficult aspects of the struggle was to convince lawmakers and opinion makers, overwhelmingly white and overwhelmingly male, that the legal obstacles they created and enforced to "protect" women—what Justice William Brennan would call "romantic paternalism"—actually imprisoned women, denying them full participation not only in society but in their own lives.[5] There was widespread bewilderment, even anger, that so many weren't grateful for these "protections" but instead supported efforts to remove them.

This was a revolution *in mind* ("their perception of the world") as well as in law, and it affected every aspect of the society at large and the culture in general:

Our Bodies, Ourselves, published in 1970, is a groundbreaking work on women's health and sexuality.

The Equal Rights Amendment passed both houses of Congress in 1971, setting off a bitter twilight struggle over ratification.

The Supreme Court, in 1971, ruled for the first time ever that a woman had been denied equal protection by state or federal law.

The launching of *Ms. Magazine* in December 1971.

The approval by the United States Printing Office in February 1972 of the use of "Ms." in official government documents.

The Supreme Court's decision in *Roe v. Wade*, in January 1973, which seemed a culmination of sorts but which proved that legal victories, like revelations, can be equally illusionary and that any battle worth fighting will likely have to be fought again.

And again.

Chattering Young Men

I went to law school because I believed it promised entree into the world of men, the only world, I thought, of any real consequence, but even during my first semester, it became clear that the world I was preparing myself to enter was vanishing—changing in ways that would have seemed unthinkable only a short time before. It didn't change fast enough, because it never does, and it didn't change thoroughly enough, and it still hasn't—and perhaps it never will. But it was impossible to mistake the fact that it was changing, in ways that were both visceral and apparent.

When I began my studies in the fall of 1971, I was one of ten women in a class section of 100 students—10 percent—and the school had hired its first female faculty member, Professor Nancy H. Fink. These steps, small as they may appear in retrospect, seemed momentous at the time and provided a comforting backdrop to a student, like me, eighteen years out of graduate school, anxious about the reception I would receive and fearful about my ability to cope.

But as it turned out there was nothing to worry about. I was treated, all the Returnees were treated, like royalty—encouraged and supported by our fellow students, welcomed into an academic world of the highest standards, and taught by professors who were brilliant, dedicated, inspired, and inspiring. The work was, at times, daunting—as was the entire academic atmosphere—but the faculty seemed to take us under its wing, giving us every opportunity to succeed as students and prosper as professionals. In part, I think this was because our teachers recognized how important this was for the three of us. We worked, we studied, as if our lives depended on it—as, indeed, in a very real sense, it did. No one worked harder than the three of us, no one was more prepared or determined. By our presence and by our example, we changed Brooklyn Law School forever. And the school, in turn, changed us.

The students as a whole, 90 percent young men, saw the Returnees at first as a curiosity and then as an object of fascination. They asked to be part of our study group, to join us at lunch, and flitted about us constantly; when I think about that time, the never-ending soundtrack is always the same: chattering young men. Coming from a household of females it wasn't unpleasant, and the occasional—

and sometimes more than occasional—sexual propositions were, in their way, flattering. Not at all feasible, for a variety of reasons, but flattering.

The attention I received from both students and faculty, my ability to thrive in an atmosphere of academic competition, and the sheer joy of learning, of being, for the first time in a long time, in control of my own life, added up to a feeling of confidence and freedom. The freedom, the sense of release a mother can feel when she knows that the children are being cared for by somebody else. Even if, in my case, the somebody else was the other children.

The Home Front

Every morning, five days a week, I left our home in the Rockaways and drove to law school on Joralemon Street in downtown Brooklyn. I'd spend the day in classes, or working with my study group, or doing research in the library. These were pre-internet days and if you wanted to use the library or any of the other school facilities you couldn't just open a laptop and log-in, you had to be there, turning the hard copy pages of a law book or flipping through the card catalogue searching for the corresponding Dewey Decimal numbers that would tell you where you needed to go. If you wanted to read a law journal you had to hold it in your hands. If you wanted to take notes on an obscure legal ruling from the nineteenth century, you had to hunt it down in the stacks. Most evenings I arrived home around dinner time, at least that was the plan, but there were occasions when that was not possible, when I was working late in the library or attending an evening lecture. At this time, when I began law school in the fall of 1971, Marti was eighteen, Amy was sixteen, Susie was going on thirteen, and Patti, the youngest, was eight years old.

Phil came and went as he chose. That was the agreement I had made with him in order to keep the marriage intact: I would make no demands on his time and would ask no questions. He would disappear for a day or so, come home, then be off again. I'd examine his closet, sort through the clothes he left behind, to try to divine how long he might be gone and whether he intended to keep his promise and eventually return. It was nerve-wracking when he was away, but it was worse when he was home. His anger at me, his unhappiness with himself and near total disinterest in his children, was something palpable, you could feel it within you, a presentiment of regret and disaster. And yet when he was gone, I anxiously waited for his return, as did my daughters, his children, dreading and longing.

There was never enough money; it was a constant worry. Phil contributed when he felt like it, but it was never anything you could count on. His parents were very well off, and once I went to them, explaining the situation, and asking if they might help with the household expenses for the well-being of their granddaughters. They more or less slammed the door in my face, telling me that this was something for a husband and wife to deal with; it was no concern of theirs. They never contributed a penny. My own parents were paying for my education and for part of everything else, including the salary of a woman named Kitty Covington, who lived with us, did much of the cooking—my daughter Amy did her share, as well—and helped keep things running when I was away at school.

At that time, and in the community in which we lived—and other, similar communities—it was unusual for a mother not to be home all day. There were working women—but they were few and far between—none of my friends had a job—and for a woman to return to school in her forties was almost unheard of. Patti remembers being at a friend's and being served tuna noodle casserole and thinking how nice it would be to have a mother who was home and made a hot lunch. A working mom is now a commonplace, and there are all types of programs—preschool, after school, intramural—that both ease the burden and normalize the choices that are made. No child is made to feel odd or "different," much less abandoned, because a parent isn't always at home. There were none of those programs back then; the idea of putting a two-year-old into daycare would have seemed like child abuse. You were very much on your own, and whatever difficulties you encountered were yours to solve while, at the same time, the culture seemed to suggest that a working mother or an ambitious mother was a bad mother and was failing her children.

When my daughters and I talk about that time, we tend to focus on those factors that drew us together. Patti remembers how nice the Brooklyn Law School students were to her when I had to bring her to class because there was no one at home to care for her. Amy remembers cooking a well-received dinner. All of us remember those times when the five of us sat at the dining room table together, doing our homework; and there are other shared moments of support and encouragement, of can-do/ourselves alone enthusiasm. Happy memories tend to be communal; less happy memories are an orphan, and because our story ends happily we tend to focus on the former rather than the latter, on those memories we can celebrate together, as a close and loving family. But I know my daughters have other memories of that time, moments of anger and confusion, wounds that have never fully healed, memories of grievance and guilt and sacrifice that are never fully shared either with myself or with the other sisters. I know some of those angers and some of that collateral damage and recognize myself as the cause of those grievances, but others remain a mystery.

Even the happy stories, the comforting tales that have become part of our family legend, contain mysteries. Patti's story about being taken as an eight-year-old to Brooklyn Law School has changed over the years, softened in the telling, until the focus has become how nice everyone at the school treated her. But contained within that story is a second story, this one about a mother so determined not to miss a single day of school, or bend to circumstance and take a day off to care for her daughter, instead takes the child, woozy with fever, with her. She leaves her in the back of the drafty classroom with a notebook and pencil, some toys to amuse her, while the mother attends class in the front. This version of the story is less about the child than about the mother, and the gravitational force of personality and will, and all those whose orbit is determined—and distorted—by that force.

Everything is a double, including perhaps most particularly, the stories we tell ourselves.

Last Tango

I was never going to divorce Phil. Divorce was a failure, and I was determined not to fail; determined as well not to be *seen* as having failed. In the socially conservative community in which I was raised, divorce was not a private affair but was an occasion of public shame, a *moral* failure, and I didn't want either myself or my daughters to be shamed. Among all my family, my friends, and acquaintances, I knew of only one woman who had been divorced, and when someone spoke of her, they lowered their voice. It was considered a scandal.

I had no illusions about regaining my husband's love or his desire, but we had four beautiful daughters, and it seemed to me tragic that he couldn't see what he had in them, which was the world. I'd known since shortly after Marti was born that Phil wasn't cut out to be a father, that he was deeply unhappy in that role, but what could I do with that knowledge? I went, as many women do, from: *Why doesn't he see,* to *What can I do to make him see?* And the answer is always: nothing. But you can't be told that. You have to live it. And I did.

Randall Jarrell, the poet and critic, once wrote that there is nothing so uncomfortable that someone won't sit in it if you call it a chair.[6] To paraphrase: there is no relationship so toxic that *someone* won't stay in it if you call it a marriage. I know this is true from decades of family law practice, but I also know it is true from my own life. I was that somebody.

The arrangement I'd reached with Phil—no demands, no questions, no accountability—proved too difficult for me to honor. I was anxious all the time, never knowing where he was, never knowing when or if he might come home, never knowing how to reach him—this was before cell phones, and there was no way to find him. We were all suspended between one type of life and another, and the apprehension and uneasiness were unbearable. When I spoke with Phil, he expressed a degree of weariness with some of his own choices, and when I asked him to return home, he agreed. And so we resumed the simulacrum of a marriage. Father went to work each morning and came home each night. Mother and the kids went to school. We occasionally managed to have dinner together as a family. It couldn't last.

Phil's weariness was short-lived. At some point he began a relationship with a woman who considered herself my friend. I don't believe it was anything serious. Suburban shenanigans. By this time, I wasn't all that easy to hurt, but Phil never lost interest in trying.

The end came in May 1973, two weeks before my second year final exams at Brooklyn Law School. At Phil's suggestion we went to see "Last Tango in Paris," a *succés de scandale* that was, at the time, considered a landmark of world cinema, one critic predicting that it would have a lasting cultural impact comparable to Stravinsky's revolutionary *The Rite of Spring.*[7] No one remembers it now except, perhaps, for its abundant nudity and the vigorous simulated sex scenes between 48-year-old Marlon Brando and 22-year-old Maria Schneider that include anal sodomy via the aid of a stick of butter and a scene where Brando slams Schneider against a wall while they pretend to have sex. The middle-aged protagonist played by Brando is seen as the progenitor of a type of sexual violence that protects his wounded heart and pales in comparison to the emotional violence he is subjected to by la belle dame sans merci. The sensitive, potent male undone by the unfeeling female—pure fantasy that spoke to the cultural moment and was right up Phil's alley. He was fascinated by the film, aroused and psychologically stimulated. It seemed to crystallize for him all that he was missing, all that he had given up, everything he had wanted once and found that he still wanted. Phil was tired of pretending to be a husband, tired of pretending to be a suburban dad. It was time to pretend to be something else. The next day he left me.

He came out of the bedroom into the living room carrying a suitcase, a single suitcase. I asked what he was doing and where he was going. He said, "I'm leaving. And I'm not coming back." I begged him to stay. I rarely cry, but I started sobbing, imploring him to change his mind. I fell to my knees and grabbed onto his leg. He kept walking, dragging me along the floor. When he reached the front door, he leaned down and disengaged my hands.

"What's going to happen to us?" I said.

He looked down with absolutely no expression on his face.

"You'll be just fine," he said.

* * *

I looked after my daughters, and I studied for my finals. That was my salvation, immersing myself in work. Two weeks later I took four exams and received straight A's.

It was hard to see a path forward, and I struggled to provide for my daughters and myself. It was the most harrowing time of my life. During the three months from May to September, when I started my final year of law school, I lost over twenty pounds.

I didn't see or speak to Phil again until the fall, when he stopped by the house to see the girls. When he saw me, the first thing he said was, "You look terrific." Then: "You're so thin."

I graduated from Brooklyn Law School the following May. I was eighth in my class. *Cum Laude*. Law Review.

I applied for various jobs. I was forty-one years old, alone, with four daughters, a mortgage, and very little money.

The next month, in June 1974, I met Arthur Feinberg, and everything changed.

Case 1: No Disgrace to Be Poor

I

At the time I graduated from Brooklyn Law School I don't think any of my professors or teachers or lecturers had ever written a prenuptial agreement. I *know* that I never wrote one in the five and a half years I practiced law between my graduation and the passage of marriage reform legislation in New York State, the state in which I practice law, in 1980, and none of my mentors or the other lawyers with whom I worked in those years had ever written one, either. The only prenuptial agreements that were then permissible involved the waiver of death rights, because the genesis of prenups involved elderly, sometimes infirm men, who, upon the death of their first wife, married the housekeeper or the nurse. It was thought in the public interest to protect the children of the first wife, the "real" family, from the mercenary designs of the predatory new woman, and these women were encouraged to sign away their death rights in exchange for paltry financial settlements. So prenups were never written by matrimonial attorneys—it went against public policy to even *mention* divorce in a prenup prior to 1980—they were written by estate lawyers. And they had to be written up with great formality and with great care.[8]

All of this began to change after the reform passed by the State Legislature. Where previously a prenuptial agreement could only deal with financial matters linked to *death*, the post-reform prenup opened things up and could explicitly address finances related to the other two "d's" of married life: *during* and *divorce*—that is, how the marriage will work while it is intact and presumably happy; and what will happen when the marriage is over. About the only issues you can't address in a prenup have to do with children: child custody, child support. Everything else is fair game and it can get extremely detailed, covering everything from macro issues like penalties—sometimes extraordinarily high penalties—to be paid in case of infidelity or desertion, to micro issues like who gets the dog if the marriage is dissolved. Or sometimes—who doesn't get the dog. I had one client whose husband agreed to pay her a penalty of a quarter of a million dollars just to make sure he wouldn't end up with a biting Alsatian named Hub. And my client wasn't all that happy, telling me later we should have held out for half a million.

Reform took divorce out of the hands of estate lawyers, whose work in this matter was legally restricted and largely by rote, and into the hands of matrimonial attorneys, who could be much more creative and who learned to maneuver within the corners and shadows of the new law. But one thing didn't change: a prenuptial agreement is a contract and, as such, subject to the same regulations, disciplines, and strictures as all other contracts.

This traces back to the fact that a prenup has to be executed with great care and formality, "in the manner of a deed," and that's important because deeds transfer real property and real property is the bedrock of our common law. Things that are done in writing, having to do with real property, have to be completed in a difficult, exact, and sanctioned manner because something very important is happening: someone is getting something and someone is giving something up and the law wants to make sure that everyone involved understands what is happening. In real estate contracts there is what's called a "to have and to hold" clause. It might sound romantic, but it is anything but—it refers to the transfer of a property and any accompanying restrictions. And a prenup has to be executed in exactly the same manner, with the same formality, as a transfer in real property—every word matters, every comma has to be in the right place because if it isn't there is a chance the prenup will not be upheld.

But if a prenup is a contract, it's an unusual one, and you don't have to possess a law degree to begin to understand just how unusual it actually is. To begin with: I wouldn't hazard a guess as to how many millions of contracts are brokered in the United States each year, but I am confident that relatively few of those contracts involve parties who are in love with one another; or are operating under a restrictive, time constraint: i.e., the date of the wedding. These two factors contribute to an atmosphere—a combination of love, anxiety, anticipation, regret, fear, and greed—that is, to put it mildly, unconducive to straightforward discussion and quick agreement. In a long career I can probably count on one hand the number of prenup negotiations that have gone simply and smoothly—by and large they are difficult, emotionally wearing, and unpleasant; and most matrimonial attorneys, in my experience, would say the same.

Obviously, intense negotiations about finances between two emotionally connected individuals, conducted in the shadow of romance, with a self-imposed time limit, are never going to be easy, but there are additional complicating factors that seem peculiar to prenups. As with any contract there is a good deal of boilerplate in these agreements that serve to emphasize that the signatories understand their responsibilities, are not under duress, are competently represented by counsel and on and on—the purpose of which is to clarify to the parties themselves and, if eventually and unhappily necessary, to the court that everyone involved understands the terms to which they are agreeing. But there is in prenups additional boilerplate designed not to clarify but to obscure: clauses that typically begin: *Whereas we want a harmonious marriage without any misunderstanding; Whereas we want to demonstrate the love we have for one another; Whereas, with love and respect, we want to show each other the high regard with which we enter this marriage . . .* Anytime you see this type of phrase you can be sure that someone is getting robbed. It's the legal equivalent of saying: *With all due respect.* No one ever follows that up with: With all due respect, you're a genius. They say: With all due respect, you're a dope. The words, and there are a lot of them in a prenuptial agreement, are used as a cover for what is actually happening, a ritualized choreography of misdirection. It can be an education, a brutal education, for someone with romantic ideals about partnership and fairness: what used to be called, in the nineteenth century, the College of Talk and Take.

The 1980 reform was part of the "Divorce Revolution," a nationwide effort to reimagine marriage, acknowledging the romantic foundation of the institution while, at the same time, bringing to it a measure of fairness that had hitherto been absent.[9] The prenuptial agreement hollows out the central premise of reform, marriage as an economic partnership, and replaces it with a vision of marriage as, essentially, a business deal—but not a deal between equals; a deal in which there is a clear winner and a clear loser. Everything benefits the person with money. That's the way of things, although it can get confusing for the parties involved because it's all mixed up with ideas of love and romance. But no one enters a prenup to give. People enter into it to take, or to take away. Or to protect, to conserve what they have or what they believe they will have. Think of a prenup as a machine that runs forever, designed to protect the Haves from the depredations of the Have Nots. As one of my partners put it: You have to have a strong stomach to negotiate one of these.

"It's no disgrace to be poor," the saying goes, "but it might as well be."[10]

In the first decades of my practice, the Have Not was inevitably the woman who, knowingly, surrendered her rights and many of the benefits the law made available to her, in exchange for harmony, a marriage ceremony, a family, and what she believed was love. I don't doubt that in many instances this was seen as a fair trade-off. I do know that in many instances it was not. Now that most families consist of two earners, there is a greater degree of economic parity, and it is not always the man who is in a position of power and wealth during these negotiations. I represented a young woman in prenup negotiations prior to her same sex marriage, and if you mixed and matched all the assets of my client, who was in graduate school, it wouldn't amount to a fraction of the $15 million fortune of her fiancée. And the fiancée insisted on one of the more onerous prenups I have ever seen. The terms were so harsh, the woman so unshakable in her demands, that I urged my client not to sign. But my client was in love, she wanted to get married and start a family, and that made her vulnerable, and vulnerable people always give up too much. In the end, she signed, and I sent her a note to the effect that I had urged her not to.

This type of note—CYA is the term of art within the profession, and it means just what you think it does—protects the attorney and the prenup agreement itself, from potential legal challenges that may surface years later. A former client, now involved in a divorce action, might ask the judge: *How could my lawyer let me sign something so unfair?*—and it simplifies matters if the answer can be found in the case file itself. In any event it is extremely difficult to have a prenup thrown out of court—it almost never happens. Pregnancy (*I didn't want my child born out of wedlock*), the imminence of the wedding date (*My family had traveled thousands of miles; I couldn't disappoint them*) and other factors have been put forward amid claims a signature was obtained under duress—and the Manhattan courts have rejected them wholesale. It is different in every state in the union, but where I practice even the fact that the significant other has misrepresented the extent of his or her financial holdings has been ruled insufficient cause to reject the prenup. Public policy holds that people have the freedom to enter into a contract and to expect that the contract will be upheld. As a result, no matter how harsh the stipulations, in New York the legal presumption, with few exceptions, is against anyone seeking to invalidate that contract.

Like all matrimonial attorneys I have represented both Haves and Have Nots, and if asked which is preferable, I think, in a general sense, most lawyers would concur: We represent all our clients to the best of our ability. In a narrower sense it's like asking: Which would you rather be, the hammer or the nail? Obviously the former, with all the power, is easier and might be considered preferable, but the temptation, if you are a hammer, is to see *everything* as a nail and that's where things can get tricky. A wealthy client can demand so much, can force a vulnerable partner to surrender so many rights, that the resulting prenuptial agreement is not upheld because, by the standards of contract law, it is said to "shock the conscience"—that is, to be seen as grossly unjust to the observer. It's called an "Unconscionable Agreement," and what that means, in layman's terms, is that the judge has examined the prenup and concluded that no one in their right mind would sign it and no fair person would demand it. The law permits someone to take a lot, but not to take *everything*, and it is up to the attorney to make sure their client is grabbing with one hand, not with both. What can result is a series of intense negotiations to determine exactly what the Have will give *back* to the Have Not in order to assure that the contract will hold up in court. Having been on both sides of this matter, it's safe to say the Haves surrender as little as possible.

Of course there are occasions when time and chance, fate or fortune conspire to undermine the meanest intentions and provide a satisfying measure of elemental justice that the court cannot. A woman, an artist, sought my help in an upcoming divorce action she had brought against her husband. Prior to their marriage he had insisted on a very strict prenup which rigorously defined and kept separate his monies from her much more modest holdings. She hadn't wanted a prenup, hoping for some form of economic partnership. He declined, stating that he had to protect the rights and inheritance of the children from his first marriage. My client told me she had reluctantly signed the prenup, all the while worrying that power rather than filial devotion—he didn't seem to especially like his children—was the motivating force. Their marriage lasted twelve years and during that period an investment she had made—as a favor to a friend—in a small silicon valley start-up had doubled in value, doubled again, quadrupled, and then provided a multi-million dollar payout when the company was bought by a rival; a payout that dwarfed the fortune her husband had insisted on protecting. Now, during the divorce, he was exploring ways in which he might get his hands on a portion of that money by invalidating the prenup he had insisted upon. His lawyer even raised the possibility, in informal talks with me, that because he had been seeing a psychiatrist at the time of the marriage, the prenup was the product of an unsound mind and as such, could not be enforced.

The judge made short work of this argument and several others, and the prenuptial agreement provided the blueprint for the subsequent settlement.

I always caution my clients: Once you sign it, it's for keeps.

And that the only real opportunity you have to ameliorate the harshest conditions and terms of the prenup and provide for your client is before it's finalized. But that, particularly if you are representing the more vulnerable party, takes skill and nerve, a determination to see things through, a steely focus on your client's goal, and what I call "dimensional" thinking—a realistic and supple understanding of the changing dynamics of a situation or a relationship.

And luck.

II

John was a friend of one of my partners, and when his daughter, Laura, became engaged he asked if our firm would negotiate the prenup. My partner asked if I would be willing to handle the case and told me that John expected these negotiations to be "demanding" and that he was looking for a "bomber"—someone with the strength and stamina to vigorously defend his daughter's interests.

They came to my office on a cold morning in mid-February and we spoke for several hours. Laura worked as an assistant director of public affairs for an NGO involved in refugee resettlement. She was small—no more than 5 feet 1" or

2"—and slim, with open features, a friendly manner, and a cheerful personality that made her seem just a bit younger than her twenty-six years. Her father was a professor of international and public affairs at an Ivy League university. John was familiar with the broad outlines of my career and with a number of my more important cases and it was apparent within a very short time that we could work well together. In the event, he ended up participating in just about every aspect of the prenup negotiations, sometimes as a sounding board but more often as a kind of unofficial co-counsel. His advice and analysis were always to the point, rigorous and pertinent, and he possessed, in addition to a shrewd intelligence, an easy going temperament that was of particular importance in keeping his daughter calm during a very difficult period.

Laura and her fiancé, Daniel, had met about two years earlier and currently lived together in an apartment they jointly rented in lower Manhattan, not far from New York University. Daniel, a year younger than Laura, had graduated from college with a degree in graphic design and was attempting to earn a living as an artist and writer while also consulting on website design with various start-ups. He was the youngest of three children, with an older brother and sister, both of whom worked in the family business. His father, Matthew, ran that business and was personally worth several hundred million dollars. One day, Daniel was going to be a very wealthy man.

Laura told me that Daniel was apologetic that he was asking her to sign a prenuptial agreement, but Matthew was insisting and they both agreed it was simpler to acquiesce rather than create any difficulties as they made ready for their marriage. Daniel told her that the document being prepared was identical to the one his sister's husband had signed prior to *their* marriage. It had been negotiated (though I was beginning to doubt if this was the proper word) quickly and with little fuss or bother and Daniel told her he saw no reason why their prenup should be any different. Both she and Daniel were of one mind about these matters and they did not believe she would be asked to sign anything objectionable.

The idea of a "family" prenup—one size fits all—was a bit unusual, but it could simply mean that this was a more or less standard document that, with a minimum of mixing and matching, could be used more than once. Many matrimonial attorneys use a dummy "fill in the blanks" template for the most uncomplicated prenups—it saves the attorney time and the client money. But was this going to be an "uncomplicated" arrangement? Given the complexity that inevitably results from a fortune of this size, and the reputation of Matthew as a take no prisoners businessman, I very much doubted it but the path forward wouldn't reveal itself until I had the prenup in hand. Laura said she would inform Daniel that I had been retained as her attorney and that his attorney should send me the draft agreement they had prepared.

The contract that formalized the agreement between Laura and me, the retainer agreement, officially required Laura to pay my fees, but it was understood that Matthew would be picking up the entire cost of the negotiations for Laura's side as well as that of his son. This is not unusual in prenuptial cases or indeed in other matrimonial law cases, including divorce actions, where the party with the deeper pocket assumes responsibility for all costs and fees. It may seem odd or even illicit in some way, a violation of a basic principle that each side in a legal action pay their own way in order to avoid obvious concerns, including the fear that financial considerations might cause the lawyer for one side to roll over for the other. But there is an equally important policy mandate: there needs to be a level playing field, and so the deeper pocket is permitted, indeed encouraged, to pay the legal fees of the other party. It is very much in the interest of both sides, but most especially the advantaged side that is pressing for the prenup, that the other side be well and fairly represented. The more competent the representation of the Have Not, the more likely the prenup will be upheld, surviving any potential future court challenge.

The meeting was wrapping up, but before it did, I had a conversation with Laura and John about how, in general, I saw this process unfolding. I never talk down to a client, and I never sugarcoat, but no one can predict the future and I'm careful never to forestall hope. Nevertheless, it is extremely important at this point that the client and the attorney understand each other because a difficult prenup negotiation—and, despite Laura's expectations, there really isn't any other kind—can be a life-altering journey; an intense, time-limited journey from one life to another. Clients come to you one way, and the process, which can be very brutal, twists them into something else, and that is why the choice of an attorney, and the relationship between attorney and client, is extremely important. You are going to be working together, and you want to work with someone whose attitudes and principles and skills are compatible with your own.

I often represent clients in their twenties or early thirties, young men or women who are deeply in love, and what they don't understand—and what even older clients sometimes don't understand—is that negotiations about money create hostility between negotiators. Or they do understand but think it applies to everyone else but not to them. Laura can say to Daniel: *I love you for who you are. I don't care about your money.* And Daniel says to Laura: *It doesn't matter that you don't have money. Whatever I have, we will share.* And now Laura is sitting down, sitting in my office, twenty-six years old, and for the first time she has to confront what the money *really* means. It doesn't mean the flowers he buys or the jewelry or the places they go. It's like a time machine, a very slow time machine. You are looking into the future and seeing the prescription for your lifetime. You are seeing how this person, whom you love and who says he loves you, is going to treat you over the next fifty years: *This is mine. This is not going to be ours. You cannot have*

this. This is not for you. And now you know who you are going to marry. And most often, even after very ugly negotiations, they do marry but they see their intended in a different way. Of course, sooner or later the bloom is going to come off the rose, but with prenup negotiations it happens at a very poignant moment, when couples are most in love, anticipating the life they will have together.

It was February 16th. Laura was already deep into planning her wedding, which was set for early September, roughly seven months away.

* * *

The following day I received an email from Daniel's lawyers with their draft of the prenuptial agreement attached. My usual process is to open the document, give it a quick once-over, start inputting my comments, and then set aside time for a deeper, more critical read. I'll make extensive notes, highlight key passages, look for points of agreement or areas where compromise seems, if not easy, at least most likely, and try to identify those red lines that signify what the other side is actually trying to protect. I read the document, study it, but I also give myself enough time to *listen* to it, because the numbers tell a story and the organization of the paragraphs I am reading, the structure of the sentences, can provide a meaning that is parallel to and often more significant than the words themselves. I want to understand what the other side's agenda is so I can work effectively, within those parameters, to get my client as fair a deal as can be obtained without encroaching upon the other side's legitimate concerns. There are areas where it's going to be impossible to reach agreement and you want to mark those off because, especially in cases like this where I am representing the less advantaged party, it's important to keep in mind that you are going to have to give or give up—and sometimes give up a lot—in order to get. The advantaged party has it all over the less advantaged, the Have over the Have Not—in life and in the law—so it is important to develop a pragmatic strategy to serve your client's interests. That always begins with a close read of the document itself.

The physicist Ernest Rutherford said: "All science is either physics or stamp collecting."[11] That's what I'm trying to do in my analysis of the prenup: separate the physics from the stamp collecting.

That's the *usual* process, but there was nothing usual about the prenup I'd been sent. I'd never seen anything like it. It was long, twice or three times as long as any previous prenup I'd ever worked with. It just went on and on, clause after clause, each provision seven, eight, or nine pages long, extended, repetitious, prohibitive—hammering home the same elements again and again—and then once again. It was brutal and uncompromising and I actually had to stop reading at several points because I could feel my heart beating—a kind of breathless anticipation of calamity. It was, in its own way impressive, as something sleek and malign can be impressive, consciously designed to bludgeon the opposing lawyer and the client into a kind of soporific acceptance of its key and only real point: *Everything for us.*

Nothing for you. When I printed out that document and looked at the huge and forbidding stack of paper on my desk, I felt something close to despair.

The specific points of the prenup were unrelenting and detailed—all physics, no stamp collecting—but the larger narrative sent two messages:

To Laura: Agree to this or there will be no wedding.

To me, and I'll put it politely: Don't *mess* with us.

When I first began practicing matrimonial law, I would sit at my desk, with the pages of a draft prenup spread out about before me and begin marking it up in pencil. And when I was finished I'd call the opposing counsel and I'd usually have to leave a message: *There are some points we have to talk about.* And then he or she would call me back: *Returning your call. Let's talk.* This would go on for a while and then we'd eventually make contact and go over a few issues and resolve nothing and both of us would refine our proposals and the whole process would begin again. Back and forth—all this motion but no movement. And while it's true advances in technology have changed not only the speed with which we can do our work but the very nature of the work itself—how we understand it, how we go about it—not everything has changed. It is still hellishly difficult to negotiate a prenup and the ease with which attorneys can now exchange marked up copies of a document doesn't make those negotiations any simpler. It usually just means that you get the bad news more quickly and in a starker context.

At its simplest, the problem boils down to this: a couple is preparing for their wedding at the same time as they are negotiating a blueprint for their divorce. Because that is what a prenup is; while it can, and often does, deal with issues arising from an intact marriage, it is essentially a map of dissolution. Clients cope with that fact in various ways. Some dig in their heels and up their demands, believing it is important to establish, early and firmly, the guardrails of the relationship with their intended. Surrender now and you will spend a lifetime surrendering. But others refuse to battle, believing that a bitter fight about money is the worst possible prelude to a successful marriage. I had a client, a music teacher at a private high school, who was marrying the heiress to one of the more famous old family fortunes in the country. They were both in their mid-thirties and neither had been married previously. I marked up the prenup they sent me and my client returned it to me with every change I had made crossed out. He undid all my work and told me to accept the prenup exactly as written, explicitly preventing me from changing or ameliorating any section of the document. He did not want it to appear that he was marrying for money or that he anticipated any financial advantage from the union. After I sent back the prenup—with no changes—the opposing lawyer called me and said his client was willing to consider a "marriage bonus:" a lump sum, one million dollars, to be deposited in my client's account on the day of the wedding. His fiancée wanted him to feel independent and to be able to afford the expenses accruing to his new life without having to ask for money all the time or constantly feeling indebted to her. My client turned down this suggestion, telling me that the marriage would succeed or fail on "her good will."

A client may decide to fight, a client may decide to "surrender," or, as with Laura, may choose a middle way—looking for the best, most fair deal possible in a system that bends toward unfairness. There's no one "correct" way to negotiate a prenup, just as there is no one way to ensure you will have a happy marriage. In my experience there are as many people motivated by a desire not to seem greedy or venal as there are hoping to strike it rich. But the system itself makes demands and has its own imperatives and unless you opt out—as did my music teacher client—it is almost impossible not to get caught in the undertow.

"I'm not a gold digger," Laura said to me at one point, when negotiations were particularly intense. "But this process is turning me into one."

When you study a document with care and intensity, examining it for long hours, it can sometimes seem as if you're inside it, seeing it from an unfamiliar angle, able to probe arguments and assumptions in new and illuminating ways. It's similar to what chess players describe, visualizing the board they are playing on transformed—no longer flat but three dimensional, with hills and valleys and culverts where an ambush can be prepared, or an outcropping behind which a knight or bishop can be hidden. My problem with the draft prenup prepared by Daniel's family was that there was no way *in*—it was all of a piece, a solid block of text and numbers that referred only to itself, imperious and intimidating. I didn't doubt it had been put together with that in mind, but if it was so constructed why couldn't it be deconstructed? If I couldn't get in, I'd open it up, take a good look at what I saw and bring it all *out*. And that's what I determined to do.

The first thing was to streamline it. The bulk, the weight of the proposal, created a reality of its own, and plowing through it was purposefully onerous. I removed every redundant phrase, eliminated every repeated clause, cleared away all the extraneous language and the duplicate figures, and ended up with a document shorter by about a third. It was still a formidable piece of work, still hammered away at a series of assertions and proposals damaging to my client but it didn't appear quite so daunting. I began working along the margins, looking for whatever small inroad I might make to help Laura; and at the same time making notes about what was important to the groom's side. Not the groom, the groom's *side*—because the more I was able to piece together the important elements of this proposal, the clearer it became that this wasn't about Daniel's future; or even, except in the most negative sense, about Laura's future. It was about Matthew, the fortune he had made, the family he had created and his desire to secure both.

That was the purpose of the draft prenup: to protect the interests of the family as Matthew defined those interests. The method by which this was accomplished was, broadly, to gut each section of the Marriage Reform Act and replace them with a series of one-off proposals, prejudicial to my client and damaging to her interests. Every major point was contested; every major right my client possessed was undermined. Here are just some of the areas of conflict:

In the event of divorce, Laura was to waive her right to spousal support—an area where the court is traditionally inclined to be generous—in exchange for a lump sum based on the span of the marriage—so much per year for every year that Laura and Daniel remained together. There was an additional one time payout if the marriage lasted ten years and produced a child. So these provisions were based on the duration of the marriage. But how to calculate that duration? The prenup stated that the marriage would be considered over upon an "operative event"—when one party notified the other that the marriage was over or filed for divorce. Death, of course, was also considered an "operative event."

I argued that the marriage was not over until the marriage was . . . over. Legally. When the divorce decree was actually granted—signed by the judge and filed with the county clerk. This wasn't an academic argument, a distinction without a difference. It can take a long time to get from the serving of a divorce summons to the entry of the judgment of divorce and to accept the other side's time frame could cost Laura hundreds of thousands of dollars.

In addition, when a party files for divorce, a series of "inchoate" rights immediately spring up the day the summons is served, as well as a web of restrictions, entangling both partners: for instance, the sale of property may be prohibited and insurance policies cannot be terminated. The goal is to prevent either party from taking unlawful financial advantage of the dissolving union. There's also a provision in the law that permits each counsel to examine the other side's financial documents dating back years in order to gain a comprehensive and accurate picture of the financial life of the family. This will reveal if there has been an illicit pattern of spending; or perhaps dodgy transfers of funds without due consideration; or actual dissipation of funds: gambling debts, payments to a girlfriend; all the costs of a second, secret life. The law is based on this "full and fair discovery" of financial documents but Laura was being asked to sign a prenup in which she explicitly waived her right to financial discovery.

I didn't believe opposing counsel was concerned about Daniel developing a gambling problem or acquiring a mistress. In fact, one of the odd aspects of this document was that it didn't seem concerned about Daniel at all except to the extent his rights and actions might entangle Matthew and Matthew's concerns, during the divorce process. What they wanted to do was completely wall off Laura from any information regarding the family business or the family fortune. She was required to waive all the rights that came into being once the divorce summons was served and waive, as well, her ability to examine documents that might provide information regarding *Daniel's* income from trusts or accounts or any other financial instruments linked to Matthew's business. The opposing counsel noted that the New York Child Support Standards Act explicitly permits such discovery in the event there is a dispute about child support; and they vowed to follow the letter of the law—before noting that Laura's waiver would cover all aspects of imputed and other income except for Daniel's personal sweat equity wages and therefore overrode the Act. It was a classic bait and switch—cite a law only to eviscerate it. A good example of what lawyers feel they can get away with when they have brute force backing them up. Laura was essentially being asked to operate in the dark as to finances in the event of divorce.

This was an extremely sensitive issue and recognized as such by opposing counsel—which is why there were all those boilerplate provisions Laura had to sign acknowledging: "I recognize that my rights would be different if I did not sign this document." This was a sensitive matter for our side, as well, as it touched on one of Matthew's recognized red lines: his business, and the need to keep all details insulated from purview by the court. Representing the less advantaged party in this negotiation, I understood there was little to be gained by trying to cross this particular frontier, but if Laura was expected to surrender her rights, I didn't think she should do so for *free*. Instead, I proposed that Daniel pay her a lump sum, a large bonus, as it were, in exchange for her signature on the document.

I sent a copy of this draft to John, who suggested several changes of his own. There was nothing major—and I added John's proposals to the markup, reviewed the document a final time, and then sent it off to the opposing counsel—whom I will call Neal. Weeks passed while we waited for a reply. When it came, I saw that they had increased by a marginal amount the ten year marriage pay-out—perhaps to demonstrate, in a possible future court proceeding, that "real" negotiations had taken place. It was the only change. Every other suggestion, every other proposition, all my other proposals, were rejected.

* * *

Divorce is a process that can last longer than the marriage itself. A prenup is a journey, a time hounded/time limited journey. Months of negotiations had produced almost no progress and June was ending. The invitations had been sent out, and hotel rooms were being booked. Laura and Daniel's wedding date was September 8.

III

Laura felt betrayed when she saw their redraft. Daniel had assured her that the prenup would be no fuss/no bother, identical to that of his brother-in-law, but she understood exactly what she was reading and was under no illusion about what was being asked of her. The precise financial details were, initially, of no great interest to Laura, whose overwhelming concern was that she not be seen as trying to monetize her relationship with Daniel. In this she was not unlike many young women I have represented in similar circumstances and it made her vulnerable—a vulnerability of which the other side was aware and which they used to press their demands. Had they pressed just a bit less forcefully, I believe Laura might well have decided to sign whatever prenup was placed before her, but the extraordinarily restrictive nature of the document seemed to her an insult—an effort to erase her completely from this process and ignore whatever interest, however modest, she might claim. It was a paradox: on the one hand Laura recoiled from seeing her marriage on a mercenary, profit and loss basis; on the other, she wanted to be recognized as a partner in the relationship and not a wholly owned subsidiary of *Matthew, Inc.* But the only way to assert herself was through a recognition of her *financial* rights: we were negotiating a prenup and this was the playing field. There was no other.

The slow pace of negotiation was, of course, itself a negotiating tactic designed both to demoralize and to keep up the pressure—as the days and weeks slid by and the date of the wedding loomed ever closer. It was obvious, but it was also effective and, along with the lack of any significant progress, it took its toll. Toward the end of June Laura called me, in distress, explaining that the day before she had been thinking about these matters and had burst into tears. When Daniel attempted to comfort her, he also began crying; the fear and tension bubbling over. Long and difficult negotiations over money are, to say the least, rarely beneficial to a healthy relationship, and while these two young people had ignited this process by falling in love, they now felt both alienated from it—mere riders on the storm—as well as, increasingly, alienated from each other. What they wanted to know, Laura asked me, was this: "Are the lawyers going to stop us from getting married?"

The simple answer was no. Over the years I've negotiated or helped to negotiate hundreds of prenuptial agreements, and there was never an occasion, not a single one, where a couple, determined to marry, was prevented from doing so by "the lawyers." We don't have the power and, equally to the point—at least in the negotiations in which I've been involved—we don't have the purpose: a client retains me to protect or advance his or her interests and that is what I do. In Laura's case, her primary interest, as she made clear, was to marry Daniel, and all my actions were aimed at facilitating that end.

A simple answer and true, as far as it went, but most anyone who has been involved in complex and protracted negotiations will recognize that the process itself creates its own reality, generating questions and answers that are anything but simple. Interests can change, perceptions alter, and under the pressure of inconclusive and seemingly interminable talks the most innocent comment or inoffensive gesture becomes fraught with baleful meaning, and what began as romance comes to seem like something else—a love affair experienced as a hostile takeover. In such circumstances it isn't the lawyers who prevent a couple from marrying but rather the couples themselves who may come to apprehend their relationship in a different and less flattering light or, more insidiously, come to doubt themselves and the nature of their commitment. This is what Laura meant when she expressed the fear that she was being turned into a gold digger.

But her concerns notwithstanding—and in no way minimizing the heavy emotional toll these talks can take—I have come to appreciate over the course of my career that even the bitterest negotiation doesn't turn you into something you are not. It doesn't change who you are; it *reveals* who you are. I didn't doubt Laura; for that matter I didn't doubt Daniel, either, but we had been talking for months without any appreciable progress. I'd send the other side a reasonable compromise proposal and they'd send me back a brick. and my client was, understandably, despairing about whether the marriage would take place at all. It was a difficult time—the tension unending, leading to short tempers and misunderstandings. John and Daniel, who had previously got along well, had a pointless quarrel, and Daniel and Laura were constantly bickering. I had sleepless nights of my own but I was confident that the negotiations would be concluded in a timely manner and that Daniel and Laura would get married as planned because I knew that we had an ace up our sleeve.

We were going to fold.

* * *

There are reasons an attorney will suggest that a client sign an onerous prenup. One of them, and one I discussed with Laura, might be called the "Inside the Harem" option. It comes from a comment by Winston Churchill, who was asked why he talked more sharply and with more force to American officials after Pearl Harbor, when the United States and Great Britain were allies, than before, when he was trying to woo US support. He said: *You speak differently once they're inside the harem.*[12] Similarly, Laura, once she was inside the family, might possess a good deal more power and influence, as wife and mother, than she had previously as fiancée. Lying in bed with her husband, night after night, she might begin to suggest how vulnerable she felt under the terms of the burdensome prenup; and how she feared for her future, and the future of their children, should they divorce or should Daniel die. Over time, and as he came into money of his own, Daniel might agree, or might get Matthew to agree, to soften the harder edges of the prenup and amend some of its more restrictive provisions. It doesn't happen all the time but I have had clients work successfully along these lines and it was one of the few options open to Laura.

Of course, the main reason a client signs an onerous prenup is because they have no other choice. The other side has the power and the money and never takes its foot off the pedal, leaving no room to negotiate. You go back and forth, back and forth and very little changes and the client is asking why there is no agreement. And I know—and the bitter truth is—that we could end all the fighting and sign this thing tomorrow if we simply throw in the towel and give up everything. And that becomes the most likely option the closer you get to the marriage date. There have been cases where the negotiations continue into the wedding day itself, into the hours before the ceremony is set to begin. The guests are arriving, the bride has her wedding gown on, the orchestra is setting up and one side is pressing its demand that the housing allowance be upped by an additional half a million dollars or the wedding is off. These, of course, are less like negotiations per se and more like extortion; what begins in enchantment devolving into a nightmarish mélange of bad faith, bad intentions and greed.

* * *

The purpose of negotiation isn't to win or dominate but to serve your client's interests, to secure the best deal possible, and there is no magic formula that guarantees that end. In Laura's case I felt the answer was there—in the documents, in the people with whom I was negotiating—but I couldn't yet see it. I went back to the draft that had been sent to me and re-read it again, looking for anything I might have missed, anything that I might have taken for granted. For example: we'd been told this document was virtually identical to the prenup signed by Daniel's brother-in-law. But what did that mean? The circumstances, on the simplest and most obvious level, were different—and because they were simple and obvious it was easy to overlook them. The brother-in-law was a *man*; Laura was a *woman*, potentially a *mother*, the mother of Daniel's children, Matthew's grandchildren, with all that meant, not only within the family but legally—with all the rights and responsibilities and assumptions that the law and nature recognized as a mother's prerogative. I didn't know exactly how this would fit into the final agreement but I felt, strongly, that it would.

And I always kept two facts uppermost in my mind. The first was that everything ran through Matthew. He was the one with the money—he was the one who, if he were willing, could assure a better life for Laura.

The second fact was that while we possessed less power than our opposition, that did not mean that we were *powerless*, that the other side did not possess its own vulnerabilities. Because this, too, is an essential part of negotiating. You have to have an unsentimental understanding of your client and of your opponent but most important of all you have to have a clear-eyed view of your own case, its strengths and its weaknesses. Faced with the brute intransigence of the other side, my definition, my understanding, of exactly what was "the best deal possible" for Laura had changed; and was changing and might change again. But the goal remained the same and I was determined to work toward it to the best of my ability and not let the overwhelming advantages of the other side create an atmosphere of lethargy and dull acceptance. We had spent months reacting to the opposition's demands. It was time to act.

While Laura had despaired at the restrictive nature of the prenup she was being asked to sign, her father, John, had had a different reaction. He'd expected a battle—

that's why he hired me. His attitude was: *Matthew's a businessman. This is business.* Additionally, over the past year, as the relationship between their children had deepened, the two men had developed a kind of friendship. They liked each other, and John was appreciative of the personal kindnesses Matthew had shown Laura on several occasions. John was a shrewd judge of character, I'd come to depend on his counsel, and he believed that there was more to Matthew than the tough-minded businessman who couldn't abide the thought that someone was getting something over on him. There was a part of Matthew, he told me, who wanted to be thought of as generous. A giver. A pleaser. Could we tap into something that would encourage the better angels of Matthew's nature to come into play?

There's a wonderful paragraph in Beethoven's papers where he is describing all those elements that must be present in a perfect symphony. Following that list, he has a single sentence: "*And sometimes the opposite is also true.*"[13] Laura, John, and I had agreed: it was better for Laura to be part of Daniel's family, even under semi-onerous conditions, than to continue these hardline, pointless negotiations. Instead of making or pressing demands, instead of working along the edges of the agreement to no great purpose, we were going to concede, give in to the opposition's demands—and, through compliance, create an atmosphere in which Matthew could both feel generous and—it was our hope—be generous to the prospective mother of his grandchildren.

Over the past months we had held a series of face to face negotiations, all of which had been held in Neal's office as an accommodation to Matthew. Now I called Neal and told him that I wanted to set up a meeting, for all parties, this time in *my* office. I said I was confident that all outstanding issues between the two families could be narrowed and if we were in my office, I would be able to streamline the process. Neal said he would get back to me which he did, within the hour, after speaking, I assume, to Matthew. We agreed to meet the following week.

The meeting had to be in my office because, on the simplest level, it represented what is called in sports "home field advantage." My home, not theirs—where I was comfortable, where I did some of my best work. On a deeper level—since it was my "home"—I was the host, I was in charge and could create not just an atmosphere, but a physical setting conducive to the kind of relaxed give-and-take that was essential if we were to succeed.

* * *

We sat at my glass kidney-shaped "partner desk"—about the size of a conference room table. I arranged the seating so that Laura was to my right. To her right was Daniel and next to him was John. Matthew sat to John's right, next to Neal, Daniel's lawyer. That put Matthew and Neal directly in front of a large courtesy monitor. It was my plan that only the six of us be in the room—I would be the "scrivener"—as I had been when we wrote the reform divorce laws for New York State—and I would sit in front of my large computer screen and type up, in real time, every point in the prenup as we reached agreement. And Matthew and Neal could watch on the monitor, again in real time, as the prenup took shape. If they didn't like my words, they could substitute their own words. It was all out in the open. Nothing up our sleeve—isn't that the atmosphere every magician strives to create before they go to work?

As the "host," I set the agenda and we began work on a series of issues that had proved intractable during the earlier negotiations. I wanted to establish, immediately, a new kind of understanding among all parties about what we might accomplish that day. As planned, my side conceded a great deal, on issue after issue, and, as we did, I could feel the temperature in the room changing. Whatever Matthew had expected, it wasn't this and I knew his eyes were on me, studying me, as he had during the earlier meetings in Neal's office, trying to make sense of the unexpected absence of clash and conflict—and trying to work out what his response should be. I don't want to minimize the complexity of what we were dealing with or the difficulties that we faced as we went page by page making our way through issue after issue—in general accepting both their numbers and their interpretations on a variety of matters including when the marriage would be considered over—the "operative event" vs the judgment of divorce. But I did pick up some minor concessions, such as on life insurance, on yearly payouts—nothing earth shattering but encouraging nonetheless after months of: *All for me/Nothing for you.*

The real breakthrough, when it came, concerned an issue that is always of prime importance during this type of negotiation: who would live where if the marriage crumbled. If the marriage remained intact, Laura was going to lead a very comfortable life, but if Laura and Daniel got divorced, Laura would have to move out of the marital home. Where she would move and under what circumstances had remained unresolved. Now we were dealing with it again. I proposed that if there were children, a new home should be purchased for her. Provisions that are inserted into prenups regarding children are typically frowned upon by the courts, but this, I felt, being a matter of housing was well within my legitimate purview.

Neal didn't respond directly but instead raised a new matter: geographic restriction—that is, placing limits on exactly where Laura and the children would be permitted to live. In most cases where I represent the custodial parent, I resist agreeing to geographical restrictions. I typically argue that as no restriction was being placed on the father, it didn't seem fair to place restrictions on the mother. But before I could muster that argument, Matthew spoke up. The restriction, it was clear, had nothing to do with Daniel—whose concerns seemed irrelevant to the process at that moment—but rather with *Matthew,* who wanted assurances from us that his grandchildren would live in close proximity to him. In my experience this was, in regard to a *grandfather,* a unique proposal—neither before nor since has anything like it been placed on the table before me. Matthew continued: If we accepted this offer, then, in the event of divorce, he was prepared to provide Laura and the children with "comparable housing," with all that entailed, and to pay for not only the new home but the costs attendant to the move and to Laura's and the children's continuing home-related expenses.

The effect upon me was electric. As I type these words, I can still recall the feeling that ran through me, sitting at that kidney-shaped table all those years ago, when I typed the word "comparable" into the proposed agreement. I glanced up at John to see if he understood what had happened. His face was expressionless, but I could tell that he had. We were both surprised, but probably not as surprised as Neal—who appeared to have had no idea that Matthew was going to make this offer. Within the context of our negotiations, "comparable housing" was worth millions of dollars to Laura. We had secured her financial future in a way and to a degree that had seemed unimaginable when the talks began.

The rest of the meeting went smoothly as we moved through the remaining terms. There was, as is usual, some horse trading, and we had some modest successes, but I don't want to leave the impression that this was no longer a restrictive prenup. It was. But I also knew that I had achieved my goal: the best possible deal for my client.

I completed the typing of the agreement then and there, and Laura and Daniel signed it. Then the two fathers, John and Matthew, embraced. Matthew and I smiled and shook hands, his expression a mixture of relief, happiness, and respect, and perhaps something else, undefinable. He had turned out to be a "pleaser" after all, and I felt at that moment, as if, throughout the meeting, he had been courting my approval. John, who was watching, later told me, "I think he fell in love with you."

Laura and Daniel were married on September 8. They are married still, with two children.

PART II

AN ADVOCATE'S WORLD

I felt the pull of matrimonial law right away. I just liked it very much, partly because of what I was going through, but also because I was good at it. I felt I had a calling.

5 RIDING THE TSUNAMI

Arthur

While I was in my second year at Brooklyn Law School, Leo Glasser and his wife Grace were at a dinner party and met Arthur Feinberg, a physician, an internist in private practice in Great Neck, Long Island. They spoke of Arthur with the highest regard, both personally and professionally and thought we might enjoy each other's company but every time I'd say "What about that guy you met?" Grace would say "He's not ready." Arthur's wife, Jeanne, still in her forties, had died the year before and they believed it was too soon to make contact. I waited for almost a year but then decided to disregard Grace's advice.

This was in the spring of 1974. Phil had been gone a little more than a year. I had buried myself in my studies during those twelve months, a kind of refuge from the terror of being a single mother and the shame of being a discarded wife, and from the constant worry about finances and about how I might keep our household together. It was a bad time for all of us. A traumatic event tends to atomize those left behind, and we all struggled, in our own individual way, to find our bearings in the wake of Phil's departure. One of my daughters was sorrowful; another acted as if nothing had happened. A third tried to assume the responsibility of a parent, while another—rightly—resented the responsibilities that had been forced upon her.

I think the world might be full of unhappy women who thought their children were going to be their friends; certainly I see it often enough in my practice, even now. That was a mistake I made at this time, and it never happens. It never works. In any event, my daughters didn't need a friend—they had plenty. They needed a mother, and in *that* role I was only intermittently successful, despite what I believed were my best efforts. I simply wasn't present enough, either physically absent at law school or emotionally absent, overwhelmed with personal or household concerns. And in that absence, my daughters developed their own survival skills, found their own allies, and dealt with their own enmities—including their animosity toward me and toward Phil. To move from a man's world to an advocate's world—a move I knew was best for all of us—required a level of ruthlessness and a level of selfishness: you get what you want but you pay for it; and others, blameless, at times defenseless, pay for it as well.

I was largely responsible for this psychological maelstrom, but I was also a victim of it. I was lonely. I needed a friend, an adult I could talk to. That was why I took, what was for me, a bold step and stopped waiting to hear from Arthur and called him myself. We spoke briefly, and when we hung up, I held my face in my hands in abject embarrassment, so saddened, believing I had lost the opportunity to know this remarkable man.

I was still sitting on the edge of my bed when one of my daughters walked in. She took one look at me and asked, "Ma, what happened?"

I said, "I just made the biggest fool of myself."

But he called the next day and we spoke for hours. He asked me to meet him a few days later at a lovely little Italian restaurant in midtown Manhattan, "Aperitivo," at 29 West 56th Street. He said, "I'll be the bald doctor sitting at the bar with a rose in my teeth." I met him there. He was beautiful. I was coughing up a storm, dealing with a bad upper respiratory infection and pleurisy. "I don't believe in the germ theory," he said. He drove me home to the house in the Rockaways, and we walked along the beach. We kissed.

We were together for thirty-two years, twenty-three of them married, before his death on November 28, 2005.

* * *

I was just beginning my career when I met Arthur. We were together the evening I learned I had passed the Bar exam. The intelligence and commitment—the courage—that he brought to his vocation inspired, and continues to inspire, my own ideas about what it means to be a professional, to meet your responsibilities with dedication and honor; and the care, skill, respect, and empathy with which he treated the men and women who came to him helped to fashion my own conduct when dealing with what Arthur called, "people *in extremis*." I hesitate when I write *empathy* because I fear it brings to mind all those "Dr. Christian" movies of the 1930s and 1940s, full of bromides and folk medicine.[1] That was not Arthur. He was a superb clinician, and several times over the course of his career, he voluntarily had himself recertified in internal medicine, an exacting and rigorous process of study and examination. In those pre-personal computer days he created his own research library: books and magazines and thousands of articles from the top medical journals that he clipped and annotated, then cross-referenced, alphabetized, and arranged in a pair of huge steel cabinets that he called his "reprint files." He was determined to remain at the sharp end of his profession, the calmest man in the room making the hard decisions from which others, including other physicians, shied away.

Arthur understood, and by example helped me to understand, that empathy unmoored from knowledge and skill is of little use to a patient—or to a client; temporary balm, perhaps, but nothing more. His training and experience were wide-ranging—an Army physician during World War Two, later stationed overseas in the Philippines; twenty-five years in private practice; twenty plus years in academia—at Columbia and Cornell Medical Schools; founder and first director of the Center for Geriatric and Palliative Care at North Shore University Hospital—one of the first such units in the country; Vice Chairman of the American College of Physicians and Chair of the Ethics Committee following his election as Governor for the downstate region of New York. The breadth of Arthur's experience, impossible to duplicate, linked to his diagnostic skill, work ethic, intellectual curiosity, and focus, had given him an unusual understanding of the power and the limitations of the healing art that was almost spiritual in nature. He taught his students that the answer to the eternal question: *Should you tell a patient the truth?*, was another question: *Do you know the truth?* A Zen-like insight into responsibility and trust which perhaps explains why a patient once said that he would almost rather hear bad news from Arthur than good news from another physician. Because if Arthur said it, it could be believed.

I don't want to leave the impression that our relationship was one of teacher to student. It was a marriage, with the give and take, the happiness and joy, complications and challenges of any long and loving relationship. At the same time it was impossible, given our shared intimacy, not to absorb each other's influence in ways both practical and profound. Arthur had been taught in medical school that the process of learning could be broken down into three parts:

1: See one.
2: Do one.
3: Teach one.

and I adapted that method when training my associates and young partners. Arthur believed that there was no limit to what could be accomplished as long as you didn't care who received the credit—a credo I've tried to maintain both for myself and for those who work with and for me. And Arthur also stressed the necessity of doing the hard work—the day in and day out slog, the attention to detail, the discipline that can be the difference in a successful treatment or in a successful legal outcome. He would quote Pasteur: "Chance favors the prepared mind."[2]

Over the decades the practice of medicine has undergone a revolution: the tools of medicine, the instruments, the pharmacology, and even the language of healing have changed in ways that would have been unthinkable to earlier generations. But the lessons Arthur imparted remain as vital as ever: how to talk to a patient; how to listen to a patient; how to diagnose and treat a patient. This is no exercise in nostalgia or romance: those lessons form the bedrock of how a physician—and by extension any professional—might approach and understand the work that they do.

I drew so much from him for my practice that he seemed, at times, a silent partner. During our weekly staff meetings, when dealing with an especially challenging problem or trying to find a path forward after an especially difficult time, someone—and not always me—would ask: "Well, what would Arthur do?"

I was a recent law school graduate, a novice just beginning to create a professional persona, and it was here that Arthur's influence was felt most deeply. His example helped me to understand what type of lawyer I wished to be. I don't mean corporate or family or criminal law—deeper: how did I want to treat clients, my coworkers, my employees? How do I meet my responsibilities—to myself and to my clients in a sometimes slippery, sometimes morally obtuse system? How to consider those matters alongside the need to make a living, to meet a payroll, to care for my loved ones? None of the answers are easy, and some parts of Arthur's influence were absorbed more thoroughly than others. Some have yet to be fully absorbed. But the search for excellence, for a morally sustaining career is an ongoing process, Arthur believed, not a result. It was a battle worth waging every day, for every patient, for every client.

* * *

If it were possible, I would "untie" all the preceding paragraphs and take the sentences, the individual words, and thread them through and around and between every sentence to come so that his presence would be everywhere in all that follows and you might have some idea of all that he meant to me, all that he means to me.

Riding the Tsunami

I had been in a hurry to meet Arthur, but then I was always in a hurry at that time. I was forty-one years old, with four daughters to care for, bills to pay, a mortgage to meet, and a living to make. The overwhelming majority of law school graduates, the people against whom I felt I was competing, were in their twenties. Their careers—their lives—could unfold in more leisurely patterns. At the same time my contemporaries, in their forties, were overwhelmingly male and just approaching the sweet spot of their careers, on the cusp of real success and financial remuneration. I felt neither here nor there, but I instinctively knew that whatever I would be able to make of myself, there was no time to waste.

It was a period when so many of the battles of the sixties and early 1970s seemed to have resolved themselves, a moment of momentary, deceptive calm, as in the eye of a storm. The Equal Rights Amendment was continuing its swift progress through state legislatures toward what appeared to be its inevitable passage. The legal and medical challenges to the Pill had failed. *Roe v Wade* was over a year old, a permanent solution, it seemed, that garnered nationwide support, including from the evangelical churches.

A fantasy of victory and permanence: no citizen of the Dreaming Suburb ever held tighter to their illusions. A writer described this period as that moment when "the tsunami of second wave feminism" was at its apex;[3] an apt metaphor because tsunamis eventually lose their power and recede . . . and the landscape returns, if not exactly to the way it was, then to a fine simulacrum. But that apex, that singular moment, held great meaning for me. My gender, which I had always assumed would be a hindrance to my employment, was instead a benefit. Just as an evolving cultural shift had helped me to enter law school, it now helped me find a job. Law firms, the courts, and judges were actively seeking to hire women—or trying to appear that they were actively seeking to hire women. I interviewed for a clerkship with a federal judge who took one look at me and said: "I can't hire you. I could never ask you to carry my bags." At the time I believed he was paying deference to my age or, more likely, was seeking a younger, presumably more malleable, woman to employ, but I later learned he had hired a man and had never had any intention of employing a woman. The judges, the law firms, and businesses could pick and choose, and many of the hires represented a more or less unwilling bow to the social currents in play rather than to any lasting interest in gender equality.

I accepted a position as an associate at a law firm run by Howard Squadron. I was their first female associate. When I left the job two years later, they had hired only one other.

The Life

Squadron Ellenoff Gartenstein & Plesent was a mid-sized law firm with an outsized impact in its day and place; indeed, for a moment in the mid-1970s and 1980s, it seemed to be at or near the epicenter of all political and legal life in New York City. The founding partner, Howard M. Squadron, the son of a delicatessen counterman, was described by the *New York Times* as "one of those lawyers who knew how to get things done . . . who seemed to have a pipeline to everyone who mattered, from presidents and mayors to corporate chieftains."[4] He also represented major cultural figures as well, helped found the International Center of Photography, and was on the board of the Joffrey Ballet. He had studied Latin, loved the language, and could recite classical poetry—a passion we shared and, I've always believed, one of the reasons he took an initial interest in me.

Howard enjoyed his time in the public square, was often on television or radio defending a cause or advocating for a client. He relished the sense of power and mastery, overt and elliptical, that came with being a lawyer "who could get things done." Most of those who came to him for advice or representation, would-be mayors or governors or prospective cabinet officials, real estate developers, business tycoons—feared, admired, celebrated, or on the make—are forgotten now but not all. Howard was a key advisor to Rupert Murdoch when the Australian tycoon took his first, deceptively opaque steps into the US media market, with his purchase of the *NY Post* and *New York Magazine*, the latter in a hostile takeover. Howard was Murdoch's legal counsel in this country, and Murdoch later acknowledged the important role he had played in making News Corporation one of the largest media companies in the world and a dominant force in the US media landscape. [5]

I had graduated from law school in June, met Arthur one week later, took the Bar Examination in July, began work in August, and learned I had passed the bar exam in the late Fall. I was obviously inexperienced, but I felt I was where I should be, where I wanted to be, and I was impatient for more. My professional life could not have been simpler: I went in each morning to my small office and was given my assignment, or assignments, for the day. As the newest hire, the most junior associate, I was what was called a "generalist," attached to no specific department within the firm, on-call and available to all. Those first months it seemed as if I never stopped working, clacking away on my Underwood typewriter that I brought from home and kept on a small desk in a corner of my office. I spent weekends in that office, part of Thanksgiving, Christmas, July Fourth. If I was impatient for more, they always gave it to me and I never complained. I was happy.

I did a bit of everything: ran downtown and filed papers with the court; picked up or dropped off documents at other law firms; researched; prepared the lawyers for and sat in on depositions. Occasionally I was asked to serve papers on an individual, a miserable assignment, always dealing with angry people. Once I recognized a name and said: *I can serve those papers. I know this man* (they were divorce papers): *he's the brother-in-law of my best friend from James Madison High School. He knows me. He'll let me into his office.* And he did. It didn't bother me. I had to do it; it was part of my job; an education in the law that they didn't teach in law school. And all the while, always, keeping precise, meticulous records of everything I had done, all that I had accomplished that day, including the time I began a specific assignment and the time I finished working on it, down to the last billable minute. Another education, this into the *business* of law.

Often I'd be asked to *Shepardize* a legal citation. There would be a point of law being developed in a brief, and I was assigned to research all the cases which shed light on the subject, listing every time that case had been cited in other cases, and if it had ended in a favorable or unfavorable decision—was the case upheld or overturned?—thus putting its value as precedent in context. I'd sit at a long table at one of the two main law libraries—one belonging to the New York City Bar Association in midtown; the other downtown, part of the New York County Lawyers Association—ten or twenty volumes of *Shepard's United States Citations*—even now I can see the maroon color of the bindings—and the books of bound case law stacked around me. Occasionally I'd recognize a distinguished attorney—or even a partner from my firm—who liked to do their own research but generally next to me or across the table from me would be other associates or law clerks or interns behind their own towering stack of books, working, heads down in silence, for hours, like something out of Dickens or Trollope, the only sound the turning of pages and the scratching of pen on paper as we made our notes. It was exhausting, grinding work, every citation leading to another citation, every court decision to another decision, a hall of mirrors that seemed to go on forever. And every point put down by hand on a yellow legal pad called "foolscap," because I wasn't just expected to Shepardize a case but to analyze it as well, noting key points, returning to the office, and typing up a synopsis of what I'd found to be used to advantage in court.

Exhausting but, at the same time, satisfying, that same satisfaction I'd felt at Brooklyn Law School, immersed in research, the heft of the heavy law volumes as I sat in the carrels, the almost sensual feel of the paper as you ran you hand down a page looking for the proper citation, the gray, watery light coming through the library windows on a late fall afternoon, the smell of old paper and ink mixed with the sharp chemical odor of xeroxed copy; a way of working, a way of life, really, that is gone for good. Here is how a case is Shepardized now, online, using Lexus/Nexus:

1. Look up your case by entering the citation within the main search box.
2. Open the full text view of the case.
3. Use the "Next Steps" dropdown box at the top right of the case to select "Shepardize."
4. Review the Shepard's report *automatically* produced in response to your query. This report contains a list of the cases that have cited your case.

What used to take hours or days can now be accomplished with three or four clicks. Time and efficiency—it is obvious what has been gained, but harder to define what has been lost. It makes no sense to romanticize the past, to linger over old times and old ways. Nostalgia is a soporific from which it can be difficult to awake; and I run my own firm now, I hire associates and interns, and I want them to attend to their responsibilities with dispatch and accomplish their assignments as quickly and correctly as possible. But at the same time there remains a feeling, nagging, *unromantic*, persistent, that the process by which I learned had value, profligate as it now seems, as a way of understanding both my profession and, by extension, the world itself.

In any case it is all gone—as is the firm I was then working for, and the partners I knew.

Ghosts.

The Feeling Passes

When Howard Squadron began advising and formally representing Rupert Murdoch, he asked me to prepare an analysis on how the Newspaper Preservation Act might affect Murdoch's prospective plans to purchase the New York Post. And so I played my own very small part in Murdoch's relentless and successful effort to establish a beachhead in American media and burrow his way to its heart. The Act, passed by Congress in 1970, eased ownership requirements and eliminated certain antitrust prohibitions in an effort to prevent competing newspapers in the same city from going out of business, the aim being to maintain a diverse, unconstrained, and financially viable press. In the end good and bad actors used elements of the Act for reasons unrelated to, and undermining, its intentions. Murdoch, for instance, didn't want to own the Post because he thought it would make money; he owns it still and it never has. What he wanted was a megaphone in the media capital of the world and that's what Squadron Ellenoff Gartenstein & Plesent—and Cohen!—helped him achieve. He wasn't worried about losing money; in fact it was essential that he did: Murdoch later used the rackety financial underpinnings of the Post to pressure the FCC into waiving its restriction against one person owning a daily newspaper and a television station within the same municipality. It was that ruling that allowed News Corp. to break out of its tiny beachhead and begin its march of conquest across the US communications landscape that continues to this day.

Shortly after buying the Post, Rupert Murdoch gave a speech to New York financial leaders in which he decried, "demagogues playing cynical and political games," vowing to be part of a united effort to defeat "the preachers of dissension . . ."[6] There was a lot more, but, as they say, verbal assurances aren't worth the paper they're printed on.

That I had any input, however insignificant, in the dealings with Rupert Murdoch illustrates an unusual dynamic that began to play itself out at the firm. I was the most junior of associates, not a year out of law school, but the fact was that I didn't *look* like a junior associate, and I didn't present myself as one. I was a 41-year-old woman, and while I may not have had extensive *legal* experience, I did have extensive *life* experience. I was a hard worker, a fast learner, and the more responsibility I was given, the more I accepted. But I also possessed a gravitas that belied my position and engendered a certain trust and respect.

I was aware of the impression I made and determined to use this to my advantage. I was, very consciously, trying to create myself as an attorney, create the attorney I wished to become, and my age, like my gender, which I had always assumed would hinder my prospects, turned to my advantage. Clients, increasingly important clients, saw me, listened to me, made whatever assumptions they made about my background and experience, and accepted me.

I remember one afternoon, working with a client in one of the conference rooms at the firm. He was about fifteen years older than me, a handsome, distinguished-looking man with clear blue eyes and longish grey hair, who had served as an undersecretary for two Presidents; had run for Governor of the state; made tens of millions in private industry—one of those accomplished people who naturally made their way to Squadron Ellenoff Gartenstein & Plesent.

We are going over the divorce agreement that has been tentatively agreed to with his wife, the mother of his eight children. The client, who has fallen in love with a younger woman, wants to be sure that he is being generous, that his wife, and by extension his children, will want for nothing. We go through the agreement point by point, and I accommodate his suggestions, revising the document as he wishes, and making several suggestions of my own, to which he nods in agreement. And it is during one of those moments, when I am explaining some point and he is listening and nodding, that I am hit with an almost paralyzing feeling of self-doubt. I think: *If this distinguished man knew that a year ago I was still in law school, knew how little experience I have, knew the depth of my lack of knowledge, he'd stand up and walk out of the room.*

I think: *What a fraud I am.*

The client is explaining some minor changes he wishes to make and I find myself noting it, then offering a further revision to which he agrees. Through the large glass window of the conference room I can see the life of the firm going on around us.

The feeling passes.

Falling Soldier

The International Center of Photography opened in New York City in November 1974, about two months after I began work at Squadron Ellenoff Gartenstein & Plesent. Howard Squadron, on the Board as the founding member and trustee, was a close friend with the Center's founder and driving force, Cornell Capa, whose brother, famed photojournalist and war photographer, Robert Capa, had been killed in May 1954, when he stepped on a land mine in Thai Binh, Vietnam, while covering the first Indochina War. ICP was dedicated as a memorial to his life and work, along with that of two other photojournalists killed on assignment in the 1950s: David Seymour (Chim) and Walter Bishoff. ICP was, at the time, one of only two museums in the United States devoted exclusively to photography, and its gala opening was considered a major cultural milestone in the life of the city. Jacqueline Kennedy Onassis celebrated it, and Cornell Capa, in an unsigned "Talk of the Town" article she wrote for the January 13, 1975, issue of *The New Yorker.*

It must have been about this time that Cornell Capa spoke to Howard about a book scheduled for publication later in the year. *The First Casualty: The War Correspondent as Hero, Propagandist and Myth Maker*, raised questions about the authenticity of Robert Capa's most famous photograph, "The Falling Soldier."[7] The author, Phillip Knightley, was a respected journalist, and *The First Casualty* was no hit-and-run affair; the issues it raised about "The Falling Soldier" were serious and well researched. Cornell Capa had corresponded with Knightley while he was writing the book, but now he was having second thoughts about his cooperation—concerned that the author was about to claim that the photograph had been staged. Howard was reviewing Cornell Capa's options—whether to consider legal action, so fraught in the area of First Amendment rights and the rules against prior restraint or—as seemed more likely—framing a public response to whatever damaging conclusions Knightley had reached. He was looking for information that would inform his decision, and he asked me to go over to the ICP and look through any documents, photographs, or negatives that might pertain to "The Falling Soldier." It would all have to be done by hand—there was no "online" then—and while it may all seem hopelessly old-fashioned, it still occasionally happens like this. A client will come to my office with a shoebox jammed full of photographs or documents and I'll have an associate go through them, explaining what I am looking for. That's essentially what I was assigned to do at the ICP, in the winter of 1975.

"The Falling Soldier" is considered to be among the finest photographs of war ever made. The black and white picture is said to depict the moment of death of a Loyalist (anti-fascist) militiaman killed during the battle of Cerro Muriano on the Cordoba front during the Spanish Civil War, September 5, 1936. The militiaman is not wearing a uniform—he's in a white shirt and dark trousers, a cartridge belt around his waist. He is falling backwards, half twisted to the left, his right arm outflung, letting go of a rifle. There is no blood, no sign of any wound. The image was published in two small French magazines in 1936 and then reproduced in *Life Magazine*, the July 12, 1937 issue, a half page spread accompanying an article entitled "Death in Spain: The War Has Taken 500,000 Lives in One Year."[8] The caption under the image read: "Robert Capa's Camera Catches A Spanish Soldier The Instant He Is Dropped By A Bullet Through The Head In Front of Cordoba." This was the only mention of Robert Capa, and the image itself was not referenced in the accompanying article. The photograph appeared on page twenty of the magazine. It did not make *Life's* cover. That honor went to "Grace the Dummy"—one of a new generation of lifelike, plastic mannequins.

The image was an immediate sensation, reproduced in hundreds of magazines around the world. To this day it retains its historic, aesthetic, and commercial value: a print is part of the permanent collection of the Metropolitan Museum of Art. Robert Capa, a courageous and indefatigable photojournalist, took a lot of great pictures—in Spain, on D-Day on Omaha Beach, in Israel during the War for Independence—but he never took a better one. By the time I headed over to the ICP the photograph had reached iconic status—a symbol of the terrible cost of war and of the "low dishonest decade" of the Thirties that had seen the triumph of fascism.[9] Though much about the photograph was mysterious, Phillip Knightley was the first to question its authenticity, to suggest that it might have been staged. He did so gingerly, admitting that "at this distance in time it has so far proved impossible either to confirm or disprove" key facts about the photograph.

My assignment was to work with Cornell Capa and staff at the ICP to provide documentation supporting the photograph's authenticity—as a prelude to whatever action Cornell Capa was considering. I went through papers, old receipts, documents, film canister, labels, and calendars, looking for anything that might establish a timeline or provide context. ICP staffers, some wearing white gloves, were carefully handling old negatives. Capa was sure the photograph was "real" in the sense that it was a document, that it depicted a genuine, tragic moment in time. And he strongly believed in his late brother's rectitude. I had full access to the material at the ICP, and I never felt any pressure from Cornell Capa or anyone else to reach a specific conclusion. Capa wanted the truth out because he believed the truth would vindicate his brother and "The Falling Soldier" from any charges that might be made.

The problem, as I began to discover when going through the material at the ICP, was that "The Falling Soldier" had no provenance whatsoever. That is, no one was able to determine exactly when the picture was taken, or where or under what circumstances, or even what it actually depicted: without the caption in *Life Magazine*, written by an anonymous photo editor in New York far from the action, the picture, as has been remarked, might well have been entitled "Clumsy Soldier Falling Down a Hill." There was no negative—every image of "The Falling Soldier" is a copy of a copy. Nor was there any paper trail; Capa was, understandably—given that he was reporting under fire—sometimes lax about labeling his rolls of film, and he gave very few descriptions of how he came to take the picture; even these were often contradictory and later described as "tongue in cheek." There were several photographs taken by Capa of Spanish militiamen, including what appeared to be the man who was the subject of "The Falling Soldier," posing for the camera and pretending to storm a trench and aim their weapons at the enemy.[10] Where and when these were taken is unclear, but they are so clearly staged, photographer and subjects having some fun during a quiet time at the front, that it was reasonable to assume that no deceptive purpose should be inferred.

In the end I was unable to provide any important new evidence supporting the authenticity of Capa's photograph. Most everything I found only deepened the mystery, and that was what I reported back to Howard Squadron. I was disappointed in myself because I wanted to find what I had been sent to find, but it was all part of the education of a young lawyer: sometimes you work to the limit of your ability and the result isn't what you had hoped for. Sometimes, as I learned from Arthur, you lose the patient. Looking back, I think I was taught an inadvertent but very valuable lesson for a future matrimonial attorney: how to deal with compelling contradictory narratives that both pose as "true."

Cornell Capa took no legal action regarding *The First Casualty* or Phillip Knightley. The book was published—it's become a classic and is in print to this day. Capa continued to defend his brother and the authenticity of "The Falling Soldier" until his death in 2008. As he feared, the book ignited a controversy that is ongoing, although in the decades since no one has come any closer to a definitive answer. The photograph continues to exist, as it always has, in a flickering, shimmery space that is all its own, timeless, forever moving into focus and out, simultaneously real and fake.

The Other World

As the only female associate at Squadron Ellenoff Gartenstein & Plesent I was in a unique position. The only other women employed by the firm were secretaries and a receptionist but I was never made to feel uncomfortable, never placed in any awkward situation. Howard Squadron, the senior partner, was responsible for setting the tone of the office and he created a working environment that was accommodating and professional.

Of course, a professional working environment as it was experienced in 1975 was a good deal different from the professional working environment of 2026. The changes—in permissible office language, permissible (or tolerated) office behavior and mores—even the physical environment, which, back then, was often enveloped in a fug of cigarette smoke—are all encompassing and much to the good. But given all that, Squadron Ellenoff Gartenstein & Plesent was a wonderful place to work, a wonderful place to begin to learn my trade, and within the world of the firm I was always treated with care and respect.

Outside the world of the firm, in this other professional world. . . . There was no question the times were changing, but the change wasn't uniform, and you were always running up against these areas of resistance and hostility. The courtroom still belonged to men. The judges were almost all men; I think there was only one female judge in the court that handled divorce. The lawyers, all my adversaries, were men. They made the rules, they enforced the rules, they'd done so forever, and they let you know, in ways both subtle and overt, that they weren't going to change. I'd walk into a courtroom and they refused to see me, refused to acknowledge me as an attorney. If I happened to walk in with a man, whether colleague or client or stranger, I was assumed to be the client—assumed to be anything or anybody but who I was. I know so many female attorneys who had a similar experience back then, and twenty-five years later, my own daughter, Patti, went through it in a courtroom in Madison, Wisconsin—a miserable rite of passage experienced by generations of accomplished, professional women.

Of course, sometimes they'd see you and you wished they hadn't. They would invade your space, stand so close, they were right on top of you. All these foolish games, these misogynistic bullies. Once an adversary put his hand on my butt, and when I confronted him, I received a shrug and a smirk. He knew that within the courtroom there would be no consequences. It wasn't about sex, it was about power: a way of letting you know that this is not your place, that this will *never* be your place. Another time a lawyer began berating me in language so abusive, I called over the guard. I said: "You have to get him out of here. He can't talk to me like that." And so often the judges were loath to intervene. You were on your own.

Things are rarely that blatant anymore, but the attitude has not disappeared. All women have had to deal with it: the sly comment, the not-so-witty double entendre. *I was just joking.*

And sometimes more than words: the unwanted hug, the lingering pat on the back. The assumption that your sensibility, your idea of appropriate conduct and comment, doesn't count.

The "Me, Too, Movement" shone a needed spotlight on the most terrible transgressions, but there remains a large territory of indeterminate behavior, a sort of no-man's land of innuendo and subtle intimidation, that has been left for women, those of my generation, but primarily my younger colleagues, to negotiate and endure. And it is not easy because human behavior and motivation can be ambiguous, and our most intimate feelings and actions subject to different interpretations. We may not even fully understand them ourselves. I represented Harvey Weinstein's first wife and his brother Bob's second wife. I also represented Andrew Cuomo, former Governor of New York, in his divorce from Kerry Kennedy. It is hard for me to reconcile the men I dealt with, courteous and professional, with later accusations of blatant and inappropriate or coercive behavior. But I do recognize that cultural shifts, harsh restrictions on abortion rights, even mainstream attacks on access to contraception, seem to have sparked a rebirth of some of the cruder attacks on women's rights and abilities.

I would think, back then: *They won't intimidate me. I won't be bullied.* I may have been an inexperienced lawyer, but I wasn't a kid. I was an adult woman, with an adult's perspective and, I felt, an adult's reserves of power and endurance. If they wouldn't change, they would *be* changed. And, over time, they were.

Two Clients

I: The Darkroom

Stanley Plesent, an elegant worldly man with a very distinctive style, headed up the matrimonial department at the firm. I admired and tried to emulate the focus and deep attention he paid to every client with whom he came in contact. That admiration has lasted my whole professional life, and at my own firm, my partners and associates are expected to provide the same encompassing level of attention to *our* clients. Early on I felt the pull of matrimonial law, partly because of what I was going through but also because, watching Stanley, I felt I could be good at it. I felt I might have a calling. We became close and later he helped me with my own divorce. I basically handled it myself—by that time all I wanted was *out*—but Stanley was always there, advising me, supporting me.

There was a lot to admire about Stanley: he was a war hero, awarded the Silver Star, Bronze Star, and Purple Heart while serving as a rifle platoon leader in Europe during the Second World War. He was a Chevalier of the Legion of Honor, a distinction awarded by the President of France; served in the administration of John F Kennedy; and was for sixteen years president of the Alvin Ailey Foundation. I don't think a young lawyer ever had a better example or a better teacher. In later years Stanley and I often found ourselves on opposite sides of a divorce action. We battled in court and at the negotiating table many times, but I like to think that, even in the midst of hard and demanding disagreements, he never regretted how well he had taught me. I know I never regretted what a good student I had been.

Stanley brought me into the first divorce case I ever handled. Our client was Elliott Erwitt, the celebrated American photographer, who was divorcing his second wife, Diana Dann.[11] The couple shared a large apartment on the upper west side of Manhattan that also doubled as Erwitt's studio and office and was the source of increasingly strained negotiations between the two as they struggled to reach an agreement on the terms of their divorce. Both Erwitt and Dann were claiming the apartment in the settlement, and as neither would move out, they both still lived there during this difficult period. For that reason Erwitt became concerned about protecting his property and had begun an inventory of his papers, archives, and photographic negatives. I was asked to assist him in that inventory.

In the course of a career that had begun in the early 1950s, Elliott Erwitt produced some of the most iconic images of the twentieth century. He had photographed everyone, from JFK and Jackie to Marlene Dietrich, Jack Kerouac, Gable, Brando, Marilyn Monroe, Montgomery Clift, Che Guevara; startling and immediate black and white photos of the American landscape; the famous photograph of Richard Nixon poking an index finger into Nikita Khruschev's chest during the notorious "kitchen debate" in Moscow in 1959 was his. A 1953 photo of his first wife,

Lucienne Van Kan, gazing lovingly at their six-day-old daughter Ellen, the family cat Brutus keeping an eye on both, was a centerpiece of the Museum of Modern Art's epochal exhibition and book *The Family of Man.* His work had tremendous value both as art and as commodity; his son, Mischa, once joking that the single "Family" photograph of mother, daughter, and cat had sent him and his siblings through college.

At my request Stanley arranged with opposing counsel a specific day and time to allow me to visit Elliott's apartment. We wanted to avoid any misunderstanding or unpleasantness with Diana Dann or her legal team. I wanted to go to the apartment because I thought it would speed up the inventory process but I also wanted to go because . . . I wanted to go. I thought it would be important, in ways difficult to explain, to *see* the focus of the dispute between Elliott and his wife. Arthur had talked to me about the importance of house calls, of visiting the patient outside the office, because it permitted a unique perspective, a new opportunity to understand the case with which he was dealing. He said patients, feeling comfortable in a less formal environment, often spoke with more candor about what they were experiencing and might reveal, consciously or unconsciously, important information that would aid his treatment. There are, of course, important differences between lawyers and physicians but I was curious if I might be able to adapt some of his techniques to my own work, and to my own advantage and that of my clients.

Erwitt's apartment, as I recall, occupied the entire eighth floor of the building, and as soon as I walked in and saw various artifacts collected during his peripatetic career, I thought: *He'll never leave here.* Then: *We're going to have to pay a lot of money to move her out.* Elliott let me into his darkroom, which was to the right, just off a foyer that was lined with framed photographs. It was a huge room, very clean, very organized, with workspaces, scores of photographs along the walls, an enlarger to the left, several cameras, negatives drying in strips hanging over a long narrow sink and additional negatives still in their trays. I remember the sharp chemical smell of developing fluid and I had that very strong feeling again: *He'll never give this up.* This was his office, the focus of his creative life, of everything he had accomplished and still wished to accomplish. But I also had another insight, based on the due diligence I had undertaken when I was asked to join the case. Elliott Erwitt's parents had fled Russia following the Bolshevik Revolution. They lived briefly in Rome, then moved to Paris, where Elliot was born in 1928; then moved to Milan and then back to Paris to avoid the strict anti-Jewish restrictions Mussolini had begun to impose. Visas in hand, the family sailed from Paris for New York on September 1, 1939, the day Germany invaded Poland. They lived in New York City, then moved to Los Angeles, where the marriage ended, and Elliott lived with his father for a time. His father then left for New Orleans, and, at sixteen, Elliott was on his own. He lived in L.A. for a year or two and then moved back to New York, then was drafted into the army for two years, where he served in a unit based in France.

The wanderings of Elliott and his family were like following a fever chart of the first half of the troubled twentieth century. He'd been on the run all his life, and now he'd found a home. I knew in my bones he was never going to leave.

You could probably have reached the same conclusion while sitting in an office or sitting around a negotiating table trading proposals for weeks on end. But you wouldn't have understood, wouldn't have felt the truth of it all unless you'd seen the apartment. I *knew* how this case was going to play itself out; I knew that whatever the cost, our client was going to insist on an arrangement by which Diana Dann would agree to move out. And, in suitable lawyerly language, I conveyed the essence of those findings to Stanley.

It's not magic; it has more to do with hard work, with "chance and the prepared mind," but in the hundreds of house calls I've conducted during my career I've almost always found something valuable, even if that something never made its way directly into court or into negotiations. I still call it a "house call"—and I do often go to houses or apartments—but I also go to schools, or places of business or I'll drive the route a client has to drive to work or to an ex spouse's home to deliver their child for a weekend's unsupervised visit. Anywhere or any place that might have relevance and offer insight into an ongoing legal battle; and there are times, in court, where I can say: *Your honor, I've been there* or *I've seen that* or *I've driven from X to Y and it isn't at all like the opposition is contending.* There's a psychological, almost ineffable understanding at times but there is also, often, a real world, hard-nosed advantage as well that can make itself felt before a judge or before an arbitrator.

Robert Capa, who befriended the young Elliott Erwitt and was an early champion of his work, once described his own profession in words that have, I feel, a direct application to mine, in the effort to tease out meaning and advantage in a complex legal environment.

"If your pictures aren't good enough," he wrote, "you aren't close enough."[12]

II: She/Her

One afternoon Howard Squadron came to my office and introduced me to a woman named Heather.

He said to me: "She's having a problem with her birth certificate. See what you can do."

He said to Heather: "This is Harriet. She's going to be your lawyer."

Then he turned and went back to his own office.

It was abrupt, but it was often that way when you were a generalist, the most junior associate. A partner or more senior associate would bring a client or a problem to you and basically say: *We need you to work this out.* Then they'd leave you to it. Sink or swim.

Heather was a woman about my own age, taller than me, bigger, very pretty, conservatively dressed, with a low steady voice. She handed me a manila envelope which contained a number of documents. There was what appeared to be an original birth certificate, noting the birth of a male child named Kenneth at a hospital in New York City. There was a completed, notarized, and processed name change petition that had been filed in civil court in New York City, indicating that the petitioner's name had been changed from Kenneth to Heather about a year previous. There were also blank New York City forms dealing with the correction or emendation of a birth certificate. The story could not have been clearer, but I had never met a transgender person before, had only a hazy understanding of what transgender *meant*, and despite the fact I had the documents in front of me, and Heather speaking to me, it took more than a moment for me to connect that *that Kenneth* was *this Heather*.

This is what she told me:

Heather had been born with male sexual organs but had never felt male. She had known she was female almost from the time she was a toddler, and through school, college, and two years in the army, that feeling had never changed. She was not considering what was then called "sex change" surgery and is now called gender affirming surgery; she was open to the idea of hormonal treatment but had not yet made up her mind. What she had made up her mind about was that she was determined to live the "truth" of her experience. She had dressed as a woman for a number of years, had legally changed her name, and now wanted her New York City birth certificate to be corrected to reflect her actual gender.

On Heather's original birth certificate the "sex" question was the second blank space that was filled in, right after "name" and right before "color." Heather would accept, if she had to, that an amended certificate would leave that line empty, but she no longer was willing to accept the "male" designation.

She had been put in contact with Howard Squadron through Howard's work on civil rights and civil liberties. Her background and personal details had been verified, and Howard had agreed to take the case pro bono. The two might have met for the first time the very day he walked Heather to my office and said: Get it done.

It was a revolutionary bit of lawyering he was asking for, and yet . . . it did not feel revolutionary.

Heather was unhappy, but her unhappiness was singular, attached to no cause, intensely personal. She had no desire to mount a barricade or wave a flag, and she expressed no particular interest in others who might be suffering as she felt herself to be suffering. What she wanted was for *her* birth certificate to be changed to reflect who she really was and, as she made clear to me, that was *all* she wanted. Howard was always on the lookout for a case or a cause he could display before the city or the state or the nation, and this may initially have looked like one of those. But the client had her own specific interests, and I think Howard may have realized that she was not on board for anything else—which was why, perhaps, he handed off the case to me.

There are those cases, few and far between, where you feel you might actually be walking with history, and that the decisions you make, the precedent you help establish, could have an impact that lasts for a generation. And then there are those cases, like this one, that feel as if you are *sleepwalking* with history, following the client's lead, focusing on that single goal and deliberately shutting your eyes to any possible wider implications. At the time Heather came to Squadron Ellenoff Gartenstein & Plesent, New York City and State law, to the extent that it even noticed that transgender people existed, criminalized them, often confusing transgender with homosexual or cross dressing or other so-called "deviant" behavior, mixing it all together into a legal and social mélange of "ick," that society preferred not to recognize except as a threat, as something to punish.[13] Heather, for instance, simply sitting across the desk and talking to me, faced arrest on a variety of charges in New York City, one of which was "impersonating a female"—a charge that wasn't fully taken off the books until 2011.[14]

In essence, the law, as understood and enforced, was arrayed against Heather, and it would have created quite a different case had she wanted to battle it head-on. But she didn't. I had been tasked with getting her a corrected birth certificate. That was something that *happened*; it was more or less routine. There were forms to fill out, documents to notarize, a place to go—The Department of Health, Office of Vital Records, at 125 Worth Street in lower Manhattan—where you filed your request and a clerk processed it. There was a $25 fee and, if I remember correctly, a nominal additional fee for each copy that you wanted made. This was the process. People used it all the time. Instead of amending the date of birth or the location or the name of mother or father, we were requesting a change from M to F, something that surely *didn't* happen all the time. But the process was identical.

We faced the imposing, hostile edifice of the law or the relatively friendly confines of a clerk's window. Why, as they say, bang your head against an open door? It is a violation of the law to amend a birth certificate for purposes of criminal impersonation. But if Heather was impersonating anyone, it was herself, who she really was, and that is no crime. We gathered the documents—which included a photograph of Heather—had them notarized, and I brought them down to Worth Street where a clerk accepted them and issued the amended certificate. From what I have been able to find out, there may not have been another one like it issued for over forty years.

In 2014 New York City passed a law permitting transgender people to change the gender affiliation on their birth certificate upon request.

In 2018 New York City law began permitting people who did not identify as male or female to select the gender neutral designation of X on their birth certificates.

Snapshots

Arthur told me, from the beginning, that he wouldn't marry me; that he had no intention of ever marrying again. I believed this was partially out of loyalty to his first wife, Jeanne; on the other hand, Arthur had no intention of being a "professional widower"—he loved life, good food and drink, books, theater, and film. Family. I told him that I didn't need to be married, that it wasn't important, but I did worry about Morris and Marion's opinion. They had grown to love Arthur, but they were about as socially conservative as it was possible to be and believed that a proper life followed certain protocols, one of which, perhaps the most important to them both, was marriage. I was an adult woman, but I was nervous when I sat them down.

"Arthur told me he doesn't want to marry me," I said. "He doesn't want to marry again. You should know that because you know how close we are."

Morris was silent for a moment, considering.

"That's all right," he said. "Don't worry. He's a good man. A decent man. It's okay. You don't have to get married."

I was a bit taken aback and turned to Marion.

She was nodding her head in agreement. *Listen to your father.*

* * *

At Patti's sixtieth birthday celebration, Susie gave a speech. She said that she was proud of her younger sister and added that she had reason to feel pride.

"Because, you know Patti, I raised you."

There was truth in this—during those years Susie had been forced to sacrifice much and to assume a heavy responsibility—but it was not the whole truth. Kitty Covington had come to live with us the day I brought Patti home from the hospital. She stayed with us until the day Patti left for college, seventeen years later. Kitty helped raise Patti, as well.

And me. I had the greatest claim on raising Patti even if, at times, it seemed as if I took the least responsibility.

Remember the book *Heather Has Two Mommies?* Patti had three.

* * *

I knew what I was doing. My eyes were wide open. I'd been warned by my mother when she tried to dissuade me from going to law school: *It isn't your time. It's the children's time.* But I believed that if my marriage was going to end, I would have to be able to support myself and the girls, and that meant not only getting into law school but graduating with honors. That was why I worked so hard, why I offloaded so much onto my daughters. I had started late, and if I was ever going to catch up, ever going to make anything of myself professionally, I knew I had to get on the Law Review; that was the key upon which my future turned, the object of a singular focus, and everything else, including my daughters, was in second place. I could imagine a future in which I would be able to care for all of us, but now, in the present, I depended on the girls to take care of each other, with help from Kitty Covington and from my mother.

The lines, which once seemed so carefully delineated, so clear, now blur and join across the years, and it becomes harder for me to know where my personal ambition ended and my hopes for my family began. My daughters knew; they could *feel* that my studies came first, and they resented it. I was aware of that resentment, but I didn't focus on it, choosing not to consider how this might shape them as they grew older, how it might shape our relationship in the years to come. I focused on the work at hand.

You default on some obligations and meet others. I made the Law Review and was recruited by Squadron Ellenoff Gartenstein & Plesent. There were additional factors in their decision, of course, but had I not made the Law Review, none of them would have mattered and the future would have been very different.

* * *

Every divorced parent, man or woman, has likely dealt with the powerful pull of a new love affair—or simply an affair—and the complex and troubling emotional ramifications this can have not only on children but on their own idea of what it means to be a good and loving parent. As a matrimonial attorney, I often have to guide my clients through these dangerous waters where questions of child custody and care—and parental responsibility—have legal, as well as emotional consequences. In my case there were no legal matters to consider, but it must have been apparent to everyone, including my daughters, that Arthur had quickly become a center of my emotional life.

It was natural that the girls at first saw Arthur as an interloper, usurping attention and affection that should have been directed toward them. But those feelings didn't last. He had the ability to speak to anyone and the rarer ability to *listen*, to engage with interest and without condescension, and all my daughters developed a personal, confidential relationship with him because he saw them and treated them as individuals, not as appendages of me—not as Harriet's girls. They were all crazy about him, so much so that if they had a particular concern—emotional issues or worries—medical issues—they'd speak to him, privately, and he'd talk to them and help them. All the types of trouble young women can get into. . .

If it was something he thought I should be made aware of, he'd explain to them why, urging them to talk to me, offering to be there when that happened. He knew how to keep a secret, never broke a confidence, never betrayed a trust. I think some of this was because he was a physician and had seen so much over the course of his career. He had a strong moral code, a sense of personal ethical conduct that he never violated, but he also understood that human beings are . . . human beings, with all their strengths and frailties. He was never judgmental, and my daughters never feared that anything he learned about them, anything he was told by them, would affect how he felt about them. And it never did.

* * *

As part of our separation agreement, Phil and I committed ourselves, in writing, to each pay half of Patti's college tuition. In the spring of 1980, when Patti was accepted into Bryn Mawr College, she excitedly told Phil the good news. Days later he responded with a long handwritten letter to his seventeen-year-old daughter:

> *I have to do this. I know what I promised and what is in the contract but I have the right not to give my consent, although it is not to be unreasonably withheld. I have my own financial needs . . . and based on those needs and that Brooklyn college is near to your home and free, I do not give my consent to your attending Bryn Mawr College.*
>
> *If that is to be the end of our relationship, so be it.*

The "financial needs" Phil spoke of included his purchase of two homes, one in Aspen and the other in the Berkshires.

We were at Arthur's apartment in Manhattan when Patti came over and handed the letter to Arthur to read. I was heartbroken for my daughter and also sad, in part, for Phil, and the enormously wasteful choices he had made in his life.

So be it.

Arthur was sitting in his favorite swivel "barrel" chair sipping an iced tea. When he finished reading, he said, "You're going to Bryn Mawr, Patti. Don't worry. I'll pay the tuition."

It was one of the many kindnesses he showed my daughters, part of a generosity of mind and heart expressed to four young women he had come to love.

Years later, when she married, Patti asked that Arthur walk her down the aisle. Arthur was loath to take Phil's place, to assume this traditional role, and he tried to demur. Patti insisted and that was what happened.

* * *

Robert Benjamin had been a patient of Arthur's who had become a good friend and, through Arthur, I also became a friend. Benjamin was chairman of United Artists Motion Pictures, but he was also a partner in the prestigious New York City law firm of Phillips Nizer Benjamin Krim & Ballon. The senior partner was Louis Nizer, one of the most famous lawyers in the country. Benjamin told me about an opening at the firm, working directly with the head of the matrimonial department, a woman named Julia Perles, and he suggested I give her a call.[15] This would be an important move up for me, a big step for an attorney barely two years out of law school. It would also situate me in the matrimonial department of an important and glamorous law firm.

It was obvious when we spoke that Julia had been expecting my call—Bob Benjamin had put the word in and I was as good as hired. She had a deep throaty voice, a cigarette and whiskey voice, I thought, though I later learned a gin martini was her drink of choice. We talked in general terms about the matrimonial department and what my responsibilities would be. She emphasized that at first, for an indeterminate period of time, I would mostly be working directly with her on a project of considerable importance. I waited for her to provide more details, but she didn't. Instead, she offered me the job. We had been speaking for about ten minutes.

When I accepted, she said, "Good." And then she added, in that phlegmy cigarette voice, no dramatics, no particular emphasis,

"We're going to change the world."

6 REFORM . . . AND ITS DISCONTENTS

The World as It Is: III

In 1976, when I joined the firm of Phillips Nizer Benjamin Krim & Ballon, New York State matrimonial attorneys were still laboring in the backwash of some of the most restrictive and antiquated divorce laws in the nation, the genesis of which dated back to the turn of the century, or even earlier.[1] There had been periodic attempts at change over the years, but these had been jerry-built atop an unsteady, outdated structure whose twin foundations remained *fault* and *title*. It was, in many respects, as if the fears, assumptions, and sex-based prejudices of the nineteenth century had been preserved in amber, like one of those fossilized insects, and dropped whole into a twentieth-century courtroom.

New York State viewed marriage as a contract between two people, in some essential points no different from a contract concerning property, although one major variance being the state's presumption that *this* contract would last a lifetime: until death us do part. The emphasis of the law, the force of public policy, was that it was in the state's interest, for the good of society at large, that the marriage remain intact. If the contract was broken, someone was at *fault* and part of the services, the preparation and the presentation of a divorce lawyer was to demonstrate to the court who that someone was and what had been done. This last amounted to an enormous hurdle because the grounds for divorce were limited and strictly construed. Of course, the intimate life of a couple, their lived experience, often contains mysteries, even to the two people involved, and is rarely so easily expressed or neatly defined. Nonetheless, New York State law demanded that the grounds for divorce be tailored to fit one of four categories:

Abandonment: one partner must leave the other, physically leaving the home for a year with no intention of returning. Abandonment later came to encompass *constructive abandonment*, the willful, unjustified, and continual refusal of one spouse to have sexual relations with the other.

Cruelty: originally defined actions that threatened the physical well-being of the spouse. This was later amended to include mental cruelty.

Adultery: sexual misadventure.

Imprisonment: For three years in a row.

Title was the second pillar of New York State's divorce laws. Basically this meant that upon the dissolution of marriage you were entitled to take from the wreckage only that which was in your name. Title controlled everything and title—of real estate, stocks, bonds, almost anything of real value—was almost always in the husband's name; in the name of the earner who had generated those stocks, bonds, real estate; who had generated the value. In practice this meant that the wife usually ended up with no property whatsoever. She was the "little woman," the stay-at-home wife and mother, and wasn't supposed to know about finances because that was above her head. Her husband kept her in the dark about such matters, paying the bills, treating her as one more decorative object in the home, as a child or as a maid. And the husband was able to claim: "I'm not taking anything from my wife. I'm just taking what's mine."[2]

Of course there were anomalies. I ended up with the home in the Rockaways, for instance, because I had title—Phil had put it in my name so as, in the event of getting sued for business-related debts, to avoid seizure of the home by creditors. This was not uncommon business practice, but most often the wife only ended up with what was then called alimony and is now called spousal support.

These were the divorce laws I had studied in law school; the world of divorce as it was understood by Stanley Plesent and other matrimonial attorneys I watched and admired. A bleak legal landscape that appeared to have been there forever and was, for both legal and cultural reasons, peculiarly resistant to change. This was the world Julia Perles knew, and she hired me to assist her as she worked, piece by piece, to dismantle it.

Garbage Men

Once, when raiding apartments and peeping through keyholes were tricks of their trade, divorce lawyers were known as the garbage men of the profession. Many entered the field only because more lucrative, cushy areas of practice were off limits to people like them: self-made children of immigrants, many of them Jewish, some of them women, raised in places like the Lower East Side or Coney Island, educated at places like Fordham, Brooklyn or New York Law School.—New York Times. December 15, 1991[3]

This was also the world of divorce that Stanley Plesent and Julia Perles and just about every other matrimonial attorney understood.

The law, which twisted the most intimate aspects of a couple's life into four neat categories, also twisted many of those who had to deal with it. Louis Nizer wrote that over the course of his career he had handled murder cases, extortion cases, inheritance battles between fathers and sons, custody disputes between daughters and grandparents, libel cases, and that:

All these litigations evoke intense feelings of animosity, revenge and retribution but none of them, even in their most aggravated form, can equal the sheer unadulterated venom of a matrimonial contest . . . Litigations between husband and wife exceed in bitterness and hatred those of any other relationships.[4]

And Nizer noted that in divorce cases, unlike the others, *"the lawyer is often caught in the fires that rage about him . . .* [the clients say]: *it's the lawyer putting him up to it . . . it's the lawyer's scheme. There is no end to this blazing hatred."*[5]

The low esteem in which matrimonial attorneys were held was, in part, a by-product of the low esteem in which *all* lawyers were held, but the law, particularly concerning sexual misadventure, added a sense of the disreputable, a sense of sordidness, that seemed to envelop the profession. Adultery might seem the simplest, or perhaps the most clear-cut of the fault categories, but it was actually a quagmire into which the reputation of matrimonial attorneys disappeared. In the 1930s, grounds for adultery included issues like criminal seduction and alienation of affection, the naming of co-respondents—matters that almost seemed to encourage blackmail. These and some of the worst of the other excesses had been abolished by the 1970s; some but not all. Adultery still had to be proven, and matrimonial attorneys did employ private investigators who did stake-out hotels and hotel rooms for illicit lovers: "They weren't in there saying their *Paternosters*," was the testimony in one notorious case. This and other factors seemed to link matrimonial attorneys to a kind of unhealthy sexual inquisitiveness: court-encouraged voyeurism.

Divorce lawyers who offered discounts to attractive clients in return for sexual favors; who stoked animosity rather than working to end it; who manipulated evidence or made it disappear if the price was right; who collaborated with the other side in order to prolong cases and increase fees—all the collective folk wisdom in popular culture—novels and movies—all the smutty stories and off color anecdotes seemed to trace their origin to an intrusive and out of touch legal system that legislators and attorneys across the nation were working to reform in what became known as the Divorce Revolution.[6]

Start the Revolution without Us

In September 1969, California governor Ronald Reagan signed the Family Law Act, making California the first no-fault divorce state in the nation. He said that while "*divorce is a tragic thing,*" the new law

is a step towards removing the acrimony and bitterness between a couple that is harmful not only to their children but also to society as a whole . . . and will do much to remove the sideshow elements of many divorce cases.[7]

Governor Reagan was said to be particularly enthusiastic about no-fault because he still resented having been accused of "mental cruelty" during his divorce from

Jane Wyman in 1948. Later, when the politics of reform took a darker turn, one conservative analyst wrote that, "with the stroke of his pen Ronald Reagan wiped out the moral basis for marriage in America." Reagan himself later said that signing the Family Law Act was one of the two or three biggest mistakes of his political life.[8]

At the time, however, reform, or at least the *idea* of reform, enjoyed general support from both political parties. Ronald Reagan was far from the only person, in California or elsewhere, who felt victimized by the necessity to fabricate grounds for divorce. But fault, traditionally, did more than just determine which partner was in the right and which was in the wrong—or, perhaps more accurately, which partner, in terms of behavior, was innocent and which was guilty—it divided marital assets according to the court's evaluation of that behavior—the "innocent" party awarded a larger share of the assets. The elimination of fault made such questions irrelevant. Where previously judges in California held enormous power in determining who got what—based on a determination of who *did* what—the new law turned California into a community property state: marital assets were divided *equally*, 50–50, and the power of judges was strictly limited. It was also hoped that reform would curb perceived excesses by matrimonial attorneys by rendering the legal environment of divorce "neutral" and draining it of the "hypocrisy and perjury that resulted from the use of marital fault as a controlling consideration in divorce proceedings."[9]

There has always been a moral factor in matrimonial law, a sense that society at large was "keeping score"—as even Ronald Reagan noted when he said that pre-reform divorce law in California created bitterness and acrimony that was "harmful" not only to those involved but to "society as a whole." By eliminating fault, largely removing personal behavior and misbehavior from the determination of who got what in divorce settlements, critics charged that the state of California was essentially creating a kind of marital nihilism that was bound to boomerang to the detriment of society. These voices became louder, the debate more bitter, as the years passed and as the effects of reform were more closely studied—although it often seemed as if this battle was a proxy for other, even more divisive debates about the role and rights of women, the responsibilities of men, the essential meaning of masculinity and of equality. What could not be debated was that the Family Law Act of 1969 was transformative, sparking a revolution that changed the nature and practice of family law, as well as in the understanding of the nature and practice of marriage itself.

In the years immediately following implementation, forty-three states moved to reform divorce law, most choosing some form of equitable distribution, which viewed marriage as an economic partnership and mandated a fair, though not necessarily equal, division of assets; fairness decided by a judge, assisted in some cases by a mediator appointed by the judge or agreed upon by both parties. In any event, the vast majority of states, including traditionally conservative states like Alabama, Mississippi, Idaho, and others, enacted some version of reform. It was as if a wildfire had come out of the west and burned to ashes the existing framework of matrimonial law.

But not in New York State.[10] There are reasons why this most progressive of states was one of the last to enact divorce law reform, why the Divorce Revolution was continually stalled and reform efforts stymied. A powerful Catholic Church, linked to strong conservative political forces that dominated the state legislature, resisted any effort seen as weakening the traditional ties of family and marriage. And a "divorce industry" of judges, politicians, lawyers, law enforcement, and tabloid editors prospered, as during Prohibition, by navigating the space between what the law decreed and the way people actually thought and behaved. As one observer put it: "a statute designed to prevent divorce in New York did not suppress the desire of New Yorkers for divorce."[11] The system may have been hypocritical, even corrupt, but it suited both sides:

Conservatives took comfort in the strictness of the law, while liberals noted the evasions by which marriages were frequently dissolved. Legislators of both stripes were loath to awaken "sleeping dogs" and risk heated debates about family breakdown.[12]

The revolution then, if it was to come, was not going to originate in the legislature in Albany. It was going to originate in a huge conference room on the 32nd floor of 40 West 57th Street, in the offices of Phillips Nizer Benjamin Krim & Ballon, presided over by a partner in the firm, Julia Perles, assisted by her "scribe."

Me.

Julia Perles

One afternoon I was in Julia's office and we were discussing the details of a divorce case on which I was assisting her. Julia was, to put it mildly, not particularly interested in small talk with associates, but our conversation began to drift into other matters. I knew she was a graduate (1937) of Brooklyn Law School and assumed, like me, she held the School in affection and high regard. There was an upcoming event for alumni, and I was planning to order a ticket and asked if she'd like me to order one for her, as well. Immediately the temperature in the room, which was never very high, dropped.

"I'd never go to one of those," she said.

Then:

"Everything I am, everything I have accomplished, is *in spite* of Brooklyn Law School, not because of it."

I never learned the reason she felt this way, but it was never easy to keep track of Julia's enmities. She was one of those people who, given the choice of loving or hating, chose hate.

Eventually she came to hate *me*, but that is another story.

* * *

Julia was a superb lawyer, one of the best I've ever known, and I worked for her and with her for four years, much of that time in intimate daily contact. We sat shoulder to shoulder in the conference room as the details of divorce reform in New York were hammered out, revised and revised again, and then again, as she sought, through craft and compromise, to create a bill that would attract enough support from both sides to win approval in the State Legislature. She was completely focused, forceful, and committed, a master draftsperson, measuring every word, searching for the precise combination that would unlock whatever puzzle she was trying to solve. *Sui Generis.*

She had a way of organizing her papers in these hard plastic folders, color-coded: red, green, yellow, and bright blue, and she'd stack them up on her desk so high and deep that you'd walk into her office at times and not know if she was there. Then you'd see this plume of smoke rising from behind all those folders. She was always smoking, there was always a cigarette or a cigarillo in her hand, and you knew she was at her desk. Or the phone would ring and she'd be speaking to a client and she'd shift the folders around, always finding the right one. She knew where everything was, although no one else could figure out her system. I'd dread those times she'd say, "Go to the office and find X" or "bring me Y"—there didn't seem to be any system, no rhyme or reason to those stacked folders, but she could always put her hands on exactly what she was looking for.

Julia was wonderful with clients, would spend whatever time they needed talking to them, comforting them, explaining exactly what she was doing and what might happen next. She had this deep voice, all those cigarettes, and it was like she was crooning to them, reassuring them, making sure they were happy and comfortable. They loved her. That same voice was an impatient rasp when talking to me or the other associates. She moved easily from rude to brusque and back again, always sounding annoyed and irritated. When she hired me, after a ten-minute telephone conversation, she said, "Ya want the job? Ya got the job. When can you start?" all in a rush, making a single sentence out of it, as if she'd suddenly lost all patience with this job-hiring thing and was anxious to get back to something important. That was generally how she spoke to the associates, a kind of chip on her shoulder aggressiveness that was meant to intimidate.

Part of it was her physical appearance. She was about twenty years older than me, a thickset woman, not heavy really, just *solid.* A dreadnought. When she moved through the office, you heard her—she didn't walk, she clumped, cigarette

in hand, a scowl on her face, looking for trouble. And finding it. She was always ready to be offended, to give offense. A bleak view of the world, of people.

Yet there was so much about her that I admired, that I admire still, and that I learned to emulate. She was a genius at law; there was nothing she couldn't do . . . except try a case.

Julia would not go into the courtroom, and if negotiations failed and the case moved to trial, another attorney would take over. It takes a particular set of skills to be a good trial lawyer, nothing is harder in my profession, and there are many attorneys, many superior attorneys, who just can't do it. In Julia's case I think the issue was the loss of control. She was entering a room where she didn't have the final word, where preparation, no matter how thorough, occasionally goes by the wayside depending on the manner—even the whim—of the judge: *We're not doing it that way. We're doing it this way.* And all the prep goes out the window and you have to improvise in the moment, reconstruct your questioning, take a different direction—and all this under tremendous time constraints. There was a certain doggedness to Julia's intelligence which was the source of great power during negotiations or drafting a proposal, when you argued, day after day, along familiar lines. In court those lines could suddenly disappear and you might be left vulnerable or exposed. That was not a position in which Julia would be comfortable. And while she was a skilled negotiator, capable of great subtlety as she maneuvered to reach her goal, there were times when she held on to an idea long past its expiration date. During negotiations over divorce law reform she mocked those who suggested it would lead to a rise in divorce rates or that one party might exploit the changes in the law to gain unfair advantage over the other.

"I think that's ridiculous," she said. "People don't get divorced over economic reasons. They get divorced because they can't stay married."[13]

* * *

I hadn't been working with Julia for long when the firm held a big party. I don't remember the reason, maybe a summer party, or Labor Day, something like that. Arthur was friends with Bob Benjamin and with Arthur Krim, another former patient, who was also a named partner at the Nizer firm. Krim was a mover and shaker, former finance chairman of the Democratic Party, advisor to Lyndon Johnson, chairman of United Artists and Orion Pictures. So when I went to the party, Benjamin and Krim made sure that Arthur and I were seated at the main table, along with Louis Nizer and all the named partners. It was a heady experience for an associate. Julia was at another table, and I could see from her face that she was very unhappy about the seating arrangements. There were any number of reasons why it all ended badly, but I think it all began the night of that party.

Still, I will always be grateful to Julia, not only for what I learned but for what I was able to experience. She sat me next to her at that long desk in the conference room, and we worked with these legislators, and with brilliant thinkers and law professors. There were no computers, and it was up to me to keep track of all the suggestions, all the changes; to make a record of what had been agreed to and what remained to be accomplished; collating the various drafts, suggesting changes of my own based on my deep knowledge and familiarity with all that had been proposed. I can still feel it viscerally, the emotions in that room, the excitement, and it was all because of Julia. She brought me into history.

The Life

Phillips Nizer Benjamin Krim & Ballon occupied the entire 32nd floor at 40 East 57th Street. You stepped out into this gorgeous reception area, as if you were stepping out onto a stage. There was something glamorous about it, something theatrical; you could imagine that everyone there had been silent and still, waiting for you to arrive before they resumed their activity, waiting for the elevator doors to open like a curtain rising. It was a carefully cultivated effect, designed to impress, but it was real, as well. There *was* something glamorous about the firm and about its senior partner, Louis Nizer, who represented movie, Broadway, and television stars, celebrated authors and artists, sports stars, and who was himself a celebrity: a bit of a bon vivant man about town, raconteur and toastmaster, a bestselling author.[14] He was the Mystery Guest on the popular TV show *What's My Line* and the blindfolded panel had taken only a minute or two to identify him: "*Are you a lawyer?*", Dorothy Kilgallen asked. "*Are you Louis Nizer?*" He was *that* famous and the public spaces and private offices of his firm were meant to reflect and endorse that fame. Even the fees he was awarded were headline news, *The New York Times* reporting that one divorce case had earned him "counsel fees that were the highest ever awarded in New York."[15] He was, for a time, "the highest paid lawyer in the world." This was in the *Guinness Book of World Records*, so you could take it to the bank.

And you might have to, because another message implicit in the beautifully decorated reception area, the art on the walls, the breathtaking views of Central Park and upper Manhattan, was that good representation did not come cheap. Of all the firms I've worked for—at least until I started my own—Phillips Nizer Benjamin Krim & Ballon was the most forthright about the fact that there was the law, which was handled brilliantly, and there was the *business* of the law, which was handled with dispatch and without embarrassment. Everyone who worked there was expected to keep in mind that the firm was a living concern that paid salaries, rent, upkeep, maintenance, and taxes. There was nothing sentimental about it; even the *Guinness Book of World Records* baloney was part of the firm's ethos: free publicity at a time when lawyers were forbidden to advertise; and, of course, the title "highest paid lawyer" was like catnip, drawing the highest paying clients.

Among the lessons I learned at the firm, and there were many, none was more important than this clear-eyed understanding of the *profession* of law.

* * *

The firm may have had glamour, but what it didn't have was enough office space for the attorneys who worked there. I had been hired—and hired in a rush—because Julia Perles needed urgent assistance juggling her usual heavy caseload and her continuing efforts to craft reform of the state's divorce laws. When I arrived at work that first day, I found that no permanent office was available for me—they'd run out of space. Fortunately, it was a big enough firm so that someone was always on vacation or out of the office for an extended period, and I'd be assigned that empty office for however long it was available. Sometimes I worked out of a small, cramped associate's office; sometimes I'd set up shop in a partner's office, with a big desk, plenty of room and a lovely view overlooking 57th street. When it was time to vacate, and this happened often, I'd pack up all my material—foolscap pads, pens, books, papers, and personal belongings along with my own transparent plastic color coded folders (arranged alphabetically, as opposed to Julia's to hell and gone system)—put it all in a large shopping cart—a metal supermarket shopping cart, like the ones from the A&P or Waldbaum's—and push it on down the hallway, Mother Courage Esq, heading toward my next temporary abode, where I'd park the cart outside and begin moving in. I was so happy to be at the firm and doing important work that I didn't mind any of it; and eventually I was assigned a permanent office.

One of the people who took an early interest in me was Bill Reilly, a partner in the firm, a very able attorney, and an angel of a man, who became a mentor. Bill was the lawyer who took over all of Julia Perles' cases that couldn't be settled and was the only person she trusted to bring those cases to trial. He was also the firm's "designated loser." Louis Nizer had the reputation, like TV's Perry Mason, of never losing a case; a reputation important to him personally and important to the firm as well, for economic reasons. As a selling point, "Never Loses" is as good as it gets; "Usually Wins" . . . not so much. So when it looked as if a case wasn't going as well as might be hoped, Bill Reilly would take over as the attorney of record. At that point no matter how the case went Louis Nizer's record would remain immaculate.

Bill worked closely with Julia and he understood how difficult she could be. Early on he kept an eye on me, helping in big ways and small, until I could find my sea legs. I would give him whatever I had written during the day and he would take it with him, reading it on the train ride home from Penn Station to Huntington, Long Island, where he lived with his wife Virginia and his five children. He would mark up my copy, correcting and amending it, suggesting additional ways I could make it stronger, then hand it back to me the next morning so I could rework it before handing it in to Julia. Bill made me a better writer and a better thinker and he helped me acclimate myself to the "style" of the firm—what was expected, what was acceptable. I've never forgotten his kindness and generosity and hope, over my career, I have managed in some small way to do the same when I have worked with younger, less experienced colleagues.

Bill's youngest child, James Brian Reilly, was working as a bond trader at Keefe, Bruyette & Woods, on the 89th floor of Two World Trade Center, and was killed in the terrorist attack on September 11, 2001. Recovery workers later found his company identification badge, which Bill and the family donated to the National September 11 Memorial & Museum.

James Reilly was twenty-five years old.

* * *

One of Julia's closest friends was Roy Cohn; indeed, if Cohn was capable of the emotion, I'd say they loved each other. Both were preternaturally smart; both were brilliant lawyers capable of great ruthlessness; and both shared a dim view of humanity in general and, more specifically, a deep suspicion of the motives and prospects of most of those they came across. The difference was that Julia had a heart and was scrupulously honest while Roy Cohn looked at you as if weighing the pros and cons of shaking you down. Julia may have divided the world into that small group she loved or respected and the much greater group she could run roughshod over. Cohn divided the world into those marks he could steal from or take advantage of and those he couldn't, and among the former were his own clients, for which he was eventually disbarred—the Appellate Division of the State Supreme Court finding he had engaged in "particularly reprehensible" conduct.[16] This was in 1986, shortly before his death.

But the time I am writing about is 1976–80, when Cohn was at the peak of his power as a kind of malign Prince of the City. He had his hand in everything and was "friends" with everyone, from Cardinal Spellman to mafia bosses like Tony Salerno to a young Donald Trump—a wide circle of acquaintances that, in retrospect, may not have been that wide at all. His malevolent reputation attracted at least as many clients as it repelled; people, especially those involved in a bitter divorce action, are often volubly looking for a gloves off/no limit attorney and that's what Cohn promised. "My scare value is high" is how he put it, although this itself was part of the scam and, unless he was representing really powerful clients like Aristotle Onassis or Rupert Murdoch, he always had his own agenda.[17]

In the case in which we were involved, Julia was representing Arnold Baker, a mover and shaker in the art world. His wife, Valerie, who had filed for divorce, was represented by Roy Cohn. Settlement talks were ongoing, and one afternoon Julia asked me to go over to Cohn's office to pick up some papers she needed to review.

Roy Cohn worked and lived in a townhouse on East 68th Street, just off Fifth Avenue. His offices were on the top floor, his living quarters off the stairway on the second. Cohn was counsel to the law firm of Saxe Bacon & Bolan, and the townhouse was owned by a Saxe Bacon subsidiary, as was the Rolls Royce Cohn drove, and just about everything else he used, up to the pens he wrote with and the suits he wore. Cohn himself owned nothing, had almost no assets, nothing the long list of creditors who constantly pursued him might attach or claim in a court victory. Every transaction was in cash, untraceable; everything, no matter how simple, even legitimate, seemingly on the cusp of larceny. It was an exhausting way to live, but it seemed to suit him.

A handsome young man in a suit and tie met me at the door of the townhouse and brought me into the reception area. *Mr. Cohn*, I was told, *will be with you shortly*. There were about five or six young men, not unlike the first, some making their leisurely way up or down the staircase, others just lollygagging about. There was a television on in a room just off the reception area, and atop the tv was a large stuffed frog. I thought I could see another stuffed animal in the corner of a sofa. There was a feeling of ease, of indolence, particularly when contrasted with the atmosphere of Phillips Nizer Benjamin Krim & Ballon. Was it really possible to work here, to get work done? At the same time I felt something was off, that in a way that is hard to explain, this was the *wrong* place.

Cohn came down the staircase slowly, carefully. He was wearing a long silk robe, open from throat to chest, loosely belted at the waist. There was some kind of design on the robe and like everything else I'd seen it looked at the same time both expensive and cheap. Cohn was about 5 feet 8 inches tall, with a large head and a slight body. He had a large nose pitted with scars and piercing blue eyes, hooded, dead, and when he spoke to me, he kept licking his lips. He handed me a manila envelope with the papers Julia had requested and we talked for a bit, I forget about what. He may have asked to be remembered to Julia. He was soft-spoken and courteous. Within a minute or two I was back on East 68th Street.

Several months later an issue between Arnold and Valerie Baker proved impossible to negotiate and that portion of the case was referred to a Special Referee. The Special Referee is an arm of the court, appointed by the judge to hear certain matters and his or her ruling, under certain circumstances, can have the same force of law as a judge's ruling. We were to argue before the Special Referee and Julia asked me to represent Arnold. I would be on my own, representing an important client, facing Roy Cohn, the city's most feared advocate. I don't know why Julia chose me, don't know what, if any, wheels were turning, but I do know I was both excited and apprehensive.

Arnold and I showed up early. Valerie showed up a bit later, without her attorney. We waited. Then the Special Referee arrived, a woman, an old-timer, who knew the system inside out and brooked no funny business. We waited a bit more, the Special Referee growing angry, Valerie angry and embarrassed. This was a scheduled sworn hearing. It meant something. At that moment, a comely young man entered the courtroom. He said he was from Saxe Bacon & Bolan and that Mr. Cohn would not be able to appear. He needed a continuance. The Special Referee was having none of it. She defaulted Cohn and gave me a complete recovery based on that default. Within a day Valerie Baker fired Cohn and may have filed suit against him as well.

If she did, she went to the end of a long line. When Cohn died, the beautiful limestone townhouse was sold for close to four million dollars—over fifteen million in 2026 dollars—but the Internal Revenue Service had sued Cohn for failure to pay taxes, and the money was held in escrow under court order pending resolution of the case.

Mr. Nizer

I always called him *Mr. Nizer*, and I was always *Ms. Cohen*, all through the four years I worked at the firm and in the years afterwards, an unself-conscious formality that seemed emblematic of the sometimes distant but very real friendship between us. Once, while I was still at Phillips Nizer Benjamin Krim & Ballon, he gave me a watercolor he had painted, a still life, flower and vase, by way of thanks for my work with him on a particular case. Years later, long after I left, a friend, knowing how much I admired Mr. Nizer, gave me as a birthday gift his beautiful rendering of the Western Wall in Jerusalem. Mr. Nizer was an amateur artist of no little skill and had exhibited at several galleries. I still have both paintings.

I came to the firm as one kind of lawyer, and I left as another. Mr. Nizer helped me to understand, more than any single person, the profession of lawyering, and to shape the lawyer I wished to become and did become. My husband Arthur provided a paradigm of how to act with grace and courage as a human being upon the earth, providing, as well, an example of honorable professional conduct. Mr. Nizer helped me to fill in all the empty spaces specific to the vocation I had chosen, to deal with the ethical responsibilities and the mercantile demands while providing the best possible care for a client; and understanding, without sentimentality, what that care required of you and what it took from you.

In the mid-1930s, while still in *his* mid-thirties, he'd become the chief counsel for the New York Film Board of Trade, and there was always something showbiz about him, the showbiz of Jolson and Eddie Cantor, George Jessel and Ed Wynn. He was a toastmaster of note, even wrote a book about it, *Between You and Me* in 1948, a kind of *Stop me if you've heard this one* collection of humorous anecdotes about the great film and radio stars he rubbed elbows with.[18] His list of celebrity clients was staggering, ranging from Charlie Chaplin and Salvador Dali to Mae West and Johnny Carson. In 1960 Elizabeth Taylor and Eddie Fisher, probably the most famous couple in the world, engaged him to sue six motion picture fan magazines for libeling them by printing "malicious gossip" about the state of their marriage.

The law is majestic, but lawyers have to be agile. Four years later he represented Fisher during his divorce from Taylor.

The reason Taylor and Fisher thought of Louis Nizer when they were contemplating libel actions was because he had won one of the most famous libel cases in US history, successfully representing Quentin Reynolds' lawsuit against right-wing columnist Westbrook Pegler. That case was later the basis for a hit Broadway show *A Case of Libel.* Several years later he represented broadcaster John Henry Faulk in a successful suit that awarded Faulk the highest libel award to date—3.5 million dollars—and effectively ended the decade-long right-wing blacklist against alleged leftist performers. George C. Scott played Mr. Nizer in the TV movie based on the case, *Fear on Trial.* Mr. Nizer wrote about these and other celebrated cases in a 1961 memoir, *My Life in Court.* The book sold hundreds of thousands of copies, was on the *New York Times* bestseller list for seventy-two weeks, and brought him national fame. Over sixty years after its initial publication, it remains in print.

Louis Nizer was short, perhaps 5'4", always immaculately turned out—suit, tie, polished black shoes, pocket square. He had a kind of craggy attractiveness and an engaging, shy smile, his wavy black hair combed straight back and parted in the middle, like every ambitious district attorney in those old Warner Brothers films. Two secretaries sat outside his office, two beautiful and accomplished women who ran his professional life. They sat at desks on either side of two large doors. Mr. Nizer's office was a suite, tastefully decorated, a huge space. It was a hike from those doors to his desk, which was at the far end of the room and slightly raised—the only place in the world that permitted him to look down on all those approaching him. It was like visiting the Wizard of Oz: Louis Nizer, sitting behind the desk—all 5'4" of him, dispensing advice and aphorisms, the energy, the sheer theatrical brio radiating off him like a Catherine wheel.

Of course, when you looked behind the curtain of the Great and Terrible Oz, what you found was, to Dorothy's chagrin, a fraud. When you looked behind the curtain at Mr. Nizer, what you found was a Wizard.

* * *

I had been brought into the firm to assist Julia Perles, and she was not pleased when, shortly after the office summer party, Mr. Nizer asked if he could borrow me. He told her that he wanted me to work on a custody matter that had arisen unexpectedly out of a divorce case that he was handling. I say he "asked" Julia but that was a courtesy: as Senior Partner he had his prerogatives, and his requests were always honored. I had, at this point, only spoken to Mr. Nizer once: meaningless party chatter when Arthur and I shared a table with him and the other named partners, to Julia's visible unhappiness. I was as surprised as Julia that he had summoned me and had no knowledge of the case that he was working on.

His office was about the largest I had ever been in. It seemed to me like a palace, or a theatrical designer's idea of a palace, although the impression it created was so genuine, so overwhelming that it seemed to erase the distinction between the real and the fake. During the walk to Mr. Nizer's desk—and it *was* a walk—I was both apprehensive and exhilarated: exhilarated because I was *here*, I'd arrived, and he'd chosen me to work with him; apprehensive because there was so much at stake. He was on that raised platform, and I had to look up to meet his gaze. Next to the big desk was a smaller desk with a telephone on it. I later learned that the only person who called that phone was Mr. Nizer's wife, Mildred, and when she did, he stopped what he was doing—no matter who was with him or what was being discussed—and spoke to her in a loving, syrupy voice, for however long she wished.

The case Mr. Nizer was working on was a particularly ugly one in which he represented Louisa Fairchild, the daughter of his friends Alan and Leigh Daniels. Alan was a partner and co-founder of one of Wall Street's top investment firms; Leigh was an heiress, the granddaughter of a founder of an oil and gas concern that had begun in the Texas panhandle but which now operated worldwide. Louisa's son from her first marriage, twelve-year-old William, had been alienated from his mother by his stepfather and, in a fit of anger, had physically threatened her. Mr. Nizer had two grown stepsons but no children of his own, and he felt he needed help in understanding the psychology of the child. That's why I was brought along and while Mr. Nizer and the grandparents discussed what to do next, I sat offering comfort and counsel to Louisa, who seemed bewildered at all that was happening and who needed a good deal of attention, then and later.

I wasn't chosen that day because of my abilities or legal acumen. I was chosen because I was available, because Mr. Nizer remembered me from the party, and because I was a grown woman, a maternal figure in his mind, no doubt, who probably knew how to handle children. But it turned out we worked well together. He was a born teacher; he was teaching something every minute we were together, lessons that went to the heart of the practical reality of being a lawyer—the day in and day out of it. Most afternoons Mr. Nizer and colleagues, along with whatever visiting celebrities were in town and available, had lunch at the Algonquin Hotel, a kind of muted re-creation of the original Round Table, and he got in the habit of taking me along. At first I think he liked having me around because he so obviously enjoyed being a mentor, and I was always, in whatever environment—even at lunch—an enthusiastic and quick learning student. As I began to develop, under his tutelage, my own style, I believe he came to appreciate me as a colleague, and he asked for me more often. "I'd like Ms. Cohen on this" or occasionally, "Let's bring Harriet"—to Julia's increasing displeasure. I was privileged to watch him, to work with him, on matrimonial cases, public corruption cases, everything with which he was involved. Even a murder case.

was having none of it. She defaulted Cohn and gave me a complete recovery based on that default. Within a day Valerie Baker fired Cohn and may have filed suit against him as well.

If she did, she went to the end of a long line. When Cohn died, the beautiful limestone townhouse was sold for close to four million dollars—over fifteen million in 2026 dollars—but the Internal Revenue Service had sued Cohn for failure to pay taxes, and the money was held in escrow under court order pending resolution of the case.

Mr. Nizer

I always called him *Mr. Nizer*, and I was always *Ms. Cohen*, all through the four years I worked at the firm and in the years afterwards, an unself-conscious formality that seemed emblematic of the sometimes distant but very real friendship between us. Once, while I was still at Phillips Nizer Benjamin Krim & Ballon, he gave me a watercolor he had painted, a still life, flower and vase, by way of thanks for my work with him on a particular case. Years later, long after I left, a friend, knowing how much I admired Mr. Nizer, gave me as a birthday gift his beautiful rendering of the Western Wall in Jerusalem. Mr. Nizer was an amateur artist of no little skill and had exhibited at several galleries. I still have both paintings.

I came to the firm as one kind of lawyer, and I left as another. Mr. Nizer helped me to understand, more than any single person, the profession of lawyering, and to shape the lawyer I wished to become and did become. My husband Arthur provided a paradigm of how to act with grace and courage as a human being upon the earth, providing, as well, an example of honorable professional conduct. Mr. Nizer helped me to fill in all the empty spaces specific to the vocation I had chosen, to deal with the ethical responsibilities and the mercantile demands while providing the best possible care for a client; and understanding, without sentimentality, what that care required of you and what it took from you.

In the mid-1930s, while still in *his* mid-thirties, he'd become the chief counsel for the New York Film Board of Trade, and there was always something showbiz about him, the showbiz of Jolson and Eddie Cantor, George Jessel and Ed Wynn. He was a toastmaster of note, even wrote a book about it, *Between You and Me* in 1948, a kind of *Stop me if you've heard this one* collection of humorous anecdotes about the great film and radio stars he rubbed elbows with.[18] His list of celebrity clients was staggering, ranging from Charlie Chaplin and Salvador Dali to Mae West and Johnny Carson. In 1960 Elizabeth Taylor and Eddie Fisher, probably the most famous couple in the world, engaged him to sue six motion picture fan magazines for libeling them by printing "malicious gossip" about the state of their marriage.

drove, and just about everything else he used, up to the pens he wrote with and the suits he wore. Cohn himself owned nothing, had almost no assets, nothing the long list of creditors who constantly pursued him might attach or claim in a court victory. Every transaction was in cash, untraceable; everything, no matter how simple, even legitimate, seemingly on the cusp of larceny. It was an exhausting way to live, but it seemed to suit him.

A handsome young man in a suit and tie met me at the door of the townhouse and brought me into the reception area. *Mr. Cohn*, I was told, *will be with you shortly*. There were about five or six young men, not unlike the first, some making their leisurely way up or down the staircase, others just lollygagging about. There was a television on in a room just off the reception area, and atop the tv was a large stuffed frog. I thought I could see another stuffed animal in the corner of a sofa. There was a feeling of ease, of indolence, particularly when contrasted with the atmosphere of Phillips Nizer Benjamin Krim & Ballon. Was it really possible to work here, to get work done? At the same time I felt something was off, that in a way that is hard to explain, this was the *wrong* place.

Cohn came down the staircase slowly, carefully. He was wearing a long silk robe, open from throat to chest, loosely belted at the waist. There was some kind of design on the robe and like everything else I'd seen it looked at the same time both expensive and cheap. Cohn was about 5 feet 8 inches tall, with a large head and a slight body. He had a large nose pitted with scars and piercing blue eyes, hooded, dead, and when he spoke to me, he kept licking his lips. He handed me a manila envelope with the papers Julia had requested and we talked for a bit, I forget about what. He may have asked to be remembered to Julia. He was soft-spoken and courteous. Within a minute or two I was back on East 68th Street.

Several months later an issue between Arnold and Valerie Baker proved impossible to negotiate and that portion of the case was referred to a Special Referee. The Special Referee is an arm of the court, appointed by the judge to hear certain matters and his or her ruling, under certain circumstances, can have the same force of law as a judge's ruling. We were to argue before the Special Referee and Julia asked me to represent Arnold. I would be on my own, representing an important client, facing Roy Cohn, the city's most feared advocate. I don't know why Julia chose me, don't know what, if any, wheels were turning, but I do know I was both excited and apprehensive.

Arnold and I showed up early. Valerie showed up a bit later, without her attorney. We waited. Then the Special Referee arrived, a woman, an old-timer, who knew the system inside out and brooked no funny business. We waited a bit more, the Special Referee growing angry, Valerie angry and embarrassed. This was a scheduled sworn hearing. It meant something. At that moment, a comely young man entered the courtroom. He said he was from Saxe Bacon & Bolan and that Mr. Cohn would not be able to appear. He needed a continuance. The Special Referee

He often used aphorisms as a shorthand to explain his way of thinking or his strategy. In the Fairchild case, for example, he believed that everything depended on removing the child from the malevolent and seductive influence of the stepfather. The entire case turned on this necessity, and in order to achieve this end, he was willing to take whatever steps were necessary—including using the Family Court to order a placement of the child, who was growing increasingly violent in language and attitude, in a youth care facility—in essence, a jail for children. "*Hardheaded is soft hearted*," is how he put it, meaning that sometimes a lawyer must take the responsibility to make very difficult, even harsh decisions on behalf of the client, decisions that might hurt the client in the short term but would result, in the long term, in a successful resolution of the case. And that's what happened here. The child, faced with the possibility of being sent away, reluctantly agreed to leave his stepfather, and Alan and Leigh Daniels assumed temporary custody. Years later William, a graduate of the Stanford Graduate School of Business, joined the investment firm his grandfather had helped found.

Another aphorism was "*Make your last line your first line.*" This referred to the writing of legal papers, particularly submissions to the court. Based on his long experience, Mr. Nizer believed that no judge was going to read the entire brief and that judges were often swayed by the initial argument. So, rather than wait until the end, the summing up, to present that argument, you should present it on page one, the first paragraph; that's where you were going to win or lose the case. Wikipedia called this "BLUF"—"Best Line Up Front"—and claims it was invented in 2017 by aides to Donald Trump, who couldn't get their boss to read more than one or two paragraphs. But Mr. Nizer was doing it and teaching it more than half a century ago, emphasizing that the argument had to be good; there couldn't be any ambiguity about it because you want to leave it to the court to interpret as little as possible. Every word counts, every word has to convey something powerful.

I teach this now to my young associates, who often seem prisoners of chronology, producing briefs that go on, page after page, factually correct and unreadable, before making their point. What it comes down to, in essence, is spending the time and making the effort to truly understand your case. If you don't, no amount of verbiage is going to convince a judge, a jury, or anyone else. Clear writing, as Mr. Nizer taught, comes from clear thinking.

It was all part of his effort to shape the legal battlefield to his advantage. I watched him in court, alert to every opportunity, always looking to wrong foot his opponent, to get them off balance. He'd spent long hours in the office organizing his material, marshaling his arguments, until he was completely comfortable with every issue that might arise, leaving as little as possible to chance. In court he was masterful, a showman, but a showman who delivered the goods: passionate, prepared, eloquent when he needed to be—a mixture, he said himself, of psychologist, visionary, and realist.[19] He used everything—the way he spoke, the way he dressed, his posture, his countenance—it was all part of a performance, thought out and rehearsed. Nothing escaped his attention. He knew how to use public opinion to his own ends and was unapologetic about the effort to frame the issues in the media:

> *The winning of popular support depends on intricate, psychological factors. The lawyer's art of persuasion must encompass public approval, because, whether we like it or not, it may have real impact within the courtroom.*[20]

He knew the names of everyone in court and would always address the judge by name, the court officers; a public affability that belied his celebrity status and put everyone at their ease. Or lulled everyone to their ease. Real, but also part of the performance aimed at securing even the smallest of advantages for his case and his client, a performance that never ended. The last article he wrote, published about a month before he died in November 1994, was entitled: *Finding and Selecting the Right Judge.*

* * *

Mr. Nizer had his own version of Pasteur's axiom that *chance favors the prepared mind.*

> *Yes, there's such a thing as luck in trial law but it only comes at 3 o'clock in the morning. You'll still find me in the library looking for luck at 3 o'clock in the morning.*[21]

His first drafts were always done by hand, usually using a black Sharpie. He *would* often work deep into the night before a trial, arranging his material, making last-minute preparations, assuring himself that his knowledge of the issues at hand was absolute. He would check and recheck every key point so that courtroom surprises were kept to a minimum; and that when they inevitably came he would not be thrown off his stride and could react, instinctively and forcefully, from a deep well of knowledge. I continue to emulate his method of preparation, although I'll work from home rather than the office or library, often propped up in bed the night before court, my papers spread out before me, working into the early morning hours, making sure that nothing, no matter how seemingly minor, goes unexamined. I don't claim to prepare quite as thoroughly as Mr. Nizer—I don't think anyone can—but I do my best.

And while Mr. Nizer never explicitly came up with his own version of Arthur's dictum—*See one. Do one. Teach one*—he didn't have to because that was the way he ran the office. The more I worked with him the more he came to trust me, and the more responsibility he gave me. I think the surest sign of how he assessed my abilities—and one of which I remain proud—is that when one of his stepsons was getting a divorce, he asked me to handle it.

And yet. And yet. One felt always that the affability, the mentoring, the many kindnesses were, in a way, another type of performance and that underneath it all was the resolve, the unemotional reckoning that had helped him achieve—and to maintain across the decades—such a high level of success. As much as Mr. Nizer liked me, as much as I felt appreciated and even loved by him, I was just one cog in the machine. And the machine was the office, the practice—a going concern, a business that was run for profit. He never forgot that. And I haven't either.

Reform

Divorce Reforms Gaining in Albany.

—New York Times, May 20, 1976.[22]

Fiscal "Equity" in Divorce Dies in Albany.

—New York Times, June 3, 1976.[23]

. . . the divorce bill, versions of which have been proposed without success in the Legislature five years in a row.

—New York Times, February 5, 1977.[24]

Albany Moves Toward Divorce-Law Change.

—New York Times, March 12, 1979.[25]

Bill Establishing "Equitable" Divorce Settlements Is Stalled in Albany.

—New York Times, March 9, 1980.[26]

Months passed. A year. Another year. And another. And still, the Legislature would not approve divorce law reform. Forty-two states had revised their laws, but New York remained a bedrock of anti-reform resistance, or perhaps anti-reform lassitude is more appropriate, as just about everybody *said* they were for reform but nothing ever happened.

If death came from Albany, the saying went, *we would all live to a ripe old age.*

Those of us involved in the battle for reform had to deal with a wearying cycle of hope and disappointment, but Julia was indefatigable, possessed of a dogged determination that was in part admirable and in part opportunistic. No one worked more closely with her during these years than myself, and I found that Julia was no feminist, no ideologue, and to her general suspicion of just about everyone who walked the earth (except Roy Cohn!) she added a more specific distrust of causes and those who believed in causes. She had a kind of pessimistic savvy about the ways of the world: she could be wrong, but she was rarely disappointed. I think Julia understood which way the wind was blowing and that, sooner or later (and it turned out later than even *she* expected) some kind of reform was inevitable. When that happened, she wanted her fingerprints on the legislation rather than those of some radical feminist or National Organization for Women (NOW) apparatchik.

Conservatives in the Legislature never understood that, paradoxically, they had in Julia, who spearheaded the effort they so resisted, a kind of ally, as determined as they were to prevent *radical* reform. I think that one of the reasons my hire was so attractive to her was that I was a mature woman and, therefore, in her eyes, less likely than my younger colleagues to be swayed by the winds of militant change.

The long battle over reform provided me with a second education, to go along with what I'd learned at Brooklyn Law School, where matrimonial law, as it then existed in New York State, was an important part of my curriculum. All that was very fresh in my mind—I'd graduated only three years earlier—and now I had the opportunity of participating with legal scholars, politicians, and analysts—some of the best minds in the country—as the prospective contours of reform took shape. Present at the creation.

All the meetings were held in the large conference room at Phillips Nizer Benjamin Krim & Ballon, at a long table, where Julia presided and I sat next to her, shoulder to shoulder, as every word of the new law was written. Julia was a wonderful draftswoman, precise in her writing, clear in her meaning, and able to synthesize a vast amount of material, no detail too small to escape her attention up to and including the placement of commas. What emerged was comprehensive legislation designed to replace all existing statutes governing divorce in New York State. There were obviously a lot of moving parts, and over the years there were changes aimed at attracting wavering legislators, but the basic elements remained more or less the same and concerned three main areas: Title, Alimony and Fault.

Title was eliminated as the governing principle in the division of marital property and replaced by *equitable distribution*, which promised a fair (as opposed to equal) accounting. Both husband and wife would now start from the premise that each had claims to all property, regardless of who held title. The criteria by which the claims to marital property were determined were expanded to include contributions traditionally undertaken by the wife and traditionally ignored by the court: housekeeping, childcare, maintenance of the home—and these were given value and consideration by the judge.

Alimony, which, at the time, applied only to women and which could last a lifetime or until remarriage, was replaced by what was then called "maintenance" and is now called "spousal support."

Fault: While our proposed bill did not turn New York into a no-fault divorce state—which we all believed, regardless of the merits, was a political non-starter—it did remove the use of fault grounds to disentitle women to spousal support. Cruelty, adultery—which, as a practical matter, was *only* applied to women in the existing law—and other issues could not be used as a moral cudgel to legally force dire economic results.

Overall, our proposed measure aimed at reconciling the huge differences between what was called "formal law" (the law on the books) and "living law" (actual divorce practices in the state). On a more practical level, reform was intended to remove the shame and acrimony from divorce—no more dirty linens, no more Garbage Men—which unfairly stigmatized women psychologically and financially and replace it with a level playing field in which both husband and wife would be treated as equals before the law, and marriage itself viewed by the court as an economic partnership. Politically—the most practical level of all—the measure was designed to break the logjam and pass the State Assembly and the State Senate. That was the bottom line. There was nothing "hearts and flowers" about this effort, and nothing "wish list" about the resultant legislation. It was carefully balanced between the very real need to revise the state's matrimonial laws and the equally real need to craft something that might actually gain legislative approval. In the broadest sense we all understood what was at stake. The definition of reform was whatever could make it to the Governor's desk; whatever he would sign into law.

. . . And Its Discontents

But it appeared for the longest time that *nothing* would reach the Governor's desk. The bill may have had lots of moving parts, but it was a standing target. Opponents charged that our wording was too "ambiguous;" or it was too precise, in that it ceded unlimited power to the courts: "*Discretion of the judges is the law of tyrants*," is how one emotional legislator put it.[27] A newly formed group, "Women United to Protect Existing Rights," backed by dubious financial entities, claimed reform would coerce women into the work force against their will. The American Academy of Matrimonial Lawyers said passage should be put on hold until "technical" matters were resolved; and another influential family law committee called the measure "unsound and mischievous." It was said to strike at the very heart of this grand Republic's most cherished right—private property—by eliminating title and thereby "creating an opportunity for a spouse to induce a court to find and divide property owned and held by the other spouse."[28]

There were, in addition, legislators and lobbyists for powerful institutions who claimed to believe that simply dealing with the issue was a sign of social disorder, that reform would lead to a devaluing of marriage and a concomitant loosening of the moral fibers that held society together. State lawmakers were overwhelmingly male and divorce law reform was seen as a "woman's issue"—the type of issue to which the Legislature was notorious for turning a blind eye: in 1979, in addition to reform, proposed laws dealing with sexual violence against women, sexual harassment, equal pay, and gender discrimination—twenty-one bills of major concern to women—failed to even secure a vote. It was undeniable that divorce law as it then existed greatly favored men. So, in the eyes of many legislators, the impetus to reform the law was . . . what, exactly?

It was all part of a phenomenon that I've seen many times in my family law practice. When I represent the monied party in a divorce action, I sometimes have to convince my client that the necessary concessions we make are not a sign of weakness, or that the other party is getting away with something. It's the powerful, not the vulnerable, who often need reassurance, who are most alert to the potential weaknesses of their position. They know that they have something to lose and convince themselves that if they give up *anything*, they will end up losing *everything*, imagining dire and irrevocable consequences resulting from a single misstep. It was that way with the State Legislature, especially the State Senate, whose members feared that any concession on divorce law reform would, inevitably, lead to other concessions on other issues; a string that, if pulled, would unravel their world. They weren't necessarily wrong—great change was coming whether they acknowledged it or not, and the long era of the male-dominated legislature was slouching to an end. We had written our proposal to take account of their concerns. It was, by any metric, a long delayed and *reasonable* reform. But we were unable to overcome the hesitancy and the fear, and our measure remained in limbo.

In the end it was nothing they did, no concession we made, that broke the stalemate. It was a *deus ex machina*, like the ones in Greek tragedy or, given that this was *Albany*, Greek comedy. On Monday, March 5, 1979, the United States Supreme Court ruled 6–3 that state laws that provided that husbands, but not wives, may be required to pay alimony were unconstitutional.

* * *

The *Orr* decision stated that gender-based alimony laws violated the Equal Protection Clause of the Constitution.[29] The ruling struck down an Alabama law and it invalidated similar laws in ten other states, including New York. The effect, on those of us working for reform, was electric. It meant that despite the reluctance of the Legislature, divorce laws in the state were going to have to be amended, and it calmed some conservative opponents by demonstrating that it wasn't only women who might benefit from reform. There were those who believed that state law could be changed simply—just substitute "spouse" for "wife" and call it a day. But many of us, on both sides of the issue, understood that it was like taking your car in for inspection: once the hood was raised, there was no telling what you'd find and no telling might happen next.

It took over a year, until the spring of 1980, but what happened next was that a comprehensive overhaul of the state's domestic relations laws, encompassing just about everything we had written, was on the verge of passage. Alimony, now called maintenance, was gender neutral, and could be awarded for a finite period instead of for a lifetime. Child support laws were made gender neutral as well, meaning that, for the first time, the legal path had been eased for men to both demand custody on an equal legal footing as their spouse and to be awarded maintenance and child support payments. Property division was according to equitable distribution, based on ten factors including the contributions of both parties regardless of title, as determined by a New York Supreme Court judge. As a safeguard against judicial overreach the judge would have to submit a written report detailing exactly how a "fair" division of property had been determined.

Just when the passage seemed assured there was a final wrinkle. The State Chapter of the National Organization for Women charged that the bill did not go far enough and urged that it be voted down unless significant changes were made. While they raised concerns about maintenance and custody issues, they focused on equitable distribution. Under our bill the court started from the premise that each party had *claims* to all property, while under the NOW proposal the court started from the premise that all marital property was *owned* 50–50. "When are women going to stop accepting tokens . . .?" asked one activist.[30]

It was the kind of comment to spark fury in Julia Perles, who saw her delicately negotiated compromise proposal, the result of nearly a decade of work, threatened at the last moment by "radicals" whom she held in contempt. And a good deal of her anger splashed over onto me, as the nearest target at hand. I was friends with many of the NOW activists and was in sympathy with a number of their objections; indeed, had raised similar points during some of the conference room meetings. I was clear with Julia about these matters, but she saw it as a betrayal—which was untrue. While I could imagine a better bill than the one that Julia was shepherding, I couldn't imagine a better bill actually passing the Legislature and without reservation I supported the bill we had written.

But Julia, regardless, continued to see me as the enemy within, the focus of her enmity and suspicion. Our relationship had begun to deteriorate from the moment she saw that, through Arthur, I had my own connection with the named partners; and the fact that Mr. Nizer came to favor me was another problem. In addition, over the years I had developed relationships with many of our clients independent of her, and this clearly bothered her. But the truth is that Julia never needed a reason to hate. She could see betrayal in a sunburn and conspiracy in a hangnail. Along with being a truly outstanding lawyer, it was her other great talent.

We engaged in no small talk, not even the customary, meaningless courtesies of *Good morning/Good evening.* Our conversations were strictly about client matters. When we saw each other in passing, she would fix me with a fierce and disconcerting glare. I stopped going through the reception area on the 32nd floor to reach my office but would turn left out of the elevator, using a back corridor, so I could get to my office without passing hers; without being subjected to her forbidding countenance. Julia managed to turn a place I loved into a bunker. It was hard for me to imagine a future in which we shared offices.

The NOW revolt fizzled. On June 3, 1980, the Legislature approved our measure; the Assembly vote was 131–6. The Senate vote 45–13. It was a day of

window at Il Gattopardo. Justin, Marty, and I spoke about my work at the Nizer firm, about the changes in divorce law and what it all might mean, and about their plans to build up their family law practice. They made me an offer and I accepted.

I handed in my notice to Julia, my department head, and she acknowledged it without curiosity or comment. Friends at the firm threw me a farewell party—champagne and laughter and affection. It was, in a way, difficult to leave, and in a perfect world I could imagine staying on, year after year, until I made partner. But this wasn't a time for dreaming. Mr. Nizer had provided an example of how to prepare a case and, equally important, how to present both case and client to the best possible advantage in court. He contained within himself both the romance and the stark, sometimes harsh reality of lawyering and he made no apologies for either or for the unabashed theatricality with which he conducted his public business. He helped create, in embryo, the lawyer I am today. Bill Reilly had mentored me as well, as had, almost in spite of herself, Julia Perles, who was one of the most skilled draftspersons with whom I have ever worked. If I could stack up every adjective she removed from my writing and was able to climb that tower of useless words I'd be a lot closer to heaven then I am.

The Gold Rush

The offer that Justin Golenbock and Marty Barell made was this:

Triple the salary I earned at the Nizer firm.

Head of the matrimonial practice.

An understanding that if things worked out as we all expected, I would be made a partner within about two years.

It might strain credibility that such an unexpected and lavish offer was made to a female lawyer strolling down a sidewalk, just six years out of law school, and I will concede that it did not happen every day. But the named partners at Golenbock & Barell were not giving anything away. Marty, particularly, was a shrewd businessman who understood the marketplace; in fact, if anything, he *anticipated* the marketplace. It was several months after they hired me that the *New York Times* took note of a new phenomenon: "*Law firms that wouldn't touch divorce before now find it very respectable.*"[1] And the corollary to what the *Times* reported was that the money generated for those firms by divorce work was very respectable, as well. Clean money.

Reform had removed the legal opprobrium surrounding divorce by removing fault as a way to disentitle women due to moral failure. The court was no longer interested in who slept with whom or who violated what moral tenet. And although it took New York another thirty years before it enacted its own no fault divorce laws, with the advent of equitable distribution divorce cases revolved around the new reality, namely, that if marriage was an economic partnership, the dissolution of a marriage should focus on, not soiled sheets, but balance sheets. "The entire financial history of a marriage," is how one judge described it.[2] In putting a case together matrimonial attorneys might have to hire accountants, economists, appraisers, real estate brokers, tax experts, and stock market, business, and pension plan experts. Matrimonial law became, in essence, an interdisciplinary field blending into trust and estate practice, securities, real estate practice, and other matters. The result was that the divorce process was more complicated. took longer to complete and was exponentially more expensive—an expense borne by the client and paid to the lawyer and to the firm. For the first time, said a family law expert at the Association of the Bar of the City of New York, "matrimonial law now involves real money."[3]

Reform did many things, some of which would take years to sort themselves out, but one thing it most definitely did was create huge economic opportunities for divorce lawyers. Barely half a year after the new law was enacted, the *New York Times* introduced its readers to another new phenomenon:

"*Because of the changes in the law, a New Yorker wishing a divorce must now frequently pay a lawyer a substantial advance deposit . . . .*"

This deposit, the *Times* helpfully explained, "*is called a retainer.*" [4]

A Commodity

Matrimonial law, post-reform, was described as a "New World" but no one could map the parameters of that world, could confidently predict the full implications of reform or speak with authority about what *equitable* really meant or how *non-titled property* would be valued. It was a work in progress and there were, as yet, no court cases interpreting the new law and providing guidance as to how it might be understood and applied. In the absence of case law the words of the statute, as solid as they appeared, were actually plastic, malleable. Undefined. Old assumptions might no longer be valid but what new assumptions might emerge? "*How can you know,*" said a preeminent matrimonial attorney:

"*Everyone is uncertain and no lawyers or judges have any real familiarity with the law or what any of it means. Every issue is open-ended.*"[5]

No lawyers or judges have any real familiarity with the law . . . that, precisely, was my value to Golenbock & Barell. No one knew the new law better than I did—I'd spent four years in a conference room helping to write it. I also understood, in a deep way, the changes that had to be agreed upon to secure passage in the Legislature—the adjustments, additions, and subtractions. There was nothing in it that was foreign to me and I understood not only the words themselves, the text, but the ellipses, the compromises behind those words, and the areas—*maintenance, custody*—that would likely prove most problematic, most susceptible to the twists and turns of treacherous human nature.

This "New World" of matrimonial law was a wilderness, unexplored, seemingly impenetrable. What I could offer was a way through the wilderness. It was around this time—1980—that in medicine CT technology was becoming more widely available and I remember how Arthur had marveled when he saw his first CT scan—the feeling that he was, for the first time, seeing the living human body complete, in exquisite, detailed three-dimensional imaging. That's how I felt about the new laws—I knew them whole, I saw them whole, in vivid detail and prospective. In addition, I knew the old matrimonial laws—it hadn't been all that long since I'd studied them at Brooklyn Law School. And this ability to compare and contrast the old and the new added to a body of knowledge and experience that was, I believe, almost unique among my contemporaries. It commodified me, gave me value—value that Justin and Marty were quick to recognize and to exploit.

* * *

They gave me a beautiful office overlooking West 51st Street, not as large as Mr. Nizer's office but then, other than the US Treasury building, what was? I hired an interior designer, Gloria Zalaznik, and the first thing she did was put a large mirror on one wall to give the illusion of even more space. She created three distinct areas within the single room: my large desk, where the client and I would usually have our discussions; a smaller conference room table and several chairs to one side, where discussion could continue in a more relaxed, informal manner, over lunch or coffee or tea; a couch against the far wall, what some matrimonial attorneys call the "crying couch," where clients, if they wish, would have some privacy to collect themselves as they dealt with their more emotional concerns or where I could, if appropriate, provide solace and comfort during those times. What I used it for primarily, however, was for conferences with adversaries who would come to the office for settlement negotiations. I remembered Mr. Nizer's office, how he sat slightly higher behind his raised desk, looking down on those people who approached him, and I appropriated that dynamic. Gloria had a couch built that was lower by an inch or two than the chair I sat in during negotiations; a slight advantage, I felt, but an advantage, nonetheless. Gloria subsequently designed every office I've ever had.

Lawyers and clients spend hours together in the office, and my goal was to create a space, a stage, that felt safe but also dynamic—I wanted clients to be able to move around if they so wished, to be able to breathe. And I wanted it to be homey and to look prosperous so that the client, from the moment they arrived, knew that they were engaging with a strong, successful matrimonial attorney, who could provide the legal help and emotional support that they needed.

Four years before I had been pushing my papers and supplies from office to office in a supermarket shopping cart. Now, in this setting that I had created, I went about building a matrimonial department for Golenbock & Barell. It was an enormous responsibility and I'd never done anything like it but I did not doubt that I would succeed. I've never had a problem with confidence but this feeling was something else, stronger, deeper. It touched the very essence of who I was and who I wished to become.

* * *

Years earlier, when I was still in school, Morris had told me: *Don't work for anybody. Whatever you end up doing, be your own boss. If you have partners, be the senior partner. It's the only way to do business.*

I took those words to heart and even at the beginning of my career, when I believed myself fortunate—and *was* fortunate—to be an associate mentored by giants like Howard Squadron and Mr. Nizer, I always thought of myself as on a path to something better. In the fourteen years between 1980 and 1994—the year I founded Cohen Hennessey Bienstock P.C.—I worked at three law firms and at each of them, I was a partner and the head of the matrimonial department. I established myself as a major force in matrimonial law—the *New York Times* dubbed me the "*doyenne of divorce*"—was consistently listed as one of the top divorce lawyers in the country and achieved great financial and professional success.[6] I won't say undreamed of success—because that's precisely what I did dream. That desire to excel never ebbed, it still hasn't, even if at times it has brought me grief or caused me to take a misstep or to learn the *wrong* lessons before circumstances forced me to learn the right ones. That was who I was and, tempered by the hard knowledge only experience can bring, it is part of who I still am.

In 1993 the *New York Times* profiled me, along with four others, in an article entitled: *The New Millionaires: Making It in Tough Times.*[7] It was flattering, it brought me clients, but it was tougher than even the *Times* realized: of those four, one ended up in jail, another was fired by the Board Of Directors from the company he had founded. I just kept on and came to think of those three law firms, Golenbock & Barell, Solin & Breindel, Beigel & Sandler, as rooms on a route that was taking me where I had determined to go.

My name on the door. My own firm.

Case 2: Uncoupling

I

I'd been retained by a woman I'll call Miranda Roche, a mother of two, an eleven-year-old girl and an eight-year-old boy, who was filing for divorce from her husband of eighteen years. Miranda worked for a United Nations Agency that liaised with governments in North and South America, coordinating efforts to protect endangered species. It was important work but not especially remunerative. Her husband, Steffan, was a naturalized citizen born in Austria, a chief researcher for a major chemical company, whose work focused on developing hardier types of renewable foodstuffs. He was the breadwinner and, in addition to a generous salary, he and his brother and sister owned valuable property in Austria. The parties lived in Brooklyn.

His counsel was unknown to me personally, but his reputation was of a clever if not particularly hard working lawyer, capable and intelligent but not "steady"—that is, he counted on intuition and insight rather than discipline and focus, keeping his eye on the "big picture" and leaving it to his associates to sweat the details. His record indicated that he was not averse to negotiating a settlement but only after a lot of huffing and puffing, a kind of performative belligerence, everything a fight until it wasn't—before getting down to the business of actually working toward an agreement. He was not untalented but there was a lot of chaff among the wheat.

When I telephoned, he was cordial, saying how much he admired me. He let me know that he had read and agreed with a recent article I had written for the *New York Law Journal* concerning social media and family law. And he said that he believed our upcoming case presented no obvious or special difficulties, and that, and here I am quoting directly: "We should have a great negotiation."

Whenever I am told this, I know I am in for a battle. It's usually the "this should be fun" lawyers who are the most pugilistic; always the "no problem" cases that take the longest to resolve.

As our conversation continued, I told him that as his client was the breadwinner, he'd need to pay *pendente lite* spousal support and child support while the case worked its way to trial or settlement and, in addition, pay a counsel fee to me. *Pendente lite* motions, meant to provide financial relief during the period (and it can be a long period) before the case is settled or tried, are standard practice in divorce cases, but when I mentioned it his tone abruptly changed, and he said he'd have to get back to me.[8] When I didn't hear from him for ten days I went ahead and filed my motion.

While he'd been in no hurry to get back to me earlier, his own papers were filed within forty-eight hours. He opposed the amount of child support we'd requested for the two children and said his client would pay absolutely no temporary spousal support for Miranda. No temporary support was required, the filing said, because Miranda and Steffan were not spouses. They had, the motion maintained, never been married.

II

The first phone contact between a prospective client and a lawyer can be tricky. For me, it comes down to a series of questions: Can I help this person? Is this the kind of case where I can do some good? Can this person afford the help I offer, and will they pay for the help they receive? That last is a judgment call and an important one. There's the *practice* of law and the *business* of law and there's no use being coy about it. I do take cases *pro bono*, as do other attorneys in my firm, and there are other cases, long and emotionally wearing cases, at the conclusion of which I will waive part of the agreed-upon fee. But there are many people, many very wealthy people, who will hire you, pay the retainer, and that's all they're going to pay. They love you as they walk through the door but on the way out it's: *I'll call you.* And there are some clients for whom, paradoxically, the more smoothly things go, the better you do your job, the less they want to pay you. They think: *That wasn't so hard. Why am I paying all this money for so little work?*

Divorce is expensive. There isn't a high-end matrimonial firm that doesn't have hundreds of thousands of dollars in unpaid fees. Lawyering can be a calling, but it is also a profession, with overheads and a bottom line to worry about, and that's just the way it is. Howard Dietz, who wrote all those great songs with Arthur Schwartz, *Dancing in the Dark, That's Entertainment, You and the Night and the Music*, was once asked: *Which comes first, the words or the music?* His answer: *The check.*[9] That's part of what being a professional is and why, early in that first phone call, I explain what my hourly rate charges are and what the retainer will be. And why, although any unused retainer will be refunded to them, that's likely only the down payment.

When a prospective client first comes to my office, I ask them to bring their laptop so we can examine all relevant financial documents. This initial consultation is an important and costly affair. It can last as long as two or three hours, and the bill can run into the thousands, the prospective client paying my hourly rate, and in certain instances, the hourly rate of an associate, or junior partner in my firm, and a forensic accountant. But it's worth it to the client whether they decide to retain me or not. Working from a financial point of view I conduct an extensive interview and use documents and accounting software to create a preliminary financial spreadsheet, an economic portrait of the marriage: how much money is coming in, how much going out, who is spending it and why. I once had a client who came to realize, just by going through the spreadsheet—based on papers that she provided—that her husband was supporting a second family. Seeing the numbers in black and white made clear to her what he was doing with what she always considered "his" money.

But even if the revelations are not that dramatic, the numbers provide clarity. Social history has been described as history with the politics left out; the spreadsheet permits the examination of a marriage with the *emotions* left out, and anyone who has been part of a devolving relationship, conjugal or other, will understand just how important that is. Numbers provide authenticity—or, at least, the appearance of authenticity. The figures create a visual representation of a marriage the way musical notes provide a visual representation of a symphony. In essence, they tell a story. My job as an attorney is to provide the proper setting, one advantageous to my client, in which to interpret those figures; and this is part—an important part—of the larger effort to tease out from all the available facts a credible and compelling narrative, one that will appeal with optimum effectiveness to the judge or the mediator. A *story* that will form, going forward, the bedrock of their understanding of the issues before them.

Finally, the spreadsheet offers, even in its most rudimentary form, a way for the prospective client to *begin* to understand the financial implications of going forward with the divorce. Before a client leaves my office, they will have an idea of what may lie ahead: the best possible outcome, the worst possible outcome, the most likely outcome. The three scenarios are more than a guess and less than a prediction but are always sobering.

And "sobering" is what's required because at that first meeting the people I am dealing with, understandably, are a mixture of exuberance and hope, dread and anger. Often exuberance predominates because they've taken a vitalizing first step, a step they've probably long been contemplating, to change their life. They say they want justice, justice for the lies they've been told or the cheating, or the stealing, the insults and humiliation they've endured. But to paraphrase the novelist Ross Macdonald: when people say they want justice what they most often mean is that they want mercy.[10] And in any event, neither justice nor mercy may be in the cards: matrimonial court is not necessarily equipped to deliver either of those virtues. The divorce law in New York is *equitable* distribution, not *equal*—so some rough form of fairness, as determined by lawyers or a judge, is about all you can reasonably hope for.

And it is my job to tell them about these vagaries, and to explain, carefully and sympathetically but also honestly, the great changes that are coming in their lives if they move forward; to try to help them understand that nothing may ever be the same. This is true not only in a financial sense but also in a deeper psychological sense. A client, a woman, may have a certain lifestyle, a feeling of contentment in her social circle. This is how she sees herself, how she imagines herself, in those quiet moments, positioned in the world; in the most meaningful way, how she fits in, as a wife, a mother, a woman. And all of it may go—gone for good and with it a sense of "somebodiness." And, as society has changed since I first began practicing, it is now often no different for my male clients, who may face the same uncertainties and experience the same vulnerabilities. So, every word I choose is important, a balancing act, being careful not to encourage false hope but also not to extinguish a genuine belief that a different and in many ways better life is possible.

But though I'm careful to discuss all the potential problems, I know that on this day I'm often not being heard. The client comes in when his or her courage is at its highest, and the exhilaration of having done *something* often makes them deaf to caution. You ask if they are willing to face the consequences and, of course, they say they are, but it's just words. They can envision the life that they want and believe that they have, finally, a plan to achieve it. This sweet dream rarely survives the first negotiation or court date, when it runs smack into a bracing dose of reality in the form of the very different ideas of their estranged spouse. What did Mike Tyson say? *Everybody has a plan until they are punched.*[11]

But if exuberance is tempered by reality, expectation adjusted, and sweet dreams fade, what remains is real and lasting and based on the trust between lawyer and client. It is important for a client to understand and articulate what it is they most want out of the process: what's their bottom line, and what real-world price are they willing to pay to achieve it. Because there's always a price. Sometimes the bottom line is money, sometimes a home, sometimes an object in that home—there are cases that last for years where a key point of disagreement involves a table or a couple of chairs. Sometimes it's speed: the client wants to move the process as quickly as possible, get an agreement, even accept a bad deal, so they can get all this behind them and begin a new life (and the partner in that new life is usually already in the picture, which stimulates an additional sense of urgency). Often it is custody and related questions: where will the child live and how will the child be educated? When I began practice it was almost *always* custody, especially for my female clients. To lose custody was not only a personal tragedy but carried a social stigma as well: the court judged you unfit, a damning indictment for a mother and one many women found it difficult not to internalize. There was a shadow across their lives and often this one tragedy deepened into other, darker tragedies. It is somewhat different today, when both parties are in the workforce and, increasingly, mothers and fathers are both "hands on" parents. Joint physical and legal custody has become the norm. As a result, the disgrace associated with mothers giving up some portion of their custody has largely disappeared—which is not to say that other stigmas, other burdens unique to women, do not exist.

Of course, under the pressure of court and negotiation, strategy and tactics may necessarily change; and a client, increasingly uneasy and unsure, may feel buffeted this way and that. My job then is to counsel the individual and to manage the expectations—not lecturing a client about what is right and what is wrong but reminding them of what they've told me they want—and explaining how we are trying to achieve it. This isn't as easy as it may appear—all that pressure, all that uncertainty, can cause a client to become confused about their goal or to say they want one thing but to act in such a manner that it is impossible for them to achieve it. It can be a psychological as well as physical marathon, and the fact that someone may bend to pressure at times or feel increasingly vulnerable and insecure is understandable. It doesn't make them foolish, and it doesn't make them weak. It makes them human.

III

Steffan Roche considered himself legally married to Miranda Roche for eighteen years and during that entire period they had, as the law puts it, "held themselves out" as husband and wife. They filed federal and state joint tax returns as a married couple. They purchased a home in Brooklyn and took title jointly as tenants by the entirety, as married spouses. They had two children together. Steffan added Miranda to his medical and dental insurance plans and represented to the plans that she was his spouse.

While it is impossible to know the heart of another, it is unlikely that Steffan harbored doubts about the nature of his marriage until after I had him served with the summons for divorce and he began consulting with his attorney. It was then that he became a "marriage denier."

Insurance plans, home ownership, yearly anniversary celebrations, joint tax returns, joint liability on mortgages, children of the marriage: almost two decades of unbroken marital assertions—the court took note of them all but ruled that the law mandated that Steffan's motion, nevertheless, proceed. Merely filing tax returns as a married couple would not, in and of itself, create a valid marriage where otherwise there would be none. And the court could not "create" a marriage in a case where one did not exist.

The motion turned on that single question.

Back in 1935, George Gershwin and Dubose Heyward described a similar case in *Porgy and Bess*, calling it a legal "complication" and noting:

It takes an expert to divorce a woman that has never been married.[12]

Here is how our judge put it more than three-quarters of a century later:

Husband argues that the parties are not validly married. This is a threshold issue. If the marriage were found to be invalid, there could be no action for divorce.

A complication.

* * *

Miranda and Steffan obtained a marriage license in Harrisburg, Pennsylvania, and then flew to France to be married. They went to Harrisburg because they were applying for what is called a "self-uniting" or "Quaker license"—Quakers believing that only God can join a couple in matrimony and that no intermediary or church official need be present to ensure that the marriage takes place. Under Pennsylvania law religious affiliation is not at issue and one doesn't have to be a Quaker in order to obtain a Quaker license. The couple were married in Paris, in a ceremony they wrote themselves, with no officiant, witnessed by family and friends who had received written invitations to this "destination" wedding; invitations that were key evidence that the marriage was valid. After they exchanged vows, Miranda and Steffan signed the marriage license before two witnesses, and following the honeymoon, they filed it in Philadelphia and were issued a marriage certificate. They then began their married life at their home in Brooklyn where they lived for the next eighteen years, until Miranda filed for divorce and Steffan realized that he'd never been married.

There was a lot to untangle. Steffan's motion involved four cities, in three jurisdictions, on two continents, as well as, at least tangentially, the observances and practices of a major Christian denomination that stresses the guidance of the Holy Spirit. It put the laws of France, Pennsylvania, and New York potentially at issue but, reading it over carefully, it became apparent to me that while the scope was wide it was not particularly deep. The husband's assertions were bold—*Miranda and Steffan's marriage was not legal under French law, or Pennsylvania law, or New York State law, and, additionally, it violated the terms of the "Quaker marriage license"*—but the legal underpinnings for those assertions were sketchy at best and often non-existent. The ambitious nature of the motion seemed to conspire against it; in an effort to prove everything, they were actually proving nothing. We would have to research, brief, and argue against each of these assertions, an expensive and time consuming process, navigating through the thickets of French marital jurisprudence, Pennsylvania law and New York law in order to provide the court with what was needed; focusing, sometimes broadly and sometimes more narrowly, on those issues which would be determinative in convincing the judge to deny the motion and affirm the validity of Miranda's marriage.

The first and most basic question concerned jurisdictional precedent—that is, which set of laws would be applied when examining and determining the legality of this marriage. Steffan's lawyers argued this meant either France, where the marriage ceremony was performed, or Pennsylvania, where the marriage was contracted. We argued that under longstanding principles of law, the validity of the marriage should be determined by the local laws of the state which had the most significant relationship to the spouses and to their marriage. New York State was where the parties resided and where the case was being heard. And it was here that all the material the judge could not solely consider as proof of marriage could be brought back into play to demonstrate the special relationship between the couple and New York State. The parties believed themselves to be married, resided in New York throughout the duration of the marriage, had two children in New York, filed joint state and federal tax returns, purchased a home and dental insurance as married spouses, and held themselves out as married.

Every state is free, within recognized constitutional guardrails, to write its own laws regarding matrimonial issues. In New Jersey, for instance, there is an explicit statute providing that the failure to obtain a marriage license "renders a purported marriage absolutely void" and no other issue needs to be considered. New York State also requires that a marriage license be obtained before a marriage ceremony but if it isn't, the ceremony may still be valid and the marriage deemed legal, if it is "solemnized between persons of full age." "Solemnized" in this case refers to a marriage ceremony, performed by someone authorized to do so before witnesses. As New York state also recognizes "Quaker" marriages the authorized persons would be Steffan and Miranda. The parties could "self-unite" in a ceremony before witnesses but with no separate officiant, which is what they did. In addition, New York is a state in which there is a strong presumption that a marriage is valid, particularly when the legitimacy of children is involved. And if they were legally married in New York, they were legally married in Pennsylvania and every other state in the country, under the Full Faith and Credit Clause—one of those recognized constitutional guardrails. Under comity, they were also legally married outside the United States.

We had to address numerous other issues raised by the motion to dismiss, but the heart of our argument remained the validity of the marriage under New York State law. I was confident that we had made our case, but I could not anticipate the sweeping nature of the court's ruling. Steffan's motion was denied, the marriage validated under New York State law, and we were awarded close to $100,000 in counsel fees. And there was more. The court had seen in the motion exactly what I had seen—a document that offered a prolific number of assertions and a paucity of evidence to back them up. It was a measure of the court's immense displeasure that the judge took time to enumerate and comment upon them all. On every single matter, large and small, the court found that Steffan's arguments lacked sufficient information or an understanding of the law or even a reasoned legal analysis. The ruling was, taken as a whole, breathtaking, about as thorough a victory as I have ever achieved in court.

The impact of all this, not only the decision itself but the way the court expressed its opinion, rippled outward, with implications that touched every aspect of the case. Matrimonial cases are judge cases, cases involving equity as well as law. There is no jury, and the judge is given extremely wide latitude—much more so than in Criminal Court or in other civil courts. In English common law, it was said that, in courts of equity, justice was what the judge said it was—nothing more and nothing less—and in that sense things haven't changed all that much. Here, the sweeping nature of the ruling made it clear that the judge felt that the court's time had been ill-used, and this seemed to reset the tone of the entire proceedings in our favor. You could feel it in the courtroom, hear it in the way the court addressed us, read it in the court's response to our various filings.

As an attorney, you spend so much of your time and effort working to shape your battlefield. And now the other side had shaped it for us.

It was during this period that I got my first look at Steffan Roche and began to form my impression of his character—an impression that deepened and sharpened over time but did not change in any important way. He was a handsome man, somewhat older than Miranda, who cultivated a theatrically fierce, unforgiving

look as he strode down the hallway outside the courtroom, moving with a sense of assurance and possession as if the court itself was another one of his Austrian properties. When we sat across a table during negotiations, he would fix me with that baleful glare which, I assume, he thought intimidating. Although I was skeptical, Miranda insisted Steffan was a good father and that she could handle entering into an equal physical joint custody agreement with him. But her acquiescence to his demands in that regard didn't obviate his protracted, bitter resistance when it came to the definition and amount of the so-called "add-ons"—kids' medical, kids' schooling/college, activities/lessons etc.—up until minutes before we signed the final settlement. Just about every time we thought we'd reached agreement on a point Steffan would raise new objections, which always boiled down to this: either he gave Miranda *less*, or he took from Miranda *more*. Say what you would about Steffan, he had a keen, almost aesthetic appreciation of other people's money.

* * *

The unforgiving nature of the judge's ruling had created a favorable legal environment for us, but in court every victory is a pyrrhic victory until the war is won and, in truth, the case, the *real* case, the one for which we had been preparing, was only just beginning. We were both litigating and negotiating—that is, we were in court, seeking rulings on key disputes while at the same time working to achieve an interim and an overall settlement—all under the watchful eye of a judge who encouraged, prodded and at times, through the use of the court calendar and the court's inherent powers, gently (and not so gently) coerced us into finding common ground. Some judges terrify both sides—which greatly motivates the desire to negotiate—but this judge wasn't like that. This judge was smart, hardworking, diligent, and patient—although his patience was not endless, and we were reminded on more than one occasion that it was in neither side's interest to risk the staggering costs and uncertainties of a trial.

This court was also—and I knew this from arguing before it on other occasions—very comfortable with numbers. This judge's eyes did not glaze over when a page or several pages of figures were presented, fully appreciating their importance and not being intimidated by them, understanding how significant they were in the context of negotiations. This was one of the reasons I prepared and submitted "as an aid to the court" two spreadsheets that detailed each party's view of what constituted marital and separate property. These were potential "settlement models" that listed everything: assets, such as the home and other real estate, cash accounts, investment accounts, retirement assets—even the value of the two automobiles they owned; and liabilities, such as mortgages and credit card and other debts. On one spreadsheet I listed my valuations of all the assets and liabilities; on the other, based on documents submitted to the court by opposing counsel during the course of the litigation, I listed Steffan's view of the value of the assets and liabilities. The spreadsheet had easy-to-follow columns for proposed allocations of the assets and liabilities: this will go to Miranda; this will go to Steffan. At the bottom I created an "equalizer," because one party might end up with too much and the other with too little, so one would owe the other a lump sum payment. A separate spreadsheet listed and calculated the percentage each party believed they should pay for things like the children's education, medical expenses and the like—the add-ons. I even wrote a user-friendly "split the difference" chart to demystify and make the calculations simpler. It was the story of Miranda and Steffan's marriage, told through numbers, and a roadmap to that marriage's dissolution.

Of course, it was *our* story and *our* roadmap, and that was the point. I wanted the judge to become comfortable with the narrative that we provided, the story that we were telling. It's the legal equivalent of quantum physics: the phenomenon changes when you observe it. Here, the compelling nature of the way we told our story defined, mapped, and changed the way the judge understood the case. The parameters shifted. You can't unring the bell. You can't unlearn something.

It was a similar story in our submissions to the court. You have to closely examine everything you are going to submit so that there is no ambiguity—because you want to leave it to the court, and to your opposition, to interpret as little as possible. But there is a further dimension. Louis Nizer used to say that you won or lost your case on the first page of your submission; maybe even the first sentence. Most judges, even most conscientious judges, aren't going to read through to page twelve to find out what the case is all about. So you not only had to write *clearly*, but you also had to write *well*. There is one opportunity to engage the judge, to capture and hold their attention. At that moment, in open court, the judge knows nothing about the issue under dispute but what you are telling them. There's no time to review. They are taking 15–20 minutes to read submissions from both sides, and they are going to be guided (perhaps unconsciously) by the most interesting. And the most interesting narrative becomes the most compelling. And the most compelling becomes the most "true."

In this case, the two spreadsheets not only captured our judge's attention but also opposing counsel's attention as well. With very few changes our numbers became the basis of a mutual understanding of the financial aspects of the case, the common point from which we began our negotiations. Once, as we were nearing agreement, a dispute arose over the valuation of this or that asset and opposing counsel opened the spreadsheet and offered *our* figures by way of resolution. It was a sweet moment, one of the sweetest you can have during intensive negotiations, particularly in front of a judge.

There were several occasions when opposing counsel disputed some trifling figures of ours, and we'd say: *okay, we'll put it to the side and revisit this point later.* But, of course, *later* never came. It never does. You spend all this time building a case, adding layers to it, and then you come to a point, if you are successful, where it vanishes. Just disappears. And what you are left with is maybe a couple of paragraphs that are meaningful and that will have to be fleshed out into a full fifty-page agreement; and two numbers: one number for Miranda and one number for Steffan. And the no man's land between those two numbers is where the case will be won or lost.

I was confident in the case I was building for Miranda and confident as well in my ability to show it to optimum effectiveness to the judge and to opposing counsel. There was much hard negotiating to do, but the outlines of a settlement were in view, flickering on the horizon. I trusted that opposing counsel would use his knowledge and experience to understand where the true interests of his client lay and that he would, in the end, be able to convince him. I counted on this. You need, after all, a partner to dance with.

Of course, until a settlement is signed it remains in doubt, and I've seen many agreements scuttled at the last moment because of an unexpected demand or a recalcitrant client so, with Steffan in mind, all this continued to be a matter of concern. But of even greater concern to me at this time was the condition of my client, Miranda. Steffan had waged destructive psychological warfare against her during the unhappy years of their marriage and his efforts, unrelenting and pernicious, had only increased after she filed for divorce. There were aspects of his personality clear to everyone (including his lawyers) that she simply could not see. He had only to raise an eyebrow or make a seemingly offhand remark to send her reeling. Miranda was extremely intelligent, and I think she understood, intellectually, that she was being manipulated, but viscerally she found it difficult, often impossible, to resist the pull of his temperament. Buffeted this way and that she would call me, teary and emotional, suggesting we take certain steps that completely undermined our position. We had, I believed, a strategy that could achieve a successful outcome for Miranda and her children but sticking to that strategy, while acknowledging Miranda's anguish, was no easy thing.

People who are going through an intense experience together, like a lawyer/client, doctor/patient, priest/parishioner, can develop a bond, an emotional connection of a kind. It is the job of the professional—the lawyer/doctor/priest—to inform the meaning of that connection and set the appropriate and practicable boundaries. I'm proud of the passion I bring to the law and to my battle for a client's rights; proud of the empathy I bring to my appreciation of what a client may be going through. At the same time there is a part that is—and must—remain separate, capable of rigorous analysis and an unsentimental diagnosis of what is at stake. It's not that these different qualities—sympathy and rigor—are necessarily at odds, usually they bolster one another, but achieving the proper balance is no easy thing. There comes a point in most cases when unpalatable truths have to be spoken, impossible choices have to be made, and you have to have positioned yourself so that your client is willing to heed and abide by the advice you are offering; at the same time balancing all this against the overall well-being of your client. It helps to remember that it is easier to prescribe hard medicine than it is to take it.

Miranda didn't have to be reminded that impossible choices would have to be made—she was walking that tightrope every day, still living with Steffan and the children in the family home in Brooklyn. Steffan had access, through his employer, to a company apartment not far from his place of work but he refused to move out to relieve the stress, claiming he wished to remain close to his children. He did, but for reasons that seemed, to me, less than parental. I'd always believed that his professed feelings for the children were infused, at least in part, with the knowledge that they could be used to hurt Miranda; and it wasn't long before she began expressing her fear that he was turning her son and daughter against her. Steffan also refused to move from the bedroom they shared, so Miranda moved—down to the basement, where she set up a cot and a makeshift work area. Locked in some terrible psychological drama, they seemed to be re-creating in the physical world the inner reality of the torment he inflicted upon her: Steffan as jailer, Miranda as prisoner, each morning walking up from the basement into the "family" area of the house as if leaving her cell; a co-conspirator in her own captivity. Time and again she begged me to let her move out of the family home, to find some temporary place for herself where she could heal, gather her resources, and find some peace. And time and again I told her: *No.*

A sympathetic judge, a promising and realistic strategy, an opposition that subverted its own interests—against all this had to be weighed the effect of the mental and emotional abuse that Miranda endured on a daily basis. She was seeing a therapist who advised her, for the sake of her own health, to remove herself from this intolerable situation. It was an awful moment that seemed to pit one type of expertise against another. In a general sense, we had a similar goal—what was best for Miranda—but I believed the therapist's focus and expertise had blinded them to the real stakes in play and blinded them as well to a fundamental truth about this case: the link between Miranda's emotional well-being and the successful resolution of her legal battle. The therapist saw these as separate issues or, at best, that there could be a split of the difference, but I *knew* they were braided together into a single whole, unique and unalterable.

Hardheaded is soft-hearted.

Mr. Nizer never let me forget that we are not pushing pieces around a chessboard, not arguing for the sake of arguing, not looking to score easy points in some game before the judge or opposing counsel. The choices we make, the decisions we recommend, affect flesh-and-blood people, vulnerable people like Miranda, defenseless people like her two children, and the consequences can last a lifetime. Miranda had told her therapist: "*I am dying inside*," and that bitter memory remains fresh, it always will, because I won't look away and I have to accept my

share of the responsibility for putting her, *for keeping her*, in that position. It is hard to justify the suffering of others; in fact, it is impossible. The best we can do is invest that suffering with meaning and purpose and that is what I tried to do with Miranda. I told her that if she moved out of her house, she would never get back in. If she left her children behind she could lose her children. Steffan would make her pay, financially and emotionally, before she was ever with them again. We were at that moment in the case, when "everything counted," and if I had to go before the judge and explain that my client, on her own volition, was no longer living with her children, the effect could well be catastrophic on all that Miranda said that she wanted, on the post-Steffan future she imagined for herself and for her loved ones, on every hope that had brought her to my office all these months ago.

This was the legal dilemma that Miranda faced, but there was, in addition, another side to the emotional dilemma with which she was already dealing. This was the home that her children lived in, the only home they knew, the home they loved, close to the school they went to and the friends they played with, the home with their bedrooms, their toys and books. It provided stability and comfort and would, if we were successful, continue to do so after the divorce. Miranda was part of that tapestry. Everything that was familiar, everything that she and the children most loved, was within these walls. Did she want to remove herself from this place and risk separation from her daughter and son? Did she want to allow Steffan to accomplish that end?

Miranda waived her HIPAA right to doctor-patient confidentiality and allowed me to speak to her therapist, with whom I had a long, inconclusive talk. We never saw eye to eye. Go or stay—in the end, it was Miranda's decision. And in the end, she stayed.

* * *

For my client, the house was, and remained, a psychological battlefield, but in the context of the overall case, it was something else entirely. It was a marital asset, the single most valuable asset jointly titled in the names of Miranda and Steffan. And how valuable was it? It was exactly as valuable as we said it was, and not a penny more. Of course, it was also as valuable as *Steffan* said it was, and not a penny less. If my theory of the case was correct, if my read of Steffan's character proved accurate, then understanding and resolving the differences between those two figures was the hinge upon which turned the resolution of the entire case.

It had always been my goal that in a final settlement Miranda and the children would live in the house and Steffan would move out. We would, of course, have to compensate him for surrendering to us his 50 percent share in the home and ceding complete ownership to Miranda. But for this to work, there had to be basic agreement on the value of the asset, and to determine that value each side hired its own appraiser. Since we wanted to *buy* the house, I was hoping for a relatively low valuation—it would cost us less. If, as I believed, Steffan was looking to *sell* the home, his appraisal would come in on the high end—a larger valuation meant more money. The number his appraiser brought back would tell me his intention.

I say that I was *hoping* our appraiser would bring in a low figure, but that is not completely accurate. Or accurate at all. The appraiser I hired was one with whom I usually worked and before he drove out to the property we had our usual talk. I told him I represented a client who wished to buy the home but that it would depend on whether or not it was too expensive. I said I understood that property taxes in the area were set to rise, that people were having trouble selling their properties and were having to lower the asking price. The neighborhood itself, I pointed out, was perhaps not what it once had been.

The law places no restrictions on what you can say to your own hired appraiser (although it will be subject to cross-examination if the case goes to trial), so while a specific price may not be mentioned you can easily make them understand what it is you are looking for. And opposing counsel was certainly giving similar instructions to *their* appraiser, pointing them in the direction they wished to go: buy or sell. The saying is that appraisers are MAI—"Made as Instructed." I know this feeds into the cliché about the legal profession: *It's all a game, a charade. No one can maintain an inner moral balance in an atmosphere where all facts are variable, where even the most basic truths are subject to negotiation.* But it's not a matter of morals or scruples. The house did not exist on some celestial plane in which there was a perfect and singular "real value" placed upon it. It existed on a street in a gentrified neighborhood and the figure we put on it was as "real" as any other. Just as I am permitted to speak to my own appraiser, I am permitted to emphasize certain facts over certain other facts and to emphasize an interpretation that benefits my case. As is opposing counsel.

The judge is aware of all this and understands it as a necessary step preparatory to successful negotiations. Had I come to court seeking to buy the house, with a higher estimate than my opposition, he'd have thought I'd lost my mind. The court keeps each side honest, preventing either party from coming up with an outlandish valuation of property, because it has it within its power to appoint its own appraiser, a neutral—and that's the one you *can't* talk to. It's a similar situation with negotiations. The court was giving us plenty of time to reach a settlement, and we were reporting back periodically about the progress we were making. If there was no progress, or if the court felt negotiations were in bad faith, then the case would not settle and the home would be sold and the proceeds split 50–50. None of that was in my client's best interest.

When the valuations from the two appraisers came in, we were about $200,000 apart. Steffan, as I'd hoped, had pivoted toward the money and his valuation was high. In other cases, with other clients, it might have been a relatively simple matter. You had a buyer and you had a seller—split the difference and the road to a settlement was open. But I knew it was a toll road and that Steffan would make Miranda pay dearly, one way or another, for every mile.

* * *

Once we knew Steffan's number, I called Miranda's father. He had accompanied her when she first came to my office; had paid my retainer and guaranteed my fee. Miranda had been a basket of nerves that first day. I could almost *see* the anxiety rippling across her skin but when she was dealing directly with Steffan there was an odd passivity at the heart of all her energy and movement. It was as if she were holding herself perfectly still, waiting, *hiding*, until his next outrage sent her into a spasm of intense, futile and sometimes self-sabotaging action—as when she considered moving out of her home and leaving her children behind. I came to see the relationship between Steffan and Miranda as akin to that of the snake charmer and the snake: he had only to sound a single note and Miranda would twist herself into positions destructive to both herself and her interests.

Miranda's father, Ray, by contrast, always projected an aura of calm, an attitude he tried to impart, with middling success, to his daughter. He held no illusions about Steffan and let me know, from the very beginning, that he understood how important it was that any final settlement removed Steffan's influence, to the fullest extent legally possible (they shared joint custody, so complete freedom from Steffan was not realistic), from Miranda's life. That was our bond and he never questioned me about strategy or second guessed any decision I made because he knew that our objective was the same.

Steffan was going to hold Miranda for ransom, and Ray was the only person capable of paying that ransom. And he would pay because he loved his daughter and his grandchildren; and Steffan knew that and it made us vulnerable. All the good qualities we treasure in life—kindness, reasonableness, willingness to compromise, loyalty, honesty—are vulnerabilities that can trip you up in court. And, to paraphrase *Corinthians*: the greatest of these is love.[13]

Of course, Steffan was not without his own vulnerabilities. From the beginning of this case, it had been clear to me that he was motivated by two factors: animosity and avarice. And just as the legal process can turn those treasured qualities we most admire into weakness, it can turn other, less admirable qualities into something strong and powerful; can accommodate itself to the worst impulses we possess. I once represented a woman who left her billionaire husband after eleven years of marriage, a second marriage for both of them. He had treated her terribly, had numerous affairs, belittled her; once, during an argument, he had struck her and she had called the police. It was all documented. It should have been a simple case—she wasn't greedy, she just wanted out of an abusive marriage that was making neither of them happy. But he wouldn't let go. He wouldn't give her anything. She had dared to file for divorce and he was determined to make her regret this, every day of her life. I always tell my clients: *Court is no place for vengeance, no place to settle scores*. But if you have enough money, if you are willing to burn it all down. . . . And he was. He spent millions in court rather than give her even a tiny percentage of what she was entitled to. It went on for years—he essentially bankrupted her—and I used every tactic, every argument, everything I knew to essentially tread water and keep the rights of my client in focus before the court. It was like arguing with an avalanche. In the end I did the best I could under the circumstances, but it was a terrible experience for both of us.

There's a Latin adage: *Audaces fortuna juvat*: Fortune favors the bold. In matrimonial court it might read: fortune favors the well-heeled. Not every time, not in every circumstance and I've certainly had my share of David vs Goliath victories. But I also understand, as does every experienced attorney, what usually happens when Goliath meets David.

Steffan had the attitude, but he didn't have the money, not the *real* money needed to finance that attitude and, as negotiations entered the final stage, I knew that he couldn't afford the luxury of his appetites.[14] He could give up his power to hurt Miranda and make a deal; or he could hold on to that power and forgo a payday. He could have one, but he couldn't have both. And that made *him* vulnerable.

* * *

There are negotiations that require every bit of legal acumen you possess, the use of every tool in the toolbox: a precise, yet nimble application of law, strategy, intelligence, and will. And then there are those negotiations that require little imagination, that are basically a test of endurance, the ability to sit, hour after hour, pouring over documents, revising the same paragraph time and again, reviewing with the opposition the most minute and at times tedious issues while maintaining focus and purpose.

And then there are negotiations like the one that concluded the case of Miranda vs Steffan, where every dispute, every legal entanglement, and all arguments have to be understood within the context of one of the more fundamental questions in the law and in life: *How much?*

It was, in that sense, pretty straightforward, and both sides understood exactly where we were and what came next. There were two related issues:

We were going to overpay Steffan for his 50 percent share in the family home. Negotiations centered on just how *much* we were going to overpay.

We were going to overpay Steffan to agree to and adhere to a timetable for him to vacate the home.

And that's where things became tricky. Stefan was angling for two payouts, one for relinquishing ownership of the house and a second one for actually leaving the house, and every time we seemed close to a settlement, he conjured up yet another roadblock, expecting that we would up the ante. And we were willing to do so—up to a certain point. We were buying Miranda's freedom, but we weren't going to *keep* buying it. There had to be an end.

Steffan's final ploy triggered that end. He proposed that he remain in the home for a year after the settlement, and during that time he and Miranda would do what is called "nesting." That's a co-parenting arrangement for divorced couples whereby the children remain in the marital home 100% of the time while the parents take turns being with them—for example, each parent would have two weeks each month with the kids and two weeks living away from them in another abode. When one parent rotates out, the other rotates in. It was a preposterous proposal, one that undercut our entire negotiating position. And it would keep Miranda in limbo—emotionally paralyzed.

The snake charmer and the snake.

Experience has taught me, again per Randall Jarrell, that in negotiations there is nothing so outrageous that *someone* won't consider it if you call it a proposal. In this case, that someone was Miranda's therapist.

I knew my client was in great emotional pain and I could understand why the chimera of even temporary relief would tempt her. But it was inexplicable to me why her therapist would consider this dangerous ploy a viable option. I spoke to her on the telephone again, more in bewilderment than anger, and asked what benefit she could possibly find in allowing her vulnerable patient to remain in such intimate proximity with a hostile ex-spouse. She spoke in generalities about short-term benefits. I told her that I believed another year, in and out of the house with Steffan, would be devastating for Miranda and that in twelve months we would certainly be back in court. She would not respond directly, would not commit herself, but said she would review the matter and get back to me.

In the end, we paid Steffan a bit more money and he agreed to vacate the home on our timetable. He'd tipped his hand when he proposed "nesting" and, despite our agreement, I knew he'd do whatever he could to remain in the home beyond the required leave date so I included, in the agreement, a series of escalating penalties—liquidated damages—for every day he did not comply. I think the judge recommended that we cap them at $1,000 a day. This greatly focused Steffan's mind on the need to fulfill his end of the agreement. No more bites of the apple.

It was finished, but it wasn't quite done. Steffan continued to raise peripheral issues, and we continued to argue and bargain, working on the margins to change and revise and review. The finishing touches on the agreement were concluded in the hallway outside of the courtroom just minutes before we were due in court to tell the judge whether we had settled or if we had to start the trial. It was that kind of case.

Miranda's therapist had said they would get back to me, and they were as good as their word. They wrote me a short note in which they appeared to explain, in guarded and very cautious language, why they now agreed with me that "nesting" was probably not a good idea. It was nice to have their input. By that time, the case had been over for several months.

A Room on the Route: Golenbock and Barell—1980–1986

Horse and Chariot

Golenbock & Barell focused on banking and real estate matters, and they offered a full panoply of legal and financial advice and services. The firm had woven itself into the warp and woof of New York's economic and political structure and featured a client base made up of bankers, moguls, entrepreneurs and the like. More than occasionally some of these movers and shakers had marital difficulties and because the firm had no matrimonial department of its own, Marty Barell would have to recommend an attorney at another firm to handle the problem—something he hated to do because it was like giving away money. He was a forward looking individual who operated on instinct and insight. He trusted and was willing to act upon his own intuition and never second guessed himself. When reform was enacted Marty foresaw that both divorce and the money generated from divorce would become "respectable." This being the case, why not keep it all in-house?—keep the money circulating within familiar borders. If a client needed help in these matters Marty wouldn't have to send them out of firm—he'd send them down the hall. That's when I was hired and given a budget and instructed to build a Matrimonial Department.

Marty was a brilliant man. He was the dynamo of the firm—always in motion, always talking. In some ways he reminded me of Professor Harold Hill in *The Music Man*—he had the conman's affability and line of patter and, as is said of conmen, he never met a stranger. But Marty was the real deal—a graduate of both Harvard Law and Harvard Business Schools, a sharp thinker, an innovator.

He had a unique kind of charisma of the type that I've rarely encountered. His clients were in *thrall* to him—and I use the term in its exact meaning: *the state of being in someone's power; having great power over someone.* Marty's clients trusted him implicitly, identified with him so strongly, and enjoyed being in his effervescent presence that many of them began consulting him on matters that were outside his expertise; wouldn't make a decision, even on intensely personal issues, without his say so. If he *had* been Professor Hill, all these captains of finance and industry would have learned to play the trombone. It's something every lawyer—and priest and rabbi and physician—has likely experienced—that almost obsessive kind of identification. I certainly have—and while it can in certain cases be helpful to the client or patient or parishioner, it can also foster an infantilized dependence that is helpful to neither party. In any case, it came to Marty naturally and there was nothing sinister or coercive about it. He was genuinely concerned about what was best for his clients and they were genuinely concerned that he tell them what that was.

He once sent me a real estate mogul worth tens of millions of dollars, who had decided to divorce his wife of close to twenty-five years. It was a very messy, complicated affair; the financial figures involved were staggering, and the two parties were at each other's throats. It wasn't that they weren't speaking; the problem was that they were—and we feared that, like the *Gingham Dog* and the *Calico Cat*, in the poem by Eugene Field, they "would eat each other up."[15] As the mogul was a client of Marty's I had immediate access to a good deal of financial material and was able to prepare a preliminary estimate of what divorce, under the new reform laws, might cost him. There was a lot of guesswork—no one was sure how the new laws would be interpreted by the court—but it was *informed* guesswork based on real numbers. I looked at the figures and saw a grim picture for our client. Marty looked at the figures and grew emotional.

"Harriet," he told me. "We have to save this marriage."

I don't know exactly what he told our client, but I think it was along the lines of: *You can't maintain your lifestyle if the marriage is over. You have to get back together. I know it won't be easy but for both of you, for your financial futures, you have to woo her back.*

It didn't happen immediately, but eventually the mogul and his wife did reconcile. They had a recommitment ceremony at the Plaza Hotel, inviting several hundred of their friends. They arrived at the hotel in a Roman chariot drawn by a white horse.

It was Marty's doing, his way of protecting his client's fortune, although he didn't want to take credit for *everything*.

"Not for the horse," he said. He thought for a moment. "Not for the chariot, either."

Putting It Together

I had a title, I had an office, I had a budget. Now all I had to do was create a Matrimonial Department from the ground up. It was an exciting time in the law, and I had strong ideas about how I wanted the department to look and how I wanted it to function—ideas based on the successful firms at which I'd been employed. Those ideas eventually evolved, though a kind of osmosis, into an intuitive understanding of what worked and what didn't. I also had hopes about what might be accomplished in this new legal world for less affluent women who had previously been discarded not only by their husbands but by the system, and who had been shut out from effective representation and consideration by the courts. But I always had to bear in mind—always—that Golenbock & Barell considered all this a *business* opportunity; and I was an investment; and they expected a return on that investment sooner rather than later. As it turned out, Marty Barell's foresight, combined with my knowledge, experience, and work ethic—and the changing times themselves—conspired to create a moment where the "return" came faster than anyone imagined and was greater than anyone could anticipate.

* * *

I brought clients with me when I left the Nizer firm, and Justin Golenbock, Marty Barell, and the other partners sent me a more or less steady stream of clients from their abundant pool of unhappy businessmen and emotionally dissatisfied captains of industry. Word of mouth, as it always is, was a huge generator of business: even now a large percentage of my clients continue to find me in this manner.

Mr. Nizer, Julia Perles, and all the other attorneys of that generation worked within the shadow of a nationwide prohibition on advertising by lawyers—a ban, strictly enforced, that lasted for decades before it was eventually declared unconstitutional by the Supreme Court. Prospective clients didn't have the internet to research and evaluate lawyers and law firms—they had phonebooks, the "yellow pages"—which I know for many readers is like saying they had cave paintings. It was about as low-tech as it gets, and unless your firm or your name began "Aa" in the alphabetized listings, it was pretty much left to chance. These lawyers may have been offering superior legal representation, but if no one could find them, if no one knew they were there, what difference did it make? They had to use their skill—and their wiles—to work around the advertising ban and keep their names before the public; to become part of the daily, social/cultural conversation. Again, word of mouth was the most important method, but word of mouth, it was understood, consisted of more than satisfied clients. In Mr. Nizer's case he developed a sophisticated and mutually beneficial relationship with a number of newspaper columnists, men and women who, in this pre-television, pre-internet world, wielded power and influence—not unlike the web influencers of today who can earn millions touting a product or endorsing a lifestyle choice. The names—Winchell, Lyons, Kilgallen, Sullivan, Sidney Skolsky, Hy Gardner—once so important, now largely unknown—undone by time and technology—still linger on the edge of memory with the potency of a half-remembered lyric or a long-forgotten face, able to conjure up a vanished self-referential world of power and patronage. These people cultivated Mr. Nizer. as he cultivated them by offering bits of news or gossip or humor in return for a mention and for favorable coverage. And each mention brought new clients and new business opportunities.

But Mr. Nizer didn't depend on others to keep his name in the news. He *made* news, often front-page news, through the clients he represented and the cases that he argued. This was the most passionate and serious side of his professional life, but there were other sides as well: he was a *public* personality of a kind that doesn't exist anymore: toastmaster, guest on radio and television shows; an analyst and commentator on just about every popular issue of the day. He was also a writer, author of countless articles and a string of best-selling books, including several memoirs and a controversial analysis of the Julius and Ethel Rosenberg atomic espionage case. A serious man, yes, but there was always a whiff of the Rialto about Mr. Nizer: gorgeous pressed suit, sharp creases, dark tie, colorful pocket square. He had the ruthless empathy of a successful attorney, the cold heart of a businessman, the public charm of a professional celebrity mixed with just the right touch of the boulevardier's raffishness. And all of it in service to the firm. To the business.

The clear-eyed understanding of the link that existed between the work you did, the public strategies you effected, and the business you ran was something I did adopt from Mr. Nizer. I couldn't reproduce his public charm, but I was developing a professional persona all my own. It wasn't always easy—I was comfortable in my skin and I wanted to project strength because I wanted clients to feel they were getting powerful representation but there was, at this time, a great deal of misogyny in my field and I faced—as just about every female lawyer faced—obstacles and adversities that male attorneys never had to deal with. Mr. Nizer and the others never thought twice about their right to stand in the public square or argue in court or negotiate on behalf of a client. The results they achieved largely depended on their knowledge and individual abilities but their presence, their right to be heard, was a social assumption that was based, fundamentally, not on those abilities but on their gender.

Female lawyers—and businesswomen and politicians and professionals—did not benefit from the same assumptions. I remember getting on an elevator with three female judges and a male court worker came in, looked us over, and said "How you doing, girls? Is everything okay?" There was in court, from officials—even from judges who later became colleagues and friends—a sense that you really didn't have to listen to the little lady, even if she was a lawyer, because she really didn't *belong*. It could be demoralizing—the same battle, the same patronizing words day after day. I knew I belonged and, remembering my mother's admonition—over or under or sideways, around and through—I knew that charm wasn't the answer It was important to establish myself immediately, no hesitation or "traditional" female deference, demonstrating from the moment I walked into court, from the moment I began negotiations with an adversary, that I was no nonsense, take charge, take no prisoners. It was what my clients expected and what my adversaries came to respect, and the roots of it, the foundation, begin in this period. In the process I developed some sharp elbows, and I believed then, and believe now, that this was absolutely essential in my development as a matrimonial attorney. I know that there are some who believe that those elbows were sharper than necessary and were sometimes employed in situations that may not have been appropriate. There may be some truth to that but it is a partial truth given the world as it was and the circumstances that I faced.

There is a saying, perhaps apocryphal, attributed to Arakcheyev: *One doesn't accomplish anything worthwhile by speaking softly in French.*[16] I was very much a woman in a hurry.

I have to believe that the reputation I was getting as a fierce and unrelenting advocate was one of the major factors in the rapid success of my matrimonial department. That reputation has never left me although with the passing of time and the changing of circumstances, it has softened to some degree. The inner passion is still there, the energy, the desire to achieve the best possible result for the men and women I represent, but it is often no longer necessary to display a public fierceness. Court battles remain as difficult as ever—fighting in the trenches is always hard work—but I know my adversaries and I know the judges and they know me so the elbows don't have to be quite as sharp or employed quite so often.

* * *

In the early 1980s, when I came to build my own Matrimonial Department for Golenbock & Barell, the intimate media world so skillfully inhabited—and exploited—by Mr. Nizer and my other mentors had vanished. No one was developing cozy relationships with Broadway columnists because they didn't exist anymore—their influence had splintered and, in one way or another, eventually migrated to more established print outlets; then to television, to cable tv and finally the internet, where, in the absence of the prohibition on advertising, every major firm now maintains a robust presence. But while it may have been a new world it wasn't then (and isn't now) an entirely *different* world and many of the old verities still applied. The Broadway columnists had disappeared but there were journalists and columnists of outsize ability and influence, in both print and television and later online, and I developed professional relationships with a number of them. I helped them navigate through the thickets of matrimonial—and eventually criminal and other types of law—and they helped me to establish in the public mind my own bona fides as a matrimonial attorney, and the elite quality of the department I created and the firm—Golenbock & Barell—of which it became so integral a part.

One of those columnists was Murray Kempton, whom I met through Julia Perles. He was exactly the kind of contrary personality Julia would befriend—perfectly courteous and quiet-spoken; there was, nonetheless, something cool and distant about him. Widely admired, virtually a legend among his contemporaries, he remained, in some definite way, separate from them. He was thin, and I see him in a dark suit, white shirt, dark tie and glasses, with a shock of white hair and a natural dour look, equal parts gloom and skepticism, like a Jesuit who has kept the discipline but lost the faith. His prose could be almost comically baroque, a tangle of sentences that weaved and twisted around his subject so that one sometimes wondered if his left hand knew what his right hand was typing. Kempton famously had a libel case against him dismissed by the New York State Supreme Court because the Justice couldn't figure out what he was trying to say; his prose, they ruled from the bench, was

> *written in a racy, hyperbolic style, is frequently cryptic in meaning, sometimes contradictory, and only dubiously suggestive of matters defaming plaintiff. Its meaning not being adequately clear, the necessity for a proper allegation of extrinsic fact or innuendo is evident.*[17]

It was a style uniquely his—it earned him a Pulitzer Prize—and I don't think any other writer would attempt it for fear of getting the bends. He was capable of startling, illuminating insight and a coruscating, bone-dry wit. Kempton abhorred sanctimony, that kind of public piousness practiced by politicians and religious leaders, hypocrisy, and dishonesty, but, like many in his profession, he had a soft spot for the rascals and rogues who committed such sins; though he was unforgiving when dealing with public cruelty and he consistently, sometimes eccentrically, identified with the losers rather than the winners, even if the losers were sometimes the very people he had eviscerated in earlier columns. He would call me from time to time to ask a question about a case that was in the news or a particular point of law—the questions always precise, no wasted words. He was always knowledgeable and well prepared.

We were in the courtroom in early December 1990 when the divorce of Donald Trump and his first wife, Ivana, was formalized. I was there because I had a case on the same docket before the same judge, Phyllis Gangel-Jacob, immediately following the Trump matter. There were a score of journalists covering the proceedings, though not quite as many as had been predicted because Donald Trump had indicated he would not be present, and I recognized Kempton sitting in one of the back row of benches and went over to say hello.

I no longer remember what we spoke about—perhaps how quickly things were moving. The couple had announced their separation in February, and Ivana and her attorneys were pushing to wrap things up expeditiously. This was a period when Trump's businesses were in collapse. He'd been put on an allowance by the banks that held his enormous debt, and Ivana clearly believed that if her husband had to declare personal bankruptcy—as seemed likely—she'd end up just another in a long line of creditors.[18] Whatever was left of the Trump money, she wanted her share. And quickly.

We were still speaking when the soon-to-be former Mrs. Trump and her lawyer, Michael Kennedy, entered the courtroom. She was tall, maybe 5'11", impeccably groomed with a helmet of blonde hair, expressionless. She was sitting quietly at her table when Trump's lawyers, Jay Goldberg and Stanford Lotwin, arrived.

They were big men, each around 6'3", and they swanned around the courtroom as if they owned it. Trump seems to move through life in a blizzard of self-regard, and, curiously, many of his attorneys seem to believe that imitating their client is a prerequisite of employment. Perhaps it is. Goldberg, in particular, was like a drugstore Roy Cohn albeit with a better sense of humor and less charm. He likened himself to a "killer" in the courtroom and boasted that he could "cause physical pain" when examining an unfriendly witness.[19] He was born to represent Trump.

I remember so many details of this scene because of something unusual that happened in court. Both sides had agreed to the terms of the dissolution of their marriage—all that was needed was the final okay from the judge.[20] But there was a delay and it became apparent that Gangel-Jacob was unhappy with one of the provisions in the agreement. It was the NDA—the non-disclosure agreement, insisted on by Donald Trump, that would prevent Ivana from publishing or telecasting without Trump's prior consent "any diary, memoir, letter, story, photograph, interview, article essay, account or description or depiction of any kind whatsoever concerning her marriage to Donald or any other aspect of Donald's personal, business or financial affairs."[21] Over the strenuous objections of Jay Goldberg, she used her discretion—and matrimonial judges are *all* discretion—to strike this provision from the agreement. I believe she felt that it was overly broad and especially onerous to one side rather than the other. She set a hearing on the matter for March and, sans NDA, accepted the rest of the agreement and dissolved the marriage. As Ivana left the courtroom she began to sob.

On appeal, the NDA was deemed valid by the state appellate court, thereby upholding Donald Trump and overruling the judge, but I've always felt that Justice Gangel-Jacob was prescient in finding it problematic. In the years following, Trump used NDAs to silence just about anyone who signed a contract with or worked for Trump—including White House employees. Increasingly the courts have recognized the coercive nature of these gag orders and ruled them "unconstitutional and unenforceable." And all these years later I have watched, with a delicious "shock of recognition" as these and other Trump controversies are analyzed by CNN's special correspondent Jamie Gangel, the daughter of Phyllis Gangel-Jacob.

If the judge was prescient that day, she wasn't the only one in the courtroom. I still see Murray Kempton seated on that back bench, his gloomy demeanor as he watched events unfold, as if they were more sad evidence of his assessment of fallen human nature. Trump at this time was passing himself off as an entrepreneurial genius and civil benefactor and he'd seduced a large swath of the media and public opinion into believing his fantasies of power and domination. This is what Murray Kempton wrote at this time:

Donald Trump dresses his hatred up as though it were a peacock's feathers. In any polity entitled to think itself civilized, persons with due regard for their breeding would rise up and leave the room politely but definitely whenever Donald Trump entered it. . . . We are assured that God does not make trash, which thought disposes of the impression that Donald Trump is not altogether a self-made man.[22]

* * *

Jimmy Breslin, like Murray Kempton, was a Pulitzer Prize winner and, also like Kempton, one of the few journalists who never, at any point, had any illusions about Donald Trump.

Beware always of the loudmouth taking advantage of the situation and appealing to a crowd's meanest nature. Insolent, cruel. . . . Such violent language sounds as if it were coming from someone who walks around with bodyguards.[23]

He wrote this in 1989, when most reporters, television anchors, and magazine writers were just beginning their decades long swoon that ended with Trump in the White House. Breslin, with keen understanding, was merciless regarding his own profession for conspiring to promote what he called Trump's brand of civic "thuggery."

The news business today is so utterly dishonest that the people are below taking bribes. Instead, Trump buys them with a smile, a phone call or a display of wealth that so excites these poor fools that they cannot wait to herald his brilliance. . . . The guy was buying the whole news industry with a return phone call. The news people provided Trump with the currency of his life, publicity, and he believed it was real and the news people believed him right back.[24]

Jimmy had married a friend and fellow classmate of mine from Barnard, Ronnie (Myers) Eldridge. Over time I became one of his go-to people—when he needed background on some legal matter or insight into a court proceeding or a particular judge or lawyer. He'd call. No, "Hello." No, "This is Jimmy." Just right into the topic, impatient, as if you'd purposely held him up by not answering the phone quickly enough.

"So what am I gonna do?" he'd say. "How am I gonna find out about X or Y?" He'd begin the conversation as if we'd already been talking for five or ten minutes.

I can hear myself trying to make sense of it, asking, "Jimmy, what do you need?"

"The goods," he'd say. "I need the goods."

There was a brashness to it, a touch of bullying, and it could be terrifying at times to be the focus of his attention, but there was also great good humor, often at his own expense, and he could be very funny. He had a Runyonesque sympathy (and he wrote a wonderful biography of Damon Runyon) for low-level conmen, grifters, crooks, and mobsters—once writing of a hapless mob enforcer "He dropped dead while being strangled"—and I think one reason he saw through Trump was because Trump had absolutely no self-awareness, no sense of humor about himself—his grifts and villainies so joyless, remorseless; a kind of inchoate vindictiveness aimed at the poor, the powerless—a world of suckers not named Donald Trump.[25] Jimmy's best work—during the Kennedy assassination or the New York City riots, or the death of John Lennon, always focused on the people usually left out of the story—the cops, the victims, the gravediggers, poor, struggling immigrants. A former sports reporter, he once said that the best story is always to be found in the loser's locker room, never the winner's. I think he is the only tabloid reporter honored by his own volume in the canon-defining Library of America.

Both Ronnie and Jimmy had been widowed at a relatively young age. It was a second marriage for each and between them they had eight children. Ronnie is Jewish, an Upper West Side intellectual, trim, meticulous in her movements and in her thinking. Jimmy was Catholic, heavyset, handsome, with unruly black hair and bushy eyebrows; careless in dress, he looked like a plainclothes cop. He could be florid in his speech and sometimes slid into a *dese* and *dems* idiom, an affectation I believe, since he was very intelligent and, when writing, precise about word usage and sentence construction. Jimmy was always on the streets, reporting, sometimes at great personal risk, and while he might have taken poetic license here and there, the people he wrote about, and the experiences he described, were *real*. He had no patience and little interest in those journalists who reported from the newsroom or from an office, turning out acres of turgid, unreadable prose. "Term papers," he called it.

Jimmy was good friends with Mario Cuomo, the governor of New York. Arthur and I had been drawn into the inner circle of the Cuomo orbit because the governor's daughter, Margaret, was an intern in radiology at North Shore University Hospital where Arthur, then Associate Director of the Department of Medicine and Chief of the Division of Geriatric Medicine, was one of her instructors. Margaret, like many of the medical staff, came to Arthur when they had medical problems or needed advice. She asked him if he might examine her grandmother, Mario Cuomo's mother, who was ailing following the aftereffects of a stroke. Arthur said he would and, shortly afterward, drove out to the Cuomo home. In time, Immaculata Cuomo came to reside in the facility Arthur founded and headed at North Shore University Hospital.

Years later, at Arthur's funeral, Mario Cuomo would remember that visit, and the care his mother received, with warm appreciation during his eulogy for my husband. He described watching as Arthur bent down, going to a knee so he could talk to Immaculata Cuomo, and listen as she spoke to him, quietly, face to face; and how pleased his mother was to talk to this physician and how she thereafter looked forward to seeing him as his patient. It was one of many eulogies to note the skill, kindness, and grace with which Arthur treated all his patients.

* * *

My professional relationships with Murray Kempton, with Jimmy Breslin, with James Barron of the *New York Times*, and many others were part of a conscious effort on my part to promote myself and my department, to raise the level of public awareness of those seeking matrimonial and legal help. Every mention in a column, every quote in the *Times*, every article I published, every letter to the editor that was accepted, resulted in a staggering number of telephone calls of inquiry and scores of new clients coming to the office. I never doubted that we would do right by these clients, but I was surprised; everyone at Golenbock & Barell was surprised at how fast the practice grew. I had never worked so hard and I was never so happy. The results we were seeing at the firm were astonishing—mirrored, at least in part, throughout the industry. It was clear to me that, much as I would like to claim credit for it all—and I certainly did my part—there were other factors in play and I worked equally hard to understand what those factors were and, to the extent possible, to master them.

The Divorced and Those about to Be Divorced

The Divorce Revolution that began in California in the late 1960s swept across the nation in an irregular but steady pattern and by 1984 every state except Arkansas had enacted some type of reform. There were myriad differences between these measures but broadly what linked them all was a belief that the process itself had to be made more fair; and since it was generally acknowledged that the process favored the moneyed partner—overwhelmingly male—more fair meant, in this context, more fair to women, to the wife. That was the goal—each state being left to meet or fail to meet it in its own distinctive way.

Reform was one of the enduring victories of second wave feminism, and analysts have hardly been shy about making claims upon it.[26] When Ronald Reagan said that signing the Family Law Act was one of the great mistakes of his political life he anticipated generations of conservative critics who blamed reform for the "me generation" or the "me too generation" or for, in the words of one scholar, "gutting marriage of its legal and moral ability to bind husband and wife" leading to a "magnitude of social dysfunction in much of American society."[27] In an analysis published in the fall 2009 issue of *National Affairs*, funded by the American Enterprise Institute, the argument was that by making it easier for wives to "*leave marriages that were abusive or that they found unsatisfying*" (my emphasis) reform replaced an ethos promoting "duty, obligation and sacrifice"—an ethos that strengthened society—with "a self-oriented ethic of romance, intimacy, and fulfillment"—that led to the fracturing of society because "one's primary obligation was not to one's family but to one's self."[28]

When I was a child there was a very popular radio comedian named Jack Pearl who, as Baron Munchausen, would tell outrageous tales. When someone inevitably doubted his veracity he would reply: *Vas you dere, Charlie?* And I remember that now because I *was* there and I don't think any of us in that conference room on the thirty-second floor at Phillips Nizer Benjamin Krim & Ballon were intending to fracture society. We were trying to reform a series of laws that badly needed reform. This last is now sometimes lost in the wider cultural debate, especially as we move further away from reform's enactment and fewer people remember just how bitter a battle it was; or that there was any battle at all. We stayed in that room for a *reason.* We worked as hard as we did for years, for a *reason.* And unless you start with the reason, with the cause, and not with the consequences, then you risk becoming not an analyst but a propagandist. And you risk airily conflating an "abusive marriage" with an "unhappy marriage" and suggesting that the abuser's violence is one more tie that binds society together.

Perhaps it does.

Every matrimonial attorney in practice at the time, regardless of how they understood reform, was aware of what the stakes were. For the women who came to us for help, it wasn't a matter of what it *meant*—nobody could know that at the time—but how it *felt.* I headed a matrimonial department, I dealt with the huge and unexpected influx of clients, mostly women, and I was more aware than most but it still took a series of unexpected encounters to bring home to me the scope of what was happening and why.

Arthur had been elected a Governor of the American College of Physicians, the second largest—after the AMA—physician group in the country. He would later become Chairman of the Board of Governors and finally receive the group's highest honor, that of Master. But at the time of which I am writing, he was one of about sixty Governors and, as such, attended ACP conferences and talks held in cities across the nation several times a year. The organization was family friendly—wives were encouraged to attend the conferences—but not necessarily Significant Other friendly. I wouldn't travel with Arthur to the conferences or stay with him at the hotels because he didn't want to offend the sensibilities of his socially conservative colleagues from across the country. Finally Burt Neuborne, a longtime friend and one of the great civil liberties lawyers in the nation's history, told Arthur that it was long past time to bring the ACP into the twentieth century and that, as Governor, he should feel free to travel with whom he wished.

The ACP would print a program for each conference and on facing pages would be photographs of the attendee and his wife (the organization at this time was almost entirely male). At the next conference Arthur submitted a photograph of each of us, which were duly printed as part of the program. Since we were on facing pages I was clearly with him but I wasn't listed as his wife. I was identified as a matrimonial attorney. And it was that printed and public identification that provided me with an unexpected experience and an insight into my professional purpose that has never left me.

While the governors were attending their lectures and their speeches, I began being approached by some of the wives, who recognized me from the photograph printed in the program. At first it was a single woman, then another, then two or three would come over together. They wanted to know about divorce law reform—there were so many questions—and I answered as best I could. Because they came from so many different states and each state's laws were different from the others, I often couldn't speak to specifics but I could explain many general principles and suggest ways they might find more information. Physicians are used to being approached by strangers at parties and gatherings and asked questions, sometimes intimate questions, about health, but I had never experienced this before. At first these were small and informal gatherings but they grew larger and, as I attended subsequent conferences, larger still until I was basically giving mini-seminars on divorce reform to an ever expanding number of women. They wanted to know, they explained, not for themselves but for a friend, or perhaps a sister or a daughter. But they wanted to *know* and it is that need, urgent and personal, that is often lost or forgotten in the statistical analyses and scholarly histories. All of us reformers, working in our individual way in just about every state in the union, had, in some ways unexpectedly, uncovered a vast reservoir of female discontent.

Something similar happened several years later when Arthur accompanied me to an American Bar Association conference in New Orleans. My first book, *The Divorce Book*, had just been published, and I took about forty copies with me to the conference, thinking I might hand them out to friends and colleagues.[29] But when we arrived in New Orleans, we found a street fair in progress in front of our hotel on Bourbon Street, and Arthur thought it might be fun to rent a table and offer the books for sale. While I attended the Association meetings, that is what Arthur did, and when I joined him later that afternoon, we ended up doing a brisk business.

The Divorce Book is a reader-friendly guide that—through general information and an overall sense of what the process is like and what they may expect—is aimed at helping men and women "get to the other side" of divorce with their lives and their mental health intact. Couples strolling through the fair would stop at our table, thumb through the book, and ask me a question or two and then move on. And then—more times than I could count, the woman—and it was almost always the woman—would come back without their spouse or significant other and quickly purchase a copy. "I really need to know about this," one told me. We ended up selling out.

When I thought of the women at those conferences with whom I was speaking, or the women in New Orleans and their furtive purchases; when I comforted the clients who came to my department at Golenbock & Barell in such unexpected numbers, it sometimes felt as if the entire world consisted of the divorced and those about to be divorced. Reform, to the vast majority of these women, was deeply personal—not a set of specific policy proposals but a promise, and they came to me and to our other attorneys to have that promise redeemed.

* * *

Of course, matrimonial court wasn't—and isn't—in the business of redemption. And matrimonial court judges are not, by and large, concerned with vengeance or score settling or rage or betrayal or any of the other emotions that clients understandably bring to their attorneys and to court. Even justice itself may not fall within their purview. What judges *are* concerned with is the law as it applies to the facts as *they* see them; and even that may not be as straightforward as it seems.

Uncertainty Principles

The heart of reform in New York State was equitable distribution, and the heart of equitable distribution was the new definition of marital property as "all property acquired by either or both spouses during the marriage" regardless of who, under the old law, held title to that property.[30] Judges were now required to place a value on non-economic contributions to the marriage—specifically homemaking—and factor in that value when considering how to divide the marital assets. This was the statute as it existed on the books in New York State—the law as it was understood by everyone involved in the reform effort and the legislative process, by the journalists who reported on that process and by the general public, who received their information from those journalists.

But it was not the law, or not *quite* the law, as it was being interpreted in matrimonial courts throughout the state; not quite the law on which matrimonial judges were basing their decisions. *That* law hardly existed at this time or existed in only hazy outline, its parameters impossible to delineate until *case law*—precedent derived from judicial decisions in previous cases—mapped its exact contours. As reform had only recently been approved, there was not as yet sufficient New York case law to permit anyone to confidently predict the effect the law would have on any individual case. In essence it was the legal equivalent of the famous quantum mechanics theorem *Schrodinger's Cat*—where the cat is both alive and dead at the same instant. This was Schrodinger's Reform: the law existed as the Legislature approved it, while at the same time it existed as the courts and the judges chose to define it. The text of the law appeared solid and unchangeable but absent interpretation and precedent, it was actually unpredictable and uncertain.

It is estimated that about 95 percent of all matrimonial cases are resolved through negotiations, but case law is important even for those cases that never reach court because the way the law is interpreted determines, in large part, the strategy one employs during negotiations. It's common sense: if you believe that a matrimonial judge, based on their record and established precedent, is sympathetic to your understanding of the case, it's an advantage and you'd negotiate from strength. If that judge is inclined to be unsympathetic, you might be more willing to compromise even on those points where the statute would seem to favor your client. The law we had written was clear in its objectives and expansive in its effort to recognize, and codify, for the first time, the rights of the non-moneyed spouse. But there is no jurisdiction, criminal or civil, where a judge has more power than in matrimonial court, no jurisdiction that relies more heavily on "judicial wisdom," to achieve equitable results, and during this period, when there was virtually no case law and thus no precedent, we carefully studied every case that ended up in court, like soothsayers endlessly turning over oracle bones, trying to discern how "judicial wisdom" would play itself out in the real world context that embraced all the woman who had come to us for help, and all of their hopes as well.

All sorts of imagined scenarios were considered. I remember one in particular, called the "ring around the collar" defense. At this time, there were a series of commercials on tv and radio for the laundry detergent *Wisk.* They were as formal and stylized as a *Noh* drama, all featuring a wife who believed she'd done an outstanding job with the family wash only to be told—by a friend or a neighbor, her husband, a complete stranger or, most humiliating of all, the squawk of the family parrot: *"Ring Around the Collar! Ring Around the Collar!"*—that she'd left a ring of dirt around the collar of her husband's shirts. The solution:

Use Wisk around the collar. It beats ring around the collar every time.

There was fear that matrimonial judges, tasked with putting a value on the non-economic contributions to a marriage, might decide to not only value housework but *evaluate* it as well—that is, assign a value based on how well a wife carried out her appointed tasks. Yes, she did the laundry, but a good job was worth more than a merely adequate job. (*Ring around the collar! Ring Around the Collar!)* And if judges were now considering housekeeping, why shouldn't their scrutiny include meal preparation—should the court award full value when the pot roast was underdone or the turkey was dry?

While it never quite reached that extreme, there were numerous cases where a wife was penalized monetarily in the final settlement because the family had employed a housekeeper or a nanny. For generations the courts had refused to value the "traditional" work undertaken by wives. Now, under the umbrella of reform, some of those same judges were reasoning: why reward a wife for something she didn't do?

* * *

My own sense as I read the decisions coming down was that the judiciary wasn't applying the law in the way it had been intended, but a more rigorous examination was needed. Someone had to look at all the reported cases, look at the numbers and the percentages in a precise and sophisticated way and build the analysis from the ground up rather than relying on the easier anecdotal approach. That was the problem: the cases were coming in, piecemeal, from all over the state and you could focus on a decision here, or part of a decision there and create a false picture of what was happening, based on prior assumptions or biases. And this was not an academic question. Real lives were at stake, real women—I dealt with them every day at Golenbock & Barell. They came to me and to the other attorneys in my department because they believed the new law guaranteed a measure of fairness, but it remained unclear if this was really the case. All we knew for sure was that more women were filing for divorce, the process took longer—approximately three times longer according to one survey and because it took longer it was exponentially more expensive. The courts were busy. Accountants and appraisers had more work than they could handle. Matrimonial attorneys were getting rich. But were the forgotten women whose needs were at the heart of reform, any less vulnerable than they had been?

When no one stepped forward to do the kind of professional analyses I knew was needed, I decided to do it myself—along with Adria S. Hillman, a friend and fellow attorney. Adria has had a long and distinguished career in matrimonial and divorce law, both in private practice and on numerous legislative and governmental advisory committees. She has a fine, analytical mind and we worked well together. The report we produced was published in 1984 under the auspices of the New York State Task Force on Women and was reprinted and cited countless times over the next decade.

It had a long official title but is generally referred to as the *Cohen-Hillman Study*, an analysis of the first seventy decisions after trial under New York State's equitable distribution law.[31] It's difficult at this distance in time, to recreate the impact that the report had but our findings were so startling that a second study was commissioned to examine our results (it found our figures were accurate) and Adria and I were asked to write another report for the Task Force which we published a year later, giving it the emphatic let's-end-this-foolish-controversy-once-and-for-all title: *Diagnosis Confirmed.*[32]

Our original paper found that in the seventy cases available for review, judges had consistently misapplied or ignored the new law. In only *five* cases was there a roughly equal division of marital assets—in general, court awards of marital property averaged about 30 percent to the wife and 70 percent to the husband. A similarly bleak picture emerged from an examination of maintenance (formally alimony) awards: of the forty-nine long-term marriages we examined, we found that wives received either short-term awards of negligible economic value or no awards at all. It was clear to us that "equitable distribution [was] ailing" and that despite what the law required, many judges were reluctant to consider the wife's contribution as homemaker in any suitable way. As one analyst put it:

> *Rather than recognizing the economic partnership theory of marriage, some judges appear predisposed to ensure that the equitable distribution law does not "make reluctant Santa Clauses out of ex-husbands."*[33]

And we also demonstrated that the grim picture extended well beyond the cases under review because these seventy decisions "set the parameters for the 90 percent of matrimonial decisions that ended in negotiated settlements."

Our work offered an unvarnished picture of the real state of reform and while it is always possible to argue policy, it proved impossible to argue with the data-based facts as we presented them. We set off a debate, at times a firestorm of a debate, with some of the most impassioned support coming, naturally, from those who had worked hardest to pass reform legislation "Women are getting the short end of the stick," said one assemblyman a view elaborated on by a top New York State Bar matrimonial expert: "Judges are completely misconstruing it, and women are being treated unjustly. The answer is to make some very, very substantive changes in the law."[34]

"I do not say the law is a bomb," Julia Perles responded, even as she acknowledged that the data made it clear that some changes were needed.[35]

During this entire process, Adria and I co-wrote a series of articles and op-ed pieces aimed at keeping the pressure on those attempting to "reform" reform.[36] At its most basic the question seemed to come down to:

Did we need new judges or new laws?

In the end, we got both. A largely male judiciary aged out and retired, replaced by a much more diverse set of judges who were, in general, sympathetic to the aims of reform and more willing, on a consistent basis, to give due weight to the contributions of the spouse who wasn't the main breadwinner. And within two years of the publication of our work the State Legislature had passed two laws, one dealing with sanctions on fathers who failed to make child support payments, the other dealing directly with efforts to more fairly distribute income during divorce. The work Adria and I did played an important part in both these efforts because it provided the factual bedrock which made all these changes possible.

So many years have passed, so many changes in matrimonial law have occurred, that the specifics of our work are now probably of only academic or historic interest. But it remains, I believe, as relevant today as the day it was written, if not as a cutting edge examination of policy and the law then perhaps as a parable of reform and its discontents. The controversies we wrote about all occurred after equitable distribution had become state law, so the message is a cautionary one: Whether you are dealing with matrimonial law or family planning or abortion or health care in general or any issue in which the Haves continue to press their cruel advantage over the Have-Nots, the toughest battles, the most difficult and bitterest conflicts occur *after* you believe that you have won.

The Real Thing

Arthur understood the impression he made by the manner in which he carried himself, the way he related to patients and to fellow professionals. It didn't happen by happenstance, it was a conscious construction of a professional persona and he believed that my own professional persona should begin before a word was spoken—from the moment I arrived at my office and presented myself to my staff and my clients. At this time scores of women were entering the workforce for the first time—as physicians, as lawyers and businesswoman, as journalists and independent entrepreneurs. There was a clothing store in downtown Manhattan called T. Jones—one of many catering to what was then called "The Professional Woman"—and Arthur enjoyed taking me there and buying me business attire. I was creating myself as a matrimonial attorney—surely I should look like one.

I look at photographs of that period now and have to laugh at the schizophrenic nature of the fashion of those times. The suits were based on men's business clothing: two or three piece suits, wide, *extremely* wide, padded shoulders in the suit jacket—it was joked that at work women would have to turn sideways to get out of the elevator—a slim, relaxed belted waist, and a skirt below the knee. A white blouse, buttoned to the throat with a short dark cravat around the neck that looked like a soft, floppy bow-tie. A not unexciting mixture of the masculine and the feminine, it is an unforgettable (much as one might try) look—whenever I see a movie or television show from that period I instantly recognize where the female characters are coming from.

Arthur was not a religious man, but he would quote Ecclesiastes to me. *Cast your bread upon the waters . . .* it was what he believed and it was how he lived. His generosity and openness came from a place of strength deep within him, and he gave his affection freely, never asked for anything in return, never tried to bargain it away. He was emotionally open but also emotionally honest. During our nine year courtship he would tell me that he would never marry me. I think he felt great and loving loyalty to his wife Jeanne, but Arthur didn't believe he was living a leftover life; he was living *his* life—and he was determined to experience and enjoy all that was before him. Once, worried, however, that I expected him to marry me, he said "You know, Harriet, I don't love you." I believe he thought he was trying to be as honest with me as possible, for my sake, about the emotional currents within him. He didn't want to lead me on or let me build expectations he believed himself unable to fulfill, and I would tell him, "Arthur dear, don't worry. Whatever this is, it's okay with me because it's better than anything I've ever had."

It was like that beautiful song (© 1936 (Renewed) Chappell & Co., Inc. and Cahn Music Co. All Rights Reserved. Used by permission of Alfred Music):[37]

I'd gladly move the earth for you
To prove my love dear and its worth to you
If that isn't love, it'll have to do
Until the real thing comes along

I'd sigh for you and cry for you
I'd tear the stars down from the sky for you
If that isn't love, it'll have to do
Until the real thing comes along

I don't know why Arthur changed his mind. He never told me and I never asked him. Obviously our relationship had become more meaningful and our feelings for each other deeper: love, on my part, whatever Arthur called it on his. In the spring of 1977, Arthur's daughter, Nancy, married James Rheingrover and I was his date to the wedding at the Park Lane Hotel. It was, I suppose, our "coming out" as a couple and I met, for the first time, many friends and family members, including, most importantly, Sylvia Dilbert Ruderman, Jeanne's mother. She was small and very slim, immaculately dressed, with blonde hair, beautiful skin, a finely boned face and green eyes that seemed to brim with intelligence and humor. She was as pretty as a Dresden doll and appeared almost as fragile. That was a misapprehension. Sylvia had survived one of the worst blows a mother can endure, outliving a beloved child, and possessed great inner reserves of strength and courage.

Three of my four daughters chose to be married in Nancy's wedding dress: it was let in, let out, hemline raised, hemline lowered, sleeves lengthened, sleeves shortened. A beautiful dress, and they all looked beautiful in it, as did Patti, in the wedding dress we shopped for together in SoHo in lower Manhattan. She had known Arthur since she was eleven years old and described him as her "father figure." It's possible that the three earlier weddings had given Arthur ideas; or perhaps he'd just been bitten by the bug. It might have been a sudden flash of inspiration because on a Monday evening, after a dinner out, as he was driving me home to the Rockaways, he said, apropos of nothing and in a low, even voice:

Harriet, would you like to get married?

I looked at him and replied, in the same low, neutral voice.

Well, you know, Arthur, I think I would.

It was July 25, 1983. Four days later, July 29th, we were married.

* * *

As a young physician just beginning his career in private practice in Great Neck, Arthur had become friends with a young Rabbi at Temple Beth-El, Martin Zion, who was just beginning *his* career. Martin and his wife Jane, like Arthur and Jeanne, had two young children, Charles (Chuck) and Barbara. The two couples became close—Chuck and Nancy, roughly contemporaries, were playmates and there are sweet Kodak snapshots, circa 1951, of the two three-year-olds tumbling about in a local park. Martin was now Senior Rabbi at Temple Israel, and it was he who married us, in his office on 75th street on the East Side of Manhattan, about four in the afternoon of a summer Friday. There were only four of us in the office. Jane Zion served as the witness.

Arthur had insisted we elope, not telling anyone of our plans. He was, I believe, concerned about how his son, David, would take the news and so all the children learned of it as a fait accompli. It was a decision I regret to this day, so needlessly provocative. Following the ceremony and a brief toast with Martin and Jane, Arthur and I returned to his apartment, where he called Nancy and David and I called my daughters. All of them, all the kids, reacted with congratulations and grace and best wishes but, at least on my side, not with surprise. When I began the conversation by asking each of them what they thought was the most wonderful thing I could tell them that had happened to me that day, each of my daughters responded with "You and Arthur got married!"

They were happy for me, and given their love for Arthur, happy for us as a family. I knew that. What I did not know at the time was that they were also angry, very angry, that I had kept this news from them until after it had happened. I had never withheld anything from them in all their lives. We had been through so much together and had so much further to go, but this felt, to each of them, like betrayal, an undermining, a deliberate denial of the terms of our affection.

It was hard on them that Arthur was number one in my heart, in my soul, and my mind. He made me understand my life in a different and better way, made me feel there was a purpose to Phil, a purpose to Miss Campbell, to all the people and circumstances that had hurt me; and that God was saying, *There is something better. You deserve something better.*

He was a singular blessing in my life, but there are other blessings. My girls, Marti, Amy, Sue and Patti are all married to wonderful men. I have grandchildren and now great grandchildren and it is my privilege, as I grow older, to love them and feel the love they have for me.

It was a privilege denied to Sylvia Ruderman. And denied as well to Martin and Jane Zion. Their son Chuck, who tumbles forever with Nancy in a series of fading black and white photographs, was an executive vice president at Cantor Fitzgerald and was at his desk in the North Tower, World Trade Center 1, on September 11, 2001. He was fifty-four years old, survived by his wife, Carole, his son, Zachary, and his parents.

A Bloodbath

About this time I became Chair of the Matrimonial Committee of the New York Women's Bar Association. Reform remained my primary focus and I was increasingly concerned about its true implications, the experiential effects on the people—my clients and others—who actually *lived* it. I was always offering my personal support to any attempt—as I wrote in an essay published in the *New York Times*—"to alleviate devastating problems that have beset women and children since the enactment in 1980 of so-called divorce reform laws that, as applied, added to the increasing feminization of poverty."[38]

There was also in formation and in its nascency, the "Women's Bar Association of the State of New York" ("WBASNY"). The organization was the brainchild of two matrimonial lawyers, Joan Ellenbogen and her law partner Marcia Goldstein, and Sheila Birnbaum, one of the country's preeminent product liability defense lawyers. The three of them would travel around the state, Johnny Appleseeds, working to establish regional chapters of WBASNY, determined, no matter how long it took, to grow the organization and increase its influence.

All three women were exceptional lawyers, but Joan was the real power, the mover and shaker, and it was her energy upon which the organization was fueled.[39] She reminded me of Julia Perles. Joan loved her scotch, always smoked brown, evil-smelling cigarillos, one after the other, and was very direct in her manner. She was about ten years younger than me, but I became her protégé and we were, for a time, very close. It was because of Joan that, in 1985, I became president of the New York City chapter of WBASNY (the NYWBA). The work I was doing was important, and was recognized as such, but it would never have catapulted me into the top leadership seat without Joan's encouragement and enthusiasm. It was all her vision.

And WBASNY was her baby. Joan and the two other founders ran it like a trade organization. They were determined to place women in positions of power throughout the state, as judges, on prominent committees, in important positions in the state bar organizations—the male organizations in which women, at this time, were only marginally represented. This required compromise with the establishment bars—the male powers-that-be—and avoiding overt conflict. They were playing a long game and if it took ten years before women were able to access the true levers of power within the State, ten years in which the more immediate legal and social needs of women would have to be sacrificed—or subtly undermined—that sacrifice was part of the game Eventually they would be in a position to help less fortunate women—that was always their ultimate and sincere goal—but first they had first help themselves by attaining the power that would make this possible.

I was developing my own constituency, activists from NOW, others who read my articles or had seen me on television or heard me testifying before committees in the state capital; women lawyers and other professionals who appreciated a more straightforward and at times confrontational approach when defending women's rights. It seemed to many of us that WBASNY's go along to get along policy was becoming increasingly problematic when dealing with the real issues confronting women, that long game objectives notwithstanding, the policy was encouraging a kind of appeasement that harmed the women we were ostensibly trying to protect. It was fine to say that eventually we'd be able to help women, but the women we represented didn't need help *eventually*—they needed help *now* on a number of issues that were threatening to unravel many of the benefits of reform. There was for example the *O'Brien* case, which involved a wife who had worked a series of menial jobs over four years, supporting her husband while he attended medical school, paying the bulk of their expenses.[40] In 1980, several months after her husband was awarded his medical license, he told her that he had fallen in love with someone else and the marriage was over. An old and not unfamiliar story.

What made it new was that Loretta O'Brien asked the court to declare Michael O'Brien's newly acquired license to practice medicine—"the parties' only asset of any consequence"—"marital property" and subject to equitable distribution under the terms of reform. The court agreed and, relying on expert appraisers, put a lifetime value on the license at roughly half a million 1980 dollars—close to three million dollars in 2026 value. The court "*after considering the life-style that plaintiff would enjoy from the enhanced earning potential his medical license would bring and defendant's contributions and efforts toward attainment of it*" ordered Michael to pay Loretta 40 percent of the value of his license in eleven annual installments. This decision was appealed all the way up the state's highest court, the Court of Appeals, where it was upheld.

This ruling kicked off a long and high-stakes controversy. Male dominated professional organizations, medical, legal, educational—any profession within the state that required a license in order to practice—began a coordinated lobbying campaign that was ultimately successful and resulted in the Legislature changing the law, preventing courts from considering as marital property, subject to equitable distribution, a spouse's enhanced earning capacity arising from a license or degree. *Nothing to see here,* they said, because the Loretta's of the world were still entitled to 40 or 50 percent of marital property. Of course, without the valuation of the medical degree this would amount to 40 percent of nothing. And there were many similar cases in which a husband successfully attempted to hide or minimize his worth—what became known as the "instant poverty syndrome." It seemed an easy call but many of us felt that WBASNY was sitting this one out in deference to the male establishment and refusing to use the full extent of their influence to support women.

Even more disquieting was a case about the awarding of attorney's fees. Since the early 1970s, the courts had recognized the need to create a level playing field between both parties during a divorce action.[41] It was important that the non-moneyed spouse not be coerced, through lack of funds, into making or accepting questionable or harmful legal decisions. In order to prevent this, judges were given the discretion to order the moneyed party to pay all or part of the other party's legal fees and expenses. This became particularly important after reform was enacted. The spouse with money—almost always the man—could afford to manipulate the system by filing feckless motions and endless appeals, drawing out the process, refusing, as a tactic, to settle until every legal avenue, no matter how obscure and unpromising, was explored; and using a demand for child custody as an even more sinister lever. Women, who now were due a percentage of all marital property, discovered that they might go bankrupt while attempting to secure their rightful share. And that was the goal of a particularly pernicious lawsuit which argued that while judges indeed had the power to award attorney fees they should not be permitted to do so while the non-moneyed spouse had any funds at all. Only until the wife was, in the words of the suit, "indigent" would the judge be permitted to take action. The lawyer who argued this position was Joan Ellenbogen and she was successful in the lower courts before the ruling was ultimately overturned by the state Court of Appeals.

The judicial establishment and, to an extent, the male bar associations were worried that if they gave the wife what they deemed a "war chest," she would have the ability to continue to assert her legal rights and add to a backlog of cases the court was already struggling to deal with. The complexity of reform was responsible for this backlog, and the fear was that if women had adequate funding they'd keep fighting and the cases would never end. By keeping women impoverished or on the edge of bankruptcy the court could manage its calendar and give the appearance that they were handling their affairs in a timely and professional manner. Wheels within wheels and everybody had an agenda and it was all on the backs of women. When Joan lent her great skill to this effort it didn't seem like a brilliant tactical maneuver in pursuit of a worthy strategic goal. It seemed like a betrayal.

This was the atmosphere in which those of us who began to oppose WBASNY's policies were operating. We understood the goals leadership were attempting to achieve, we supported those goals but questioned the need for such cruel sacrifice. The choice between a hard working wife and a Romeo husband seemed so obvious that it was really no choice at all. The decision to approve bankrupting a wife before she was permitted to pursue her legal rights seemed an obscenity. And to the extent that WBASNY approved of or washed their hands of these matters compelled many of us to make the case that a new direction and a new leadership was needed.

I was being urged to run for president of the statewide organization by many of the grassroots attorneys in WBASNY. We put together a slate of incredible women, idealistic women. Joan Ellenbogen and the other leaders gathered their power and mounted their own slate. It was a difficult decision for me to go forward. Joan was a friend, as were other members of the leadership, and I was not unmindful of all they had done for me. I was their fair-haired girl. But I was being urged to run by principled colleagues representing the women for whom I had helped write the reform law. And I couldn't disappoint them.

At this time one of Joan's closest allies, a revered judge within the bar association, took me to breakfast. I went to a lot of breakfasts in those days, a lot of meetings in coffee shops, and the message was always the same: an unfriendly warning wrapped up in a friendly *for your own good* caution. This particular breakfast remains sharp in my memory.

I'm very worried about you, she said. *I don't think you appreciate what you're getting into, what's going to happen. You shouldn't take this on, this is not something that will be allowed to happen.*

I said that I felt enormous pressure to run. That the issues were real and I couldn't disappoint all the women who were counting on me.

She nodded, showing, I thought, that she understood and to some extent commiserated with me. But she was just impatient for me to finish.

"You're going to lose," she said. *"And it will be a bloodbath."*

Myrna Felder was chosen by Joan Ellenbogen to run against me for president of the statewide organization, the first contested election in the organization's history. Myrna is the wife of Raoul Felder, a matrimonial attorney and player in the male legal establishment of the city and state. Myrna had an unusual, perhaps unique, road to the law. She was a Broadway dancer in a revival of "Anything Goes," and Raoul was a "stage door Johnny" (Myrna's description) when they met and married in 1963.[42] Myrna continued dancing on Broadway for several years until she became pregnant. At that point, at Raoul's suggestion, she went to New York University Law School, graduating in 1971 and specializing in family law. She was much honored and highly respected, a trial lawyer of note.

We both campaigned across the state in the late summer and early fall of 1986. Once, at the airport in Albany, Myrna and I found ourselves together, victims of stormy weather, and we sat down to pass the time in the terminal with coffee and a chat. She was petite and beautiful, about five feet, with a pixie haircut and an alert, intelligent face. Amid an intense, at times bitter campaign, it was a congenial moment, two women on the road waiting for a connecting flight, talking about the things that interested them and finding surprisingly little difference in our views. I've always been haunted by that moment—a vision of a different future, one in which all the issues between us, which in retrospect do not appear all that great, might have been settled without rancor, without that sense of personal betrayal. Certainly my future would have been very different. There's that saying, *Academic politics are so vicious precisely because the stakes are so small.*[43] The stakes here weren't necessarily small but the differences between us were; they were, by any measure, certainly resolvable. There was room to deal with both agendas but there wasn't the will. At this time both sides were convinced they were right and that certainty had devolved into a kind of curdled or spurious righteousness that made compromise impossible.

Looking back, after decades of trying to come to terms with those times and those issues, I believe Joan and the leadership of WBASNY were perhaps right, or maybe *more* right than we were. The organization continues to thrive: twenty chapters, over 4000 members, it is the largest women's bar association in the country. And the goals they set, all those years ago, are being met: women make up 51 percent of all judges on the appellate level, somewhat lower but steadily increasing on the others. Gender bias, even outright gender discrimination, continues to exist but by any measurable standard it is decreasing as the courts, the state bar organizations, the legislature and legislative committees become more diverse, both in terms of gender and of race. As a result the old boy bench has disappeared and we are getting much better decisions from the courts. All this took time, as Joan understood, and it also took sacrifice—which I could not let myself be part of. I just could not accept it. Of course I benefit, as a practicing matrimonial attorney, from those painful sacrifices every day and I recognize the awkwardness of my position but I also believe there was, at the time, a better way and I believe that the issues upon which I ran were the right issues. The right issues but, perhaps on my part, not all the right decisions.

I had been urged not to make this race and in the months and the weeks leading up to the actual voting I was urged to drop out but I never stopped campaigning and, against the odds, the wonderful, idealistic women who backed me, fully understanding the ominous power they were fighting, continued to battle up until election day. We made it close—a difference of only about 80 votes out of around 800 or so cast—but we lost. And then, as predicted, came the bloodbath.

* * *

It was a terrible time. Women with whom I'd been friends for years wouldn't speak to me. Other attorneys with whom I maintained a strong professional relationship completely cut me off. There were women judges who made me pay, made my clients pay, every time I appeared before them; terrible decisions against me. And this went on for years, a corrosive, unrelenting unforgiving attack. There was the judge who had taken me to breakfast and warned of a bloodbath. To some extent, and over time, we managed to repair our personal relationship but whenever I appeared before her in court she just would not give me a break. Never. A friend once observed her in court and afterwards asked me, "What does she have against you?"

It was a long story.

Joan Ellenbogen saw my actions as a personal betrayal. We never spoke again without strain, and she worked to undermine me for the rest of her life. She died in 2001 and at her funeral a friend noted, lovingly, "She never forgave and she never forgot." I didn't need a eulogist to point out that truth. I lived it.

Arthur helped me through all this. I had to deal with the psychological effects of losing, and the very real effect that loss was having on my career. He offered a blueprint. *You stay calm,* he said, *you put one foot in front of the other and do the work in a professional way and to the extent possible don't let bitterness and anger control your decisions. Don't waste your passion on your enemies. Use it for your clients.* I also received support from activists at NOW and awards from the NOW Legal Defense Fund. Strong vocal support came from many other women, some within the court system, some at firms throughout the city, who appreciated that I had made a principled stand and who made me feel, at times, like a heroine. I remember walking into a meeting and receiving a round of applause. WBASNY was dead to me but I founded, along with these women, a group called COWLI—New York State Coalition on Women's Legal Issues and, as co-chair, continued to advocate and lobby for those issues in which we believed.

But these were bright moments in a bleak period. And the hits kept coming. I felt a change at Golenbock & Barell, nothing overt at first, but the atmosphere was just . . . different. I'd been away from the office a good deal during the campaign, and I initially believed that was the reason. But I came to understand it was because I'd been away from the office and returned a *loser*. Winners don't have to explain. Losers can't. It wasn't easy. I had created a spectacularly successful matrimonial department from the ground up, but it was time to consider my options. There was a future before me, a different one than the one I had planned, but it was waiting, just the same. And it arrived more quickly than I anticipated.

One afternoon Donald Shack came into my office. He was a managing partner at the firm and a power who was close to Marty Barell.

We spoke for a moment or two and then he said:

"You know, Harriet. We just don't feel it's a good fit anymore."

And just like that I was out.

8 OPEN FOR BUSINESS

Patience and Fortitude

And just like that I was in.

Six years I was at Golenbock & Barell, from 1980 to 1986, and the work I did at the firm brought me suitors who recognized the success I was having and wanted to hire me away in an effort to duplicate and extend that success. One of the most ardent of these suitors was Dan Solin of the boutique firm Solin & Breindel. He had plans, and he was convinced that my particular talents would help bring those plans to fruition.

Dan was distinguished-looking, handsome and trim, elegant in dress and erudite in manner. His partner, Howard Breindel, wasn't as finely drawn; not as neat, not as put together. He looked exactly like what he was: a scrappy kid out of the Bronx. They seemed like one of those mismatched detective teams on 1980s television or, going further back, a vaudeville team: a clash of opposites. Actually, they fit together perfectly. Dan was the visionary, who dreamed with his eyes open and trusted the truth and practicality of those dreams. Howard was the businessman, a superb commercial litigator, with a hard-nosed appreciation for facts and numbers that approached the transcendent in its reach and sensitivity. Dan had seen me on television, *Nightline*, I believe, the Ted Koppell show and told Howard: *She's the one.*

We had been in touch off and on, but once I realized my time at Golenbock & Barell was coming to an end the courtship became serious. They offered me a partnership, a nice bump in salary and other perks. Their offices were in 530 Fifth Avenue, second floor, right across the street from the New York Public Library, and one weekend afternoon, while I was still considering their offer, Arthur and I went over to walk through the premises. 530 Fifth is a beautiful old building, high ceilings, a perfect location. I fell in love with a particular office that had large windows that looked directly across at the façade of the public library, eyeball to eyeball with the two famous stone lions that guarded the entrance *Patience* and *Fortitude*. They'd been there since the turn of the century but only named in the early 1930s by Mayor LaGuardia, who felt that those attributes—patience and fortitude—would help New Yorkers survive the great depression.

I told Arthur, while we were standing there, looking out across Fifth Avenue, that I would accept Dan's offer if he gave me the office. If not, I'd consider other options. It was that important to me. After being told that I was no longer a "good fit" at Golenbock & Barell, I wanted to be assured that Solin & Breindel were prepared to make a serious and lasting commitment; and the best office on the floor was a symbol of that commitment. I also believed that if I was to succeed in the role they had planned for me, if I was to succeed in a way that was meaningful to me, I had to be free to perform on a stage of my own design. And it was a performance. And it was a stage. I was going to bring clients into a space that was meant to dazzle and reassure them.

Dan and Howard agreed to give me that office, and I brought in Gloria Zalaznick and she created a magnificent space. Breathtaking. My desk chair swiveled outwards, toward the huge windows where I could see both stone lions: *Patience* to the south of the main steps, *Fortitude* to the north. Sometimes I would sit back in my chair and the sun would pour in and I'd half close my eyes and imagine they were winking at me.

And more than once over the years, I'd be tempted to wink back.

Open for Business

All those many years ago, Morris had teased me, wondering if I'd ever find a job, believing everyone, man or woman, should be able to earn their own way. And Marion had drilled into me the necessity of having a goal and achieving it, no matter what.

I was their daughter. The week I left Golenbock & Barell was the same week I joined Solin & Breindel. I didn't miss a single day of work.

The speed with which it all happened, the speed with which I made it happen, precluded any serious soul searching. I had suffered a professional defeat which bled over, inevitably, into a personal defeat. That's just the nature of things. It felt in some ways like a divorce. People who'd loved each other didn't speak to each other anymore. People who'd trusted each other showed that they were not worthy of that trust. I often tell clients who are going through a divorce that they'll have to reorient themselves, rediscover what is really important to them, what they really want and what they are willing to give up to get what they want.

That's the place I was in, whether I let myself be conscious of it or not. I felt I had to work even harder to make myself credible, and while that feeling is understandable, it can also be self-defeating. You feel like you have to do *everything*. But sometimes, as Arthur pointed out, the disease cures itself. Sometimes doing nothing—not subjecting the patient to the rigor of vigorous and possibly harmful treatment—is the right therapy. Benign neglect. As with all the best insights it can seem counter intuitive, and you have to be very sure of yourself because it's hard to stay still and let things sort themselves out, but it's true.

I became tougher—or more mature, able to take stock, to sense what was worth fighting for and what the cost would be. Risk/benefit—I was better at adding it all up. I was always a client-focused attorney, but I think I became better at that, as well. The hurt that I was feeling, which at times edged into something deeper, made me able, in a more profound way, to understand the hurt my clients were feeling. I was better able to counsel them. It was empathy, yes, but something more than that. Empathy fused with knowledge and the skill that only experience can bring.

And none of this was happening in a vacuum. I had a very full life, in love with Arthur, loving my children and my stepchildren. I knew change was coming both to my practice and to the way I understood my practice, but for once I was content to let it come rather than try to hurry it along.

I wasn't yet as dimensional as I would become but I believed I was on the right path.

The Practice

Dan believed the way to grow the firm beyond its boutique roots was by entering the burgeoning and lucrative "divorce market." He envisioned building a matrimonial department with a celebrity client base because the resultant publicity would bring business to the full panoply of services that the firm offered. In essence he was following the lead of Marty Barell who'd had the brilliant idea to keep everything in-house: client problems, financial and matrimonial, all circulated within familiar borders—as did the fees associated with those problems.

Dan wanted to keep everything in-house as well—only the house wasn't big enough. Solin & Breindel didn't generate a large enough or wealthy enough or distinguished enough client base to help fuel the type of expansion Dan was contemplating. So he found another house.

Dan was friends with an attorney at the firm of Frankfurt Garbus Klein & Selz, which represented artists, writers, publishers, directors, composers, models, sports stars, and other entertainers worldwide. Lawyers from the firm negotiated contracts for everyone from the hot new actress on that weekly tv show, to the movie star returning to the Broadway stage, to the author worried about the adaptation of her latest bestseller. They made sure no one wrote an unauthorized sequel to *Gone with the Wind* or played games with royalties from a classic 1960s sitcom. They had represented the plaintiffs in a complex financial dispute about the estate of Igor Stravinsky—the settlement of which involved, in part, Stravinsky's handwritten score for "The Rite of Spring," and required a stipulation signed by attorneys in Manhattan, Paris and Geneva. High culture, low culture and everything in-between. Dan appreciated culture, being a cultured man himself, but I think he most appreciated the often piquant romantic entanglements with which these culture makers were likely to ensnare themselves and, continuing along this line, he believed Solin & Breindel and Frankfurt Garbus Klein & Selz would make a good and mutually advantageous fit.

The arrangement that was reached is called *of counsel*—basically, each firm would be the go-to firm for the other in certain kinds of cases. It was not a merger; the firms retained their separate identities, but it was a formal, legal arrangement that lawyers from one firm could represent clients of the other firm without being a partner or associate—a kind of cross-fertilization whereby we would have our name, Solin & Breindel, on their letterhead and vice versa. When they had a client who needed matrimonial help, and they had a lot of them, they would send that client to me, and if they needed any help with commercial litigation, Howard, under the same *of counsel* arrangement, would provide that help.

One reason Dan had hired me was because he believed I would not be intimidated by the type of high-powered clients he expected I would have to deal with. A lot of well-known people were going to be coming through my door and he didn't doubt that I would know how to handle them.

Dan and Howard were straight shooters, and they offered full support to what I was doing. I hired two associates, two secretaries and a paralegal and was up and running. Dan in particular encouraged a savvy and aggressive campaign designed to keep the name of the firm before the public. As a result, my media appearances began to increase and I became, at least in part, the face of Solin & Breindel, commenting not only on my area of expertise but upon wider cultural matters as well. A lot of it wasn't very deep—the *New York Times* or other outlets would ask for a comment on a controversial episode of *L.A. Law* or wonder how closely films like *War of the Roses* mirrored actual divorce cases—but it was fun, it got the name of the firm into the papers or on television and it brought in clients. Dan also encouraged me to write my first book. I found an agent, Carla Meyer Glasser, Grace and Leo's daughter-in-law and an old family friend, who in turn found a co-writer, Ralph Gardner, Jr. *The Divorce Book* wasn't published until 1994, after I had left Solin & Breindel, and, while the legal landscape has changed a good deal in the years since publication, many parts of the book dealing with the human and business aspects of divorce remain as relevant as ever. It is a work which was very important to me and to my career and I will always be grateful to Dan for its genesis.

* * *

In order to keep the in-house financial arrangement working in a legal and legitimate way, a lawyer from Franklin Garbus was deemed co-counsel on all the matrimonial cases I handled that originated in that firm. For me, practically, it meant that I had to confer with the other attorney, keeping them in the loop about what I was doing and occasionally asking for their opinion—although I was always lead counsel. It was a complicated arrangement, but it was necessary, and it generally served both our ends. The co-counsel arrangement also meant there were no confidentiality requirements, no lawyer-client restrictions that bound us in any way and information was freely shared between the two firms. I now had access to a blizzard of documents about my clients that was at times overwhelming but that ultimately facilitated a revolution in how I defined and handled every case that came my way.

Dancing with Numbers

It hadn't been all that long ago when divorce was still the province of sheet-sniffing private investigators and lawyers of questionable repute. The papers generated by a case might fit into a folder or a manila envelope: a sheet of dubious numbers submitted to an unsympathetic judge. *Fault* was still determinative and the most important documents might be part of the P.I.'s worksheet: a couple of polaroids showing the arrival of the couple at the hotel in the evening and their departure the following morning or the matchbook stuck in the door that hadn't fallen out all night. And what were they doing in the intervening hours?

And this was at a time, years before the widespread use of personal computers, when the material had to be typed up—carbon paper producing second and third generation copies of increasing blurriness until the truth in the documents seemed to vanish into the paper while you were reading it.

Not all that long ago . . . but from the perspective of some of the younger attorneys I dealt with at the firm and in court, it was as unreal as a fairy tale: *Once upon a time in a kingdom far away . . .*

Divorce was now complex.[1] Divorce now took a long time. It was expensive. It dealt with the entire financial history of a marriage, so matrimonial law became an interdisciplinary field. It might involve teams of lawyers, forensic accountants, appraisers, hedge fund managers, stock market experts, bankers, real estate brokers, all of whom produced their own documents, reams of documents; a tidal wave of paper designed to clarify but which, in aggregate, tended to obscure the reality of a case. And all of it had to be typed up and xeroxed—the digital age was still several years away. Many of the financial summaries, graphs and diagrams had to be done in hand, by pencil, because the figures kept changing: revised, updated, eliminated. The Statement of Net Worth official form, submitted to the court, with attached riders, might run 30–35 pages. And the other side submitted their own assessment at similar length. An avalanche of documents and a wilderness of numbers, all accurate but difficult, at times impossible, to digest.

And this wasn't just an inconvenience. It went to the heart of how you shaped your case, how you tried to make the court understand the case, how you sought to shade the judge's perception of the facts in a comprehensible way that was favorable to your client. And that was the point. The numbers were changeable depending on how you used them. They were a tool, like any other tool, with which to persuade the court. But no judge—and again, matrimonial court is a judge's court—is going to wade through twenty or thirty pages of figures, no matter how accurate or how well prepared. The challenge, as Mr. Nizer had taught me, was to find a way to present an easily understood snapshot that would capture the judge's attention and predispose them toward a sympathetic understanding of my arguments that would then play out through the entire length of the case.

To this end I was working with an accountant named Stanley Goodman. He'd worked on the O'Brien case, which involved the complex valuation of a professional license, specifically a medical license, and he understood the need to simplify and condense the vast amount of material that reform had made relevant to the divorce process. Stanley helped me to re-visualize the use of this material, although I think he saw it as a math problem while I saw it as a part of a radical reordering of my legal strategy. It was about this time that I was talking to Howard Breindel about this and other matters. Howard was also someone unintimidated by numbers—we spoke the same language. He knew I was involved in a couple of very big cases and he said that he had been working with an accountant named David Kaufman on some commercial litigation and was impressed by his creative approach and innovative ideas. He thought David would be useful to me going forward and offered to introduce us.

David was young, somewhat brash, just beginning what turned out to be a long career. I immediately saw what had drawn Howard to him. He had a problem-solving mind, wasn't bound by old orthodoxies and understood at once what I was trying to achieve. He was something of a genius with numbers and, working off the official Statement of Net Worth form that ran to thirty plus pages, he began to re-imagine the entire process, eliminating categories, moving figures around—he could make them dance across the page. Essentially, he was creating a spreadsheet, a pre-computer spreadsheet done by hand, in pencil, on ledger paper. Spreadsheets had existed in one crude form or another for hundreds of years—Bob Cratchit was working on one when Ebenezer Scrooge made him stay late on Christmas Eve and tally up accounts—but this was the first time I'd ever seen one used in matrimonial law. We worked together, using figures I supplied that represented assets and liabilities of both my client and their spouse. My goal was to create something I could submit to the court that was immediately comprehensible. It would be both an objective financial picture of the marriage, based on the numbers supplied by both sides in the case, while at the same time, through arrangement and emphasis, it was an argument that encouraged the judge to view the issues involved through the lens I had created.

What we ended up with was a document that had the name of the two parties at the upper left-hand corner—say *James v James*. Then the index number of the court, followed by the date of the marriage, the date of the separation, and the date the case commenced. I'd also include the names and dates of birth of the children. We were creating a cheat sheet for all the information relevant to the case—but a cheat sheet with an agenda. My agenda. Running down the left-hand side of the page were categories: personal assets, cash accounts, investments accounts, retirement accounts, insurance, and the like. That was the snapshot, as accurate as we could make it, using numbers both sides had submitted to the court. Across the top of the page were another series of categories that included the husband's separate property, the wife's separate property, and individual lines for both the percentage and the actual cash value of the marital assets that should be awarded to each party. This was argument—our proposal, our estimate, tethered to the actual figures, but an estimate, nonetheless, that encouraged the judge to use our figures when resolving the case. At the bottom, running across the width of the page, was a category entitled Net Worth: total assets/amount allocated to husband/amount allocated to wife. Again, our estimates but the likely resolution of the case—if you followed the logic of our submission, which was seductive in its simplicity.

David had managed to put all this on a single sheet of paper. In later years I would refine it even more, centering it within the heart of my practice. But even at that moment, looking at the document, I felt I was on the precipice of something new. It was in pencil and paper, a bit dogeared, figures on the page had been erased and then written over. But I thought it was beautiful. And more than beautiful, it was a revelation. And more than that. It was the future.

Clients

I was a partner at Solin & Breindel for five years, from 1987 until the firm dissolved in 1992, and during that time I represented film and television stars, Broadway and cabaret performers, producers, and directors, just as Dan had envisioned. We were a money maker from the very beginning and I was fielding offers from other firms, anxious to grab a piece of my celebrity clientele. It was a heady time.

The celebrity practice was fascinating and entirely satisfying to me. Many of the cases followed a pattern: the opposing side might do a bit of posturing, a bit of tabloid trawling but eventually we would get down to serious talks and work out a settlement. Of course, one reason for this was that when I represented a celebrity I was representing the moneyed party and that always makes it easier: there are so many more options and the financial pressure, which can limit the range of plausible legal action and often leads to missteps and bad decisions, is just about non-existent.

The celebrities I represented were smart, hardworking, focused—everything a divorce lawyer could hope for in a client. By and large they were well educated and, while obviously at different levels of accomplishment, almost all possessed a certain savviness about their public persona—and the weight that persona might bear under public scrutiny. They weren't out to "prove" anything through the legal process, weren't demanding justice or vengeance. They were looking to negotiate an agreement and move on with their lives and careers with as little fuss and public notice as possible.

But if many of these cases were of the garden variety, there were a number that I particularly remember. One of the most amiable and certainly one of the easiest divorce cases my office ever handled involved a young actress, Annette Bening, who was just at the beginning of her career. She was appearing in an off Broadway play, had garnered some favorable reviews and, as she told me, was soon off to begin shooting her first motion picture. She was sent to the office from Frankfurt Garbus to finalize the divorce from her husband of seven years, arriving alone, friendly but business-like, wearing jeans and a white button down shirt, no make-up, hair pulled back, startling blue eyes. She looked like a college senior but was brisk and professional, anxious to review the terms of the divorce, which were very straightforward. She met with Pat Hennessey, my associate. I think she was at the office for just about an hour. She signed the documents and off she went to head downtown for that evening's performance. Not even a year later I read in the newspaper that she had married Warren Beatty.

Annette Bening came to the office knowing what she wanted, absolutely clear about her priorities, something that is atypical because many clients are, understandably, not as self-assured. Years ago there was a book of short stories about divorce entitled: *I Love You, I Hate You, Drop Dead!*—and that about sums it up except for the fact that a client will sometimes feel this range of emotions simultaneously or often swing back and forth between them during the proceedings.[2] And then add sorrow, anguish, fear, uncertainty, embarrassment and just about every other emotion there is into the mix.

When Linda Lavin called, she told me she was unhappy in her marriage but was uncertain about how to proceed or, indeed, whether she wished to proceed at all. Linda, who became a friend, had just finished up her nine year run on the TV series *Alice*. She'd been a working actor with a successful career on the stage and on television, but *Alice*, a critical and commercial hit loosely based on the Martin Scorsese film *Alice Doesn't Live Here Anymore,* had made her a star. At the time she telephoned me she was about to star as Mama Rose in the acclaimed Broadway revival of *Gypsy*. We spoke for some time and I then suggested she come to my office for a more thorough discussion.

Linda sat on a couch facing me, and we spoke for hours during that first meeting, *Patience* and *Fortitude* providing silent encouragement in the background. Linda had been married for ten years to her second husband, Kip Niven, an actor with a semi-recurring role on "Alice."[3] They'd married in 1982 and lived on Linda's considerable earnings, some of which Kip used to finance a separate social and presumably sexual life with a series of young women, some of whom he'd met at parties or galas to which he had escorted Linda. Linda told me she had encouraged Kip to audition for commercial work when acting jobs were not forthcoming but that he told her that this was beneath him.

Linda did not know what to do and had not made the decision to seek a divorce. She was a very unhappy woman who seemed almost transfixed by her unhappiness. I have seen this occur with many clients; indeed, to some extent, I lived through something similar during the unraveling of my own unhappy marriage. The pain these women are experiencing becomes at times addictive, a proof of the worthlessness they have been made to feel .They feel bad because they deserve to feel bad. And their hesitancy to act, to change these circumstances, makes them in their own minds a co-conspirator in that unhappiness, which serves to validate the feeling of worthlessness. There is a song by John Mellencamp entitled, *Hurts So Good*. It is a hard cycle to break.

We spoke constantly and had a number of meetings—my office became Linda's home away from home. But she still hadn't decided what course to pursue and, although I always felt like Linda's lawyer, I also felt, at times, like her therapist. She later said that during this difficult period she knew that I stood beside her, behind her, always with her as she sought to reclaim her dignity, her self-respect, and her life. This is an area of practice that is often misunderstood and sometimes demonized: the lawyer as fireman who starts fires instead of putting them out. I know there are people out there who think: *If my spouse hadn't gone to Harriet Cohen, we'd still be married.* And they're right. And I can live with that. I can accept that responsibility. I have never talked a client into getting a divorce and I've never kept the process going longer than it should, but I have worked hard, relentlessly, in an effort to help clients see what is the most healthy path to take.

It begins, as it did with Linda, with discussion, sometimes over a period of weeks or longer. I learned from Arthur, who brought focus and intelligence to the bedside, that listening is the most important thing: training yourself to hear not only what the patient/client is saying, but what they are hesitant to say. When I was listening to Linda speak, in my office, in her apartment, over multiple conversations, I was also taking notes, in essence creating a history from her own words. And through that history and from the judgment I applied to it, I hoped she would come to understand what she should do. I'm not shy about offering my judgment or opinion in these matters—that, along with technical skill and courtroom intelligence is why they've hired me. It can be daunting, but I am not convincing anyone to do something they don't wish to do. Plutarch wrote:

Music, to create harmony, must investigate discord.[4]

And that is my role as an attorney—to pursue a resolution while investigating discord. Indeed, sometimes I feel like a musician able to instantaneously recognize a wrong note. This is something I've worked hard to develop, and in the space between the notes, the pauses, or hesitancies between the words, the case unfolds and I hear what is not being said. It's not magic or juju—it's discipline, training yourself to bring the breadth of your experience and the force of your knowledge to focus on the client who is sitting in front of you. I know the kind of a situation that has hope in it. And I know the kind of a situation that doesn't. I understand that the client may be in a bad relationship, but I also understand that it may be the only relationship they have. And they may cling to it for that reason. The devil you know . . .

How much simpler it can be to deny what you are seeing, ignore what you are feeling, and navigate the shoals of your life with a somnambulist's dexterity and unconcern.

I try to help the client see that there may be another reality out there, indifferent to their unhappiness, another path, other options, and that it may be time to "reclaim" their life, because only action wakes us from dreaming.

* * *

There are, of course, many factors to consider when deciding to end a marriage. Among the most important are physical safety, emotional well-being, and financial security. For Linda, financial security wasn't really a problem but for many of my clients it's a central concern that leads to hard questions and even harder decisions. Divorce often involves financial sacrifice, a loss of friends, a complete estrangement from a life—and a privileged lifestyle—that the client has come to take for granted. The truth is that while it may not be ideal at home perhaps the better solution is to remain married but to create a separate private life and endure. There is also what has come to be called the "death gamble"—when a spouse is older, or there is illness, waiting out a spouse may be the more reasonable approach.

In any event, Linda, because of her financial independence, had a range of options open to her. And through our discussions they narrowed themselves down to the decision that the marriage was finished. I didn't make the decision for her and I won't recommend a divorce to somebody who I believe will be worse off afterwards. But I did lead Linda, through her own words and perceptions, into that place where the choice seemed obvious; that there was a single path which might lead to the happiness and security that she now felt that she deserved. At this point, once the decision is made, it becomes a question of strategy. I wrote to Kip and had him hand delivered a letter notifying him that I was Linda's lawyer and that the marriage was over. Kip was obviously aware of the marital estrangement but he had no lawyer of his own at that time—because not only did he misunderstand—or disregard—what Linda was feeling, but he consistently underestimated her courage.

Kip refused to leave their Central Park West apartment, moving into the small maid's room behind the kitchen. They had separate phone lines into the apartment, landlines. This was before cell phones and, at night, his line would light up on Linda's telephone, indicating to her that he was chatting up a conquest or arranging to meet a new one.

During the ensuing negotiations and court case Kip claimed something unusual. He not only wanted what he thought he was due under equitable distribution, he not only wanted spousal maintenance, but he also claimed that the marital property to be divided should include Linda's status as a celebrity; that there was a value, to be determined by the court, to her existential existence as a star. It was to be treated like a medical license or law license. It had value now and it had value into the future and Kip wanted his cut. He argued that he had earned this because he had contributed to the maintenance and extension of Linda's celebrity status—a status that had a tangible value for as long as Linda should live.

It was a novel argument born out of reform and the advent of equitable distribution. In time the State Legislature would amend the divorce statutes so that the court would "*not* consider as marital property subject to distribution the value of a spouse's enhanced earning capacity arising from a license, degree, *celebrity goodwill*, or career enhancement" (my emphasis),[5] but at this time the issue was very much alive. We never argued that Kip was not entitled to a share of the marital property that was accumulated during the marriage but instead argued that Linda's celebrity existed before the marriage to Kip and that it would exist after the marriage. We told the court that basically Kip had "gotten his already." Every time he put on a tuxedo, went to an opening, enjoyed a gala and a benefit, that was his reward and his playground. He could share in marital property, including his share in the jointly titled apartment, but not in Linda's post-Alice celebrity. One bite of the apple was enough.

After a lengthy trial, Kip and his lawyers agreed to a settlement which was extremely favorable to Linda. The judge had given plenty of signals from the bench that our "he'd gotten his" argument, paired with Kip's reluctance to look for work, had been very effective and it would be in Kip's interest to come to an agreement. The day the settlement was signed, Linda, Arthur and I celebrated with a huge steak dinner at Peter Luger's in Brooklyn.

Linda and I remained close until the last day of her life. She died suddenly on December 29, 2024, at the age of eighty-seven. At the time of her death, she was working on a new series for Hulu with Nathan Lane.

Rest in peace, dear friend.

* * *

Laurence Fishburne's mother's name was Hattie, and I always thought that that was why he hired me—the similarity in first names, Hattie and Harriet. We developed a close relationship and I remained impressed by his warmth, intelligence, and humanity. He told me how he had been hired for his first film role, as Tyrone "Mr.

Clean" Miller, in *Apocalypse Now*, fourteen years old, claiming to be sixteen. He said he was reading for the part, sitting across the table from Francis Ford Coppola, when a secretary came in to drop something off. Coppola asked her: "Do you think he could play an 18-year-old?" The woman barely looked at Fishburne and said, "Why not?" and he got the part. Fishburne has won three Emmy awards and a Tony.

He once spoke about how emotionally difficult it had been to film *Apocalypse Now*, not his own death scene but the scene where Gunner's Mate Miller machine gunned an object moving under a blanket that turned out to be a child. "Traumatizing" was the word he used and he wept when telling me the story.

I was representing him during his divorce from his first wife. Laurence handled himself during this difficult time with grace and generosity. With the help of the matrimonial judge, we settled all issues, financial and custody in a timely manner. Celebrity status was an issue in this case, too.

When I represent celebrity clients, in addition to listening to them and making house calls, I also become familiar with their work. If they are movie stars, I go to their movies. If they are Broadway stars, I go to their shows. If they are writers or their spouses are writers, I read their books. In the case of Laurence Fishburne, I not only saw *Boyz in the Hood* and *Apocalypse Now*, but also his then current film, *What's Love Got to Do with It*, in which he portrayed the gifted but physically and emotionally abusive Ike Turner, husband of Tina Turner. It was an extraordinary, frightening, and painful performance to watch. Arthur and I took my mother along when we went to see it. Marion was in the early stages of dementia, and it was difficult for me to see this formerly brilliant woman struggling valiantly to retain a part of herself. She watched the movie intently, as if she were trying to work out an important question. On our way out of the movie house, she leaned into me and asked, "You don't think he was Jewish, do you?" She didn't see Ike Turner's color. It simply didn't register with her as she was reentering childhood; color no longer mattered to her. But she would have been ashamed if this brute who had beaten his wife was Jewish.

A large portion of my practice at this time involved celebrities. But the case I handled of most significance involved two unknown women and the children they shared, who found me through word of mouth. They had told their acquaintances about their situation and the legal threat they faced and been told, "You need Harriet Cohen." It was a case that would change the law and all of our lives.

Case 3: The Case of a Lifetime

I

Early in August 1991, I received a telephone call in my office from a woman named Sandra Russo.[6] She was extremely upset and spoke passionately, and with anger, about the unexpected legal jeopardy that threatened her family. Russo—no one ever called her anything else—was an attorney with Legal Aid but possessed no special knowledge of family law, and she was unsure how best to proceed, how to respond to the lawsuit that had been filed against her life-partner, Robin Young. All these years later, I don't recall how she found me, but I've never forgotten her tone or the exact words she spoke: *I was told I needed Harriet Cohen. I was told that you would help.*

It was Friday, August 9th, what should have been the beginning of a lazy summer weekend. At some point Robin joined the conversation and the three of us spoke for about half an hour during which they offered a brief outline of the case. Russo and Robin had been a couple for about twelve years. They had never married—in fact, that was not possible for them since same sex marriage was not then legal in the United States; in 1991 it was legal in only one nation in the world, the Netherlands, and that only since the previous April. They had two daughters via artificial insemination, Cade, eleven years old, and Ry, nine. The lawsuit had been filed against Robin and raised issues of parental, custodial, and visitation rights with Ry, her genetic daughter. It had been filed by Thomas Steel, a prominent Bay Area lawyer, who had provided the sperm that had impregnated Robin.

"It's an emergency," Russo told me because, among other matters, Steel was asking the court to order Young to permit Ry to visit him, regardless of the mothers'—or the child's—wishes, alone, in California, at the end of the month, including over the upcoming Labor Day holiday. This was something the couple vehemently opposed—both because they felt it would be damaging to Ry and because it might be seen as a first step in creating and acknowledging some form of parental rights for Thomas Steel. Given the time pressure, I asked them both to come to the office later that afternoon for a full consultation and to bring with them a copy of the lawsuit and any documents, checks, or photographs that they thought might be important.

Russo and Robin arrived several hours later, bringing with them not only the documents requested but also their two daughters, Cade and Ry. This occasioned a bit of awkwardness because I had to be wary concerning my interactions with Ry, so as not to create any conflicts either for myself or for the child. Ry was a minor, and the court would soon appoint—if it hadn't already—an attorney, what was then called a Law Guardian, to represent her interests. I was going to represent her mother and the law did not assume that the interests of mother and child were, necessarily, the same—so the court was extraordinarily alert to any outside attempt to influence or emotionally coerce the child. In our brief contact I found both girls to be smart, personable and, in the sense that they appeared completely unintimidated about being in a strange environment, mature beyond their years.

I found an office for Cade and Ry and brought them some books, papers, and pencils to keep them occupied. Russo, Robin and I then went to my office for the consultation where we were joined by my associate Peter Bienstock. Over the coming months and years his intelligence, legal skills, and courtroom savvy would prove essential as the case progressed.

This is what Sandra Russo and Robin Young told me that day in my office, in 1991.

In 1979, Russo was thirty-nine years old, and Young was twenty-four. They lived together, in a West Village apartment in downtown New York City, in a committed relationship, one they both believed would last for the rest of their lives. Russo had been married twice before and had always wanted children. "I wanted kids from the time I was kid," she told me, but after she committed to Robin it "was no longer on my radar."

"As a gay couple, that was just something you had to give up," Robin added. "That you would ever have a family."

In August 1979, the women vacationed in San Francisco and spent time with a friend of Russo's—Chris Arguedas. The two women had met in law school, become best friends, and maintained a close relationship ever since. Chris knew about Russo's desire to have a child—and told her she thought this was possible, that she could help make it happen. She showed them both a pamphlet aimed at lesbian couples, entitled "Women Controlled Conception." It illustrated, through simple text and even simpler pictures, how a woman might self-impregnate using donated sperm and a turkey baster. "As simple as 1-2-3," the pamphlet claimed. Neither woman had ever considered this, had thought it possible, but the more they thought it through the more real it seemed. And because it now seemed real they discussed in detail exactly what they wanted to do and how they would go about doing it.

They wanted what Young called "a traditional family." Their idea was that each woman would be artificially inseminated by the sperm from a different donor, and the children would be raised together as siblings, the offspring of both women. From the very beginning the idea was that they would create a family, *their* family—and they wanted to find donors who lived far enough away from them that being "part of the family" would not be an option. They believed they had thought everything out and this was something they were very concerned about—they were not looking for any sort of emotional connection between the sperm donor and the child. It was one of the reasons they also wanted a different donor for each child—another way to temper any potential complications. Because Russo was older, under more biological pressure, it was agreed that she would become pregnant first. If everything worked out as they hoped, Robin would stay home with the two children as primary caregiver. Russo would be the breadwinner. It was what they both wanted, as close an approximation of a straight family as they could imagine.

Chris said that she knew a gay man who might be willing to donate his sperm. He was Jack Kolb, a physical therapist, and, after talking with Chris, he agreed to see the women. Russo was too nervous to meet with him, so she waited in the car while Robin went into his home and spoke with him for a short time. She found him intelligent, handsome (both Russo and Robin admitted this was important to them—indeed, they turned down a potential candidate because they thought him unattractive) and personable. Robin was clear with him when she explained the terms: "This is our family. You have no responsibilities and you have no rights. Eventually, if the child asks to see you, you will make yourself available, as per our conditions." Kolb agreed and Robin handed him a standard health survey which he filled out and signed. When Robin returned to the car, she said to Russo: "We got a guy."

A day or so later, Kolb called Chris and said, "It's ready. Come and pick it up." As per their conversation, he had ejaculated into a jar—one that had formerly held artichoke hearts. Chris put the jar in a paper bag to keep it away from direct light, as the contraception pamphlet recommended, and brought it to Russo and Robin. Later that day, the two women used a glass syringe to impregnate Russo. Nine months later, in May, 1980, their daughter Cade Russo-Young was born.

1-2-3.

In February 1981, Russo, Robin, and nine-month-old Cade flew to San Francisco, where Chris Arguedas had found another likely sperm donor. Tom Steel, Thirty-one years old, was a well-known attorney, celebrated for a series of cases involving free speech, civil rights (he represented Huey Newton of the Black Panthers), and civil liberties. He was the go-to lawyer in San Francisco for matters involving gay rights and Chris, after sounding him out, felt that Steel, as a gay man, would be enthusiastic about helping a lesbian couple create a new kind of family. Both Russo and Robin met with him at his home and were extremely impressed, finding him smart, charming, politically aware. And very handsome. They spelled out their conditions—"no rights, no responsibilities"—and he offered verbal assurances that he understood and agreed to those terms. At the time of the visit a man was staying with Tom whom Russo and Robin referred to as "The Sailor," because his manner or his dress put them in mind of something nautical. They never knew his name. Tom and the Sailor went upstairs and shortly afterwards both came down, and Tom handed Robin an artichoke jar with his sperm.

Russo and Robin's second daughter, Ry Russo-Young, Cade's sister, was born on November 16, 1981, and for the next four years, there was no contact of any kind between the mothers and the donors.

The women had always expected that sooner or later Cade and Ry would start asking questions about their circumstances, why they had two mothers, and other matters, but they assumed it would be later—perhaps in junior high school. Instead, in 1985, when five-year-old Cade began attending pre-school, she came home one day and said that all her classmates had been talking about their fathers . . . where was hers? Russo and Robin told me they had always determined to be honest with the girls, and to treat them equally, as sisters, so, even though at this time only Cade was curious, they spoke to them *both*, providing a simple explanation about what had happened. Cade remained curious about her "father," wondering if she would ever see him. At this point, the mothers contacted both Jack and Tom, asking if they'd be willing to meet with the children. They agreed, and Russo and Robin told Cade and Ry they were all going to fly to San Francisco to see "the men who helped to make you."

That first meeting—Jack, Tom, Russo, Robin, Cade, and Ry—went very well; Russo said there was a wonderful, generous spirit about it, and Robin "felt so thankful to these guys"—and it established a pattern. They visited with each other once or twice a year, during school vacations, spending summers together, renting a home either on Long Island or on Stinson Beach in Marin County, California. It was always the six of them—the women had wanted separate sperm donors because they didn't want any one person having such a powerful biological—or potentially emotional—hold over the family. The men were expected to treat the children as if they were biological sisters, not to favor one over the other and not to assume any stronger bond existed with one of the girls and not her sister. They never saw the children except in the company of the mothers and, Russo and Robin said, they were treated as good family friends and that both seemed happy and satisfied with the arrangement.

Over time, Jack stopped coming to these vacations. He had developed a drinking problem and seemed to have trouble connecting with the others. When he did show up, his behavior was erratic, and Russo, whose estranged father had died of alcoholism, confronted him. Jack took offense and cut off contact with the family. They never saw him again.

But the relationship with Tom deepened. They saw him not only on vacation or during the summer but when he came to the city on business. During those times he would sometimes stay in their West Village apartment and, occasionally, attend school events for the girls. They showed me photographs they'd brought of Tom and their family, all of them in bathing suits by the seaside, wading out into the water, waving at the camera, Russo with her ever-present cigarette; or walking through the streets of lower Manhattan on a chilly winter day, bundled up and holding hands. As the years went by it became apparent to Russo and Robin—and most probably, they said, to Cade—that although Tom may have tried to treat each of the girls equally, it didn't come naturally to him and he was developing a special fondness for Ry. The mothers could see this in the way he treated her, the way he held her and looked at her. And that worried them and created some tension among the adults.

That tension increased when Tom began a relationship with the man who would become his life partner: Milton Estes, a Mill Valley physician. Before he'd come out, Estes had been married and he had a teenage son, Jacob; so now when they visited together it was Tom *and* Milton, and occasionally Jacob, as well. The relationship Russo and Robin had built with Tom was, by its nature, somewhat delicate and required a sense of discretion and mutual understanding. Milton either didn't understand or didn't respect the dynamic they had worked to create. He seemed to have his own idea of what the family should be and wasn't shy about attempting to impose that idea on the rest of them. He encouraged Ry to refer to Tom as "Daddy," and, to the women, it was clear that he had no regard for the boundaries they had set, inserting himself into their life and the decisions they made in ways they considered inappropriate. When they attempted to talk to Tom and Milton about this they got nowhere and eventually they told Tom: We don't want Milton around our children. We're happy to see you, but not with Milton.

Tom *did* come to visit with them—alone—in New York, but it was stressful and he had as little interaction with Russo and Robin as possible. A series of angry letters were exchanged, the women accusing Tom of trying to undo their original agreement, Tom saying that they had all changed over the years and that a new understanding was inevitable. He complained that the women were trying to control his relationship with Ry, afraid of, in his words, "the love between a father and his daughter" afraid this love would undermine their relationship with the children. He said they made *him* feel like a child, dependent on their whims, distrusted and suspected.

Matters came to a head when Tom told Russo and Robin he wanted to take Ry and Cade to a Steel family celebration to honor his grandmother's birthday, in Yuba City, California, at the end of August 1991. The mothers were not invited. It made no sense to them: Tom's brothers and sisters would all be there with *their* children . . . but Ry and Cade weren't to come with their mothers? It unsettled them that Tom would even consider this—he hadn't yet told his family that he *had* a daughter and told Russo and Robin he wasn't sure how he'd manage this, but he knew he didn't want *them* to come. The women flatly refused to allow their children to attend unaccompanied by their mothers—either all four of them would go or none of them. Tom said he was fed up, sick and tired of them preventing him from spending time with the girls alone, or with his family. He said the impasse saddened him and that the past few months had been very painful, however the three of them were still trying to work things out.

The lawsuit Tom filed came as a bolt from the blue, a sickening, staggering development that caught both women by surprise. Tom had given no indication he was preparing to go to court, and neither Russo nor Robin had ever considered legal action as a way to resolve their differences. The mothers had brought a copy of the lawsuit to my office. It had been filed in Family Court in New York County on Monday, August 5th; filed against Robin Young, as the biological mother of Ry. Russo was not named in the suit; indeed, being no blood relation, in terms of this case, the court considered her a "legal stranger" with no connection with Ry that had to be protected or even acknowledged. The lawsuit asked the court to issue a declaration of paternity, recognizing Tom Steel as Ry's father, which obviously raised potential questions of custody. It further asked the court to permit "liberal and unsupervised visitation between Petitioner and his daughter Ry," ordering Robin to immediately produce Ry so that Tom could take her to California for several weeks, as part of the court's mandate. Robin had been served with the lawsuit the previous day, Thursday, August 8th.

Both women felt betrayed by Tom, but for Russo it was a double betrayal, as she knew one of the named lawyers in the lawsuit who was representing Tom. In addition, they were incensed by a message left on their home answering machine by Milton. He said this could all be over quickly: Tom's lawyer was preparing a simple draft agreement—they could all meet in the office and sign it and it would all be resolved on paper. He added that they might pack a small suitcase and then he and Tom could take Ry with them back to California. The assurance and ease with which he spoke was unnerving; not only angering them but making them profoundly uneasy. It was clear to them that Tom, an experienced attorney, had filed the suit because he thought he would win—and win easily. It was inconceivable to them, and insulting, that he'd assumed they would fold, that they would not fight to protect what they loved and what they had created, together. At this point, Russo called me and asked me to represent them.

* * *

A good attorney must understand exactly who it is he or she is representing and that is not as simple as it might seem. In this case, my client was Robin Young. Robin had been sued and it was her rights that were being challenged and that had to be defended. Sandra Russo, who we maintained was Ry's mother and who had helped raise her since birth, was not part of the lawsuit and was not recognized by the court as having any rights in this matter at all. In the event, she was not even allowed into the courtroom during the trial—and had to watch the proceeding from the hallway, standing on a stool and looking through a tiny glass window in the courtroom door. And yet, though the court could never acknowledge it, and opposing counsel would struggle to recognize it, I was representing Russo, as well.

I had found both women very impressive during our initial meeting and that impression subsequently strengthened as the case progressed. They were not only unusually intelligent but they possessed a keen working understanding of the fight they found themselves in, the stakes involved, and what they might have to do in order to give themselves a chance to prevail. I don't remember a single disagreement about strategy—and that is unusual in a case so difficult and controversial. They trusted each other completely, understood and never deviated from their goal, and they trusted me as well. They were clear about what they wanted—that Tom never be granted parental rights, that he never be legally recognized as Ry's father—and they allowed me to develop a supple and powerful strategy toward that end. Clients can sometimes be confused about what they want and what they are willing to sacrifice in order to get it. This is completely understandable: in divorce or custody cases, for example, you are most often facing off against someone with whom you had an intimate relationship, usually for many years. That can lead to uncertainty or confusion: You might feel sorry for your ex; you might still harbor warm feelings toward him or her. Russo and Robin did have a relationship with Tom, the exact nature of which, in Robin's case, the court would decide. But the women were not conflicted about what they felt. Tom's lawsuit had acted as a bomb, severing any connection, obliterating any residual warm feelings. In terms of the case and the path forward, there was never any ambivalence, never any second guessing. So while Robin was my client, I understood that every decision made about strategy would have to be—and was—approved by Russo, as well.

There was yet another factor of some importance to the case. I liked both women. Obviously, over the course of a long career, I've had some difficult, and at times unreasonable or unpleasant clients—sometimes very unreasonable, very unpleasant. And you work just as hard to represent a client you may not think so highly of as one you do. But generally, I tend to identify with my clients, and in this case, I genuinely admired Russo and Robin and the life they had built for themselves. It had not been easy, but they had conducted themselves, as far as I could tell, with courage and, in terms of their relationship with Tom, with honor. That first consultation lasted for hours, deep into Friday evening, as we spoke and worked our way through the documents they had brought. It seemed to me they were making every effort to be as clear as possible, not to sugarcoat anything, to present the decisions and choices they had made—good and bad, helpful to the case or unhelpful—as honestly as they could.

Russo was more direct, more forthright, her language colorful—peppered with *fuck this* or *that fucker*. She was short and seemingly pugnacious—in some ways she reminded me of a Dead End Kid—forever looking for a fight, never looking to end one: a public, at times flamboyant power. But she possessed a great sense of humor, a fine analytical mind and was, notwithstanding her public persona, capable of great kindness and sensitivity. Robin, younger by fifteen years, was more reserved, quieter, and seemingly more measured. But in the brief time we had spent together I recognized that she possessed, as they say, *a whim of iron*; that she was, in her way, as tough and determined as Russo.[7] I think one of the great factors in our favor as the case moved forward was that Tom and his attorney had completely misread Robin, underestimating her and her fierce desire to protect her daughters and the family they had built around them. By removing Russo from the legal equation, they believed they had significantly reduced the power, purpose, and will of the opposition. Everyone could see how tough Russo was. It took a keener eye to recognize those same qualities in Robin, but they were there. Together, they made a formidable pair.

My relationship with Cade and with Ry was, as I've explained, necessarily circumspect. I never spent time with them alone and, beyond a courteous "Hello" or "Goodbye" never really spoke to them. I observed them of course, but just about everything I knew about them at this time came from Russo and Robin. They told me the girls understood what was happening, believed that they had two parents—two mothers—and that Tom represented a threat to a life they valued, the only life they knew. Their reality. From what I could tell they seemed extremely well adjusted, well-loved and very close to each other. They may have been aware of what was happening but, the mothers told me, they weren't paralyzed by it: they went to school, played with friends, lived, as much as possible, the life young girls lived. Inevitably some of this changed as the trial progressed but based on what the mothers told me—and what I would come to learn from Bonnie Rabin, who would be appointed by the court as Ry's attorney, her Legal Guardian—I was, in some way, representing not only Russo and Robin but the best interests of Ry and Cade, as well. At least, that was what I felt.

* * *

When I evaluated the case, as I then understood it, based on that first long consultation and an examination of the documents, photographs, and other papers that Russo and Robin had brought to my office, there were a number of factors that seemed to favor our position. The most important were the women themselves. Russo and Robin were in a stable, loving relationship and they had created a stable, loving family. We might present that family to the judge as a *fait accompli*, a mise en scene of domestic security and affection—two parents, a breadwinner and a stay at home mom, two children—that he would be loath to tamper with or to alter in any way. He could, of course, he had that power, but I already knew, at this very early stage, that it would be important for him to see this family as *real*, for us to present it to him as *real*; in a sense, upping the ante: if he ruled for Tom he would be tearing this beautiful thing apart. In addition, the close, loving relationship between Cade and Ry was also an important factor. Judges are traditionally ill disposed to separate or upset in any way the relationship of siblings; indeed, I've been involved in cases where custody is decided based on where a sister or brother lives.

Tom was now claiming that Ry was his daughter and that he loved her as a daughter. But there was the uncontested fact that for the first four years of her life he had no contact with her and made no effort to contact her or have any relationship with her. He had displayed, we might argue, indifference to her very existence and it was Robin and Russo who had initiated contact and encouraged a relationship acting, as they always did, in the best interests of their children. The terms of that relationship had been spelled out and agreed to by both parties. In essence, they had a contract. Robin and Russo had fulfilled their part of the bargain; it was Tom who was in default. In one of the documents the women had given me, a letter

Tom wrote to Russo, he seemed to acknowledge their understanding regarding Ry and how she would be raised, but to insist that now the terms must be changed.

The emotional and legal ties between the parties were important, but of equal, if not paramount importance were the financial ties—or in this case, the lack of financial ties between the parties involved. Tom came from a wealthy family but he had never been asked to contribute—and indeed had never contributed—any money to the family or more specifically to Ry's upbringing. Not a penny. The women lived a very comfortable life based on their own funds and their own earnings. They owned the building they lived in—purchased, cheaply, a decade earlier in a rundown section of Manhattan that had since become fashionable. The law is very much about encouraging someone who wants to take responsibility as a father. But that policy, in fact much of our social policy, is economically based: the state wants to ensure that the child is provided for and, in the worst case scenario, does not end up on the public dole. Our position would be that in this case, that was not a possibility and should not factor into any decision.

Finally, Ry herself was certainly going to be a key part of our legal effort. Much would depend on exactly who the court chose to represent her interests. We might hope the Legal Guardian was sympathetic to our arguments and, most importantly, sympathetic to the child herself. The mothers assured me, in that first meeting, that Ry was unusually mature, that, in their words, "she knew her own mind." But exactly what weight the court would put on a nine-year-old's testimony, how they would evaluate her stated wishes and preferences, would be determined in part by the Legal Guardian, any psychologists or psychiatrists appointed by the court, by the judge himself and, finally by Ry, her conduct and testimony in court. At this point, so early in the case with so many unknowns, the only one in whom I had any confidence was Ry.

There was one other factor that played into my thinking those first days, a very personal one. This was the case of a lifetime. I'd known that from the moment Russo had called and asked for my help. I was an attorney specializing in family law, and here was an opportunity to change, or at the least expand, the definition of family in an important and positive way. It was the type of case that made a life in the law meaningful, and it was possible that the outcome might not only provide relief to my clients but provide legal protection and comfort to others across the country as they struggled to create new families, new connections, based on new, or perhaps only newly acknowledged, realities.

So this is what I believed that second weekend in August 1991: I had the case of a lifetime, with the clients of a lifetime and, if what they told me was accurate, I had in Ry the child of a lifetime.

And I believed one other thing: We were going to lose.

* * *

We faced an inhospitable legal landscape.

It wasn't simply a question of whether the court protected—or even acknowledged—the rights of lesbian couples. It didn't.[8]

Or whether the larger legal environment, the system of jurisprudence in the State of New York and the volume of case law, was sympathetic to the arguments we might make. It wasn't.

Or whether the idea that a couple might consciously create a family in which the children were parented by two women was, within the law as understood and interpreted in Family Court, largely incomprehensible. It was.

It seemed to me, as I continued that initial evaluation, that just about every point in our favor seemed shadowed by another point, a dark twin as it were, that served to emphasize the weaknesses in our case. And so much of those weaknesses were baked in, stemming from the fact that, because of their sexual identity, my client and her partner found themselves in legal limbo. New York State would not permit them to marry. The state would not permit them to adopt. The rights routinely granted to heterosexual couples, the responsibilities that existed concurrent with those rights, were denied them because they were lesbians. In addition, the Court in which we would seek to establish and defend those rights acted from the assumption that the traditional nuclear family—with a mother and a father—was obviously, by its nature, in the best interests of the children; so, in a sense, the allegedly "neutral" guardrails by which the court operated and within which we would have to make our case seemed to conspire against us. Being a parent is a legal status, subject to interpretation by each state's laws, but there wasn't at this time a state in the union whose laws defining and governing parenthood did not reflect, in one way or another, the idea that "biology is destiny." There were accommodations to this principle: in New York, a person who legally adopted a child had the exact same rights as that child's biological parent. But, as noted, this remedy, which was called second party adoption and secured the child's legal connection to a non-biological parent, was not available to my client or her partner. And how very different this case would have played out had Russo been able to adopt Ry, and Robin able to adopt Cade—something that would not be possible for another decade, when New York finally removed prohibitions on same sex second party adoptions. And it would be a decade after that before the Marriage Equality Act legalized same sex marriage in New York.

As a committed lesbian couple, as same sex parents, Robin and Russo understood that they faced peculiar legal and social vulnerabilities. In consequence, they consciously discouraged interest in their living arrangement and in their children from those outside a close circle of friends and acquaintances, not because they were hiding something or because they were ashamed, but because they believed such interest might be, more often than not, hostile in nature. They were no different from many gay couples at the time; the self-impregnate, "women controlled conception" movement had been created to shield same sex couples from the prying, unsympathetic eyes of the medical establishment and the government. It was the reason there was almost no documentation about the conception of either Cade or Ry—indeed, about the only contemporaneous paperwork that *did* exist was the meaningless health survey Robin had given to Jack Cole. Usually, when lawyers get together, if one of them sneezes you end up with paperwork about as long as the Treaty of Versailles. Here one very smart woman, Robin, and three very smart lawyers, Tom, Chris, and Russo—all gay—had been involved in the creation of a human being and none of them had thought it prudent to write a contract detailing the agreements and understandings that had been undertaken. They believed they understood each other and *all* of them believed that what they were doing was no one's business but their own. In a way they saw themselves as pioneers, with shared interests, operating through faith and trust, beyond the boundaries of law and custom.

While this decision is understandable, it created serious legal problems. We would be arguing that Robin and Tom had an agreement—in essence a contract—the terms of which were understood and acknowledged. But as nothing had been written down, Tom might deny there was any agreement or, faced with possible evidence of such in his letters to Young and Russo, might claim that his understanding of the agreement was different from theirs, that he never had, and never would have, agreed to the terms Robin specified. It was a hellish conundrum.

But even more problematic was the fact that Robin and Russo had brought all this on themselves. *They* had invited Tom into their family—for reasons that were completely understandable, even laudable—and *they* had established a relationship with him and permitted their children to establish a relationship with him, of some intimacy. The documents and photographs the mothers had brought to my office paid proof to that and as I reviewed them that first weekend I had to assume that Tom, and his legal team, possessed photographs and letters, some from Ry, of equal or perhaps greater intimacy; and that there was certainly other material as well—birthday cards perhaps, drawings by the children, film or videotape of Tom (and Milton and Jacob) and the girls. In addition, the mothers had permitted Tom to stay with them in their West Village apartment when he came to New York to visit, or on business. There was no denying the fact that an affectionate relationship of some type existed or, we could argue, *had* existed, between Tom and Ry but the exact nature of that relationship would be determined by the court.

Tom argued in his filing that his connection with Ry was not only biological but emotional: he loved her as a daughter and, more importantly, he claimed that was how Ry thought of him. He said that when he arrived at their New York apartment, Ry would shout, "Daddy's here." The mothers denied this. They had told me that Ry thought of Tom and treated Tom as a close family friend—a friend who lived across the country and sometimes came to visit. And they said there was no emotional confusion: Ry knew who Tom was, and she knew who her parents were: Robin and Russo. Whatever mistakes the women had previously made in their relations with Tom, whatever problems they had created for themselves, they now understood the nature of the threat they faced and were determined to fight. That was why they had hired me. But, as we prepared our response to Tom's initial court filing, what concerned me was: would we be permitted to make that fight?

Estoppel is a legal principle that empowers a judge to prevent or "estop" someone from arguing something or making assertions that contradict something previously said, demonstrated, or agreed to. The sanctioned party is said to be "estopped"—forbidden to argue a particular claim. Ry was nine years old. Tom had been in her life, invited into her life, for the past five years. Could Robin's actions over that period be seen as, essentially, validating Tom's assertions and would the judge then prevent us from contesting those claims? It was a distinct possibility.

There was nothing simple about this case. Even the question of financial ties, or lack of financial ties between the parties, which seemed to favor our position, was not without its complications. Tom was asserting paternal rights and responsibilities, something the law encouraged for social and, as noted, economic reasons: the state did not want the child to become a financial burden on taxpayers. He came from a wealthy family; he was wealthy himself and just because he had not contributed any funds toward Ry's support in the *past* did not preclude him from offering such aid in the *future*. In fact, by claiming paternity. Tom was telling the court he was willing and able to assume that responsibility. We opposed his claim and if the court ruled in our favor, it would, presumably, be cutting off a nine year old child from a lifetime of financial support and a potential inheritance. And that was something a judge, charged with protecting the best interests of the child, might not be willing to do. This issue would gain a new immediacy, and a poignancy, as the case progressed.

But at this moment, that first weekend, I was most concerned with the tremendous time constraint we were under. We wanted to file our response to Tom's lawsuit when court opened on Monday morning because he and his team were asking for immediate interim relief. In the words of their filing, the court should "enter a declaration of paternity, an order of liberal and unsupervised visitation [and] an interim order permitting visitation between petitioner and his daughter Ry in California in August 1991, and for such other and further relief as may be appropriate under the circumstances." They envisioned that Ry would be handed over to Tom within days and that Tom would then be allowed to take her to California for the rest of the summer, even while the larger issues of the case were being reviewed and briefed.

This was completely unacceptable to us. Robin, Russo, and I believed that to permit Tom to take Ry would be an assertion of privilege that could do terrific, if not fatal damage to our case. It was an existential threat that might end things almost before they'd begun. The pressure we were under was extraordinary but we had to respond quickly and forcefully, addressing a series of issues while at the same time letting Tom and his legal team know, in no uncertain terms, that they were in for a fight and that any "shock and awe" effect they'd hoped the lawsuit would have, had failed.

Therefore, our initial filing had to accomplish a number of goals. The Family Court judge who would be hearing the case was Edward M. Kauffmann, and, in these days before widespread use of the internet, it wasn't immediately possible to determine his background and past rulings. All I knew about him at this time was that he was a respected jurist with a reputation of being intelligent and fair minded. I was counting on the latter, because there was absolutely no settled case law that supported our position.

As I've mentioned, I'm not one of those lawyers who will wait for the end of a brief to make my key points. My mentor, Louis Nizer, had taught me that you should never assume—indeed it is unlikely—that a judge is going to read your complete filing, and it did your case, and your client, no good to make a killer point on page twelve if the judge never got that far. So you want to make your strongest argument right up top and, at the same time, you want to make it as easy as possible for the judge not only to understand that argument, but, more importantly, if not to sympathize entirely with it, at least to sympathize with the manner in which you are presenting it. By introducing your case this way, clearly and forcefully, you are demonstrating respect for the court—and beginning a process of creating a favorable environment in which to make your arguments. The military call it, "shaping the battlefield." Ideally, you are looking for "home field advantage" and, as there are usually no juries in matrimonial court, the only way to achieve this is through the judge.

I wrote the papers that weekend and in that first paragraph we disputed every assertion made by the opposition. Tom was not Ry's father. The relationship between Tom and Ry was not parental—she never deemed him her father and never *understood* him to be her father. Ry did not wish to go away with him to California. What Tom was doing, by asserting paternity, was a complete betrayal of trust, breaching all the understandings he had reached with the women. Tom had helped create this family; that is what they all agreed to and that is *all* that they agreed to. This was a nuclear family of two children, Ry and her sister, Cade, and two parents, Robin and Russo. When a physician asked for parental consent, when a principal invited parents to attend a school event, those were the names that were given. Russo went to work; Robin stayed home; the family was financially secure.

The only threat they faced was from Tom. He was the only factor that could tear apart everything Robin and Russo had built, the happiness and security they had created for their children. And I added that biology was not destiny—if it was, what was going to happen to all the adopted children in this world?

There was nothing left out. If I'd learned that Tom cheated at pinochle, and found some way to make it relevant, I'd have put that in, as well. When you are fighting in litigation of this sort, it would be professional malfeasance not to use everything that you have.

It was, I believed, as powerful an argument for our case as I was capable of making in this first filing. But, reading it over, I believed it wasn't enough. We had to find some way to slow the process down. It is understood in court that plaintiffs, seeking relief, want speed, and defendants, more or less satisfied with the status quo, seek delay. But even within this context, there was something about Tom's case, the sheer brute force of the unexpected lawsuit, that indicated they didn't expect a fight, didn't want a fight, and believed this would all be over quickly. Milton's taunting "pack a suitcase" phone call to Russo seemed to underscore this. I began reviewing again everything Robin and Russo had told me, every document they had given me, looking for anything I had overlooked that might be helpful to us. And when I found it, like the man on the stair, it wasn't there.

We were arguing that Tom had broken an agreement that he had with the women, and I had understood the lack of documentation about that agreement as a burden we had to overcome. But in a much more fundamental way it was also a burden for Tom, who was claiming to be Ry's father based on . . . what? There was nothing written down, no order of filiation, his name was not on the birth certificate. There was no paperwork of any kind regarding Ry's conception and there was simply no reason why we had to accept Tom's claim at face value. And there was the question of the Sailor: the "strapping young man"—as Russo described him,—who had been with Tom when the women had received the sperm used to impregnate Robin. They had both expressed a mild unease about his presence. The Sailor had gone upstairs with Tom and who could say that it wasn't his semen that they'd been given. Tom was Ry's biological father? Let him prove it.

And, after consulting with Robin and Russo, that was the relief we requested in our filing: "an order requiring the mother, the child and the alleged father to submit to one or more blood grouping tests by a duly qualified physician or laboratory . . . to determine if the alleged father can be excluded as the father of said child." Tom's lawsuit had exploded like a bomb; now we had one of our own. But unlike theirs, we had a smart bomb.

* * *

The reaction to our motion from opposing counsel was a kind of baffled surprise. They appeared unprepared, openly wondering why we would challenge something—Tom's paternity—that was so obviously true—and this reinforced my belief that, despite my reputation as a fighter, they had expected an easy time of it in court. Tom was reportedly furious, and I know he called Chris Arguedas, in California, to complain about our actions. Chris then called Russo, and asked, "What are you doing? Why are you forcing a nine year old to get a needle in her arm to prove what you already know?" It seemed to me that Chris wasn't confused, she was angry, as if she was the one who had been betrayed. Russo, her close friend, was taken aback. "No one knows what we know," she told her.

Even at this early stage I felt an uneasiness about Chris' role in all this and about what she claimed was her divided loyalty between Tom and Russo. It has been my experience, over a long career in family and matrimonial law—and life—that *no one* is neutral in a divorce or custody case and that those who most profess their neutrality are often the most dangerous, the most likely to betray. If someone tells you they're neutral, it's best to assume they're on the other side. I didn't know much about Chris at this point and perhaps she was the exception but I did feel that sooner or later, like everyone else in this process, she would fly her true colors and we could only hope to limit the fallout.

But, whatever her motivation, Chris had raised an important issue with Russo, one that appealed to both mothers at their most vulnerable: we *were* demanding a lot from a nine-year-old, and, if the case played out the way we hoped it would, we would be demanding even more. Parents have rights and those rights have to be considered and weighed in the balance, but primarily this was a case centered on what the law called "the best interests of the child." That phrase was repeated a great deal during the trial—as it is during most cases involving simple custody or parental rights—but so often, it seems to me, those mouthing the phrase don't stop to consider what it really means, and the sometimes harsh choices that it may dictate. Chris didn't feel it was in the best interests of the child to have blood drawn; presumably, the alternative, *the real life* alternative, the *only other option*—that Ry be forced from her home and taken to California with a man she did not wish to go with—was preferable. And one of Tom's lawyers, talking about the case in a documentary film made by Ry (*Nuclear Family*/2021), said that she never believed it was in the best interests of the child that the case ever went to court at all—overlooking the fact that it was her own action, on behalf of Tom, that landed us, nine year old Ry included, in court in the first place.

Robin, Russo, Peter and myself didn't have the luxury of pholosophizing about the best interests of the child, because we were singularly dedicated to protecting and securing the best interests of *this* child, Ry Russo Young; a child, yes, but not an infant and, according to her mothers, one who knew that she was at the center of a bitter legal battle. It was never a matter of *wanting* to stick a needle in her arm or *wanting* her in court; and there were times, understandably, when Ry was upset, even scared, but she remained throughout determined to have her voice heard by the court. Every decision Peter and I made, every strategic choice, came only after consultation with Robin and Russo, and the wellbeing of Ry and Cade, and the survival of their family, was always uppermost in their minds.

But this focus by the mothers on *their* child and *their* family came at a cost. The broad support they might have expected from the gay and lesbian communities was not, by and large, forthcoming because many within those communities saw this defense of the nuclear family—children, two parents—as profoundly conservative and out of step with the broad imperatives of the gay rights movement. Indeed, neither Robin nor Russo was a revolutionary. They were manning no barricades, seeking no "newer worlds"—at the most basic they were asking for the same rights and protections enjoyed by heterosexual couples. This was radical enough for some—and they had their supporters—but not for many others, for whom the terms "normative" and "homosexual" or "heterosexual" were themselves cultural constructs, and who envisioned new kinds of family with new kinds of familial connections. At the same time, Tom, who was a star within the gay community—charismatic, widely known and respected—had his own detractors, who felt his lawsuit was an attack on the entire lesbian community. In fact, the split within these communities did not break down along any simple lines—gay men for Tom, lesbians for Robin and Russo—but seemed to reflect a wider split between moderates and progressives, or radicals, concerning tactics and ultimate goals. It was a dispute that would be mirrored years later in the battle for same sex marriage, between those who saw this as an end in itself and those who saw it as only a beginning.

But if my clients enjoyed only splintered and, at times, desultory support from the gay and lesbian communities, they faced a united and increasingly powerful opposition from those who viewed gay rights as a threat to home and family—indeed to American civilization. The landmark children's book, *Heather Has Two Mommies*, by Leslea Newman, was published in 1989; self-published because no established publisher would touch it.[9] The story of Mama Jane and Mama Kate received a mixed response from the lesbian community, where some, in a preview of the criticism Robin and Russo would receive two years later, believed it was a misguided attempt to graft a mild lesbian sensibility onto an essentially heterosexual paradigm. (In the first printing of the book Mama Jane becomes pregnant the same way my clients did—the self-impregnate, "turkey baster" method. Later editions of the book dropped all details of artificial insemination as "not age appropriate.") Among others who broadly supported gay rights there was also considerable unease about the book—the concept of same sex parents being viewed with a sort of bemused incredulity. Indeed, for a time "Two Mommies" became a kind of national punchline.

Among those opposed to gay rights, *Heather Has Two Mommies* touched off a firestorm, sparking protests nationwide from New York to California, a virulent, vociferous wave of homosexual panic.[10] In 1999, the American Library Association would list it as one of most banned books in the United States over the previous decade—higher up on the list than the perennially controversial *Catcher in the Rye. Heather Has Two Mommies* was read into the Congressional Record during the debate over a bill to ban federal aid to school districts that "carry out a program or activities that has either the purpose or effect of encouraging or supporting homosexuality as a positive lifestyle alternative."[11] The bill passed 63–36. The idea of same sex parents was seen as especially threatening, undermining support for traditional, "normal" ideas of marriage and parenthood. This imagined threat became a key issue during the debate over the Defense of Marriage Act, which defined and protected marriage, on the federal level, as an exclusively heterosexual institution. DOMA was approved by Congress—342–67 in the House; 85–14 in the Senate—and signed into law by President Clinton in 1996.[12] And much of the debate about the measure centered on protecting children from the so called "homosexual agenda."

Ry of course didn't need protection by the House of Representatives, or the Senate, either. She had her own lawyer, appointed by Judge Kaufmann, to protect her "best interests." I met her that first day in court, in August 1991, when she came up to me and introduced herself.

"I'm Bonnie Rabin," she said. "And I've been appointed as Ry's Legal Guardian."

Her voice was cool; her tone off-putting.

"I don't want you talking to my client," she told me.

I had been scrupulous about not speaking to Ry, and I fully understood my legal responsibility to avoid influencing her in any way. This woman's manner seemed both presumptuous and hostile. I reacted in kind.

"Who do you think you're talking to?" I said, and we glared at each other for a moment before she walked away.

It was the beginning of a beautiful friendship.

* * *

Court remained dark while we waited for the results of the DNA tests, but the case proceeded on. We hoped that the blood work would prove that Tom had no biological connection to Ry, that he had no standing to bring legal action of any type, but we couldn't count on it. It was like that period of the "Phoney War"—both sides aware that a major conflict is brewing and both sides preparing for that conflict amid a volatile stew of anger, suspicion and increasing rancor. Someone began calling Robin and Russo's home and hanging up. They believed it was Tom and while their suspicions were never confirmed, they worried that Tom might follow Ry on the street or come to her school. They changed their phone number and unlisted it; notified the school of their concern and left Tom's picture with the guards: *Don't let this man near Ry. Don't let Ry go home with anyone but us.* That was the atmosphere in which we were preparing our case.

* * *

My first priority was to visit Robin and Russo's home. Arthur often talked to me about the importance of the house call, a vanished art now, but one that he believed provided unique clinical and social insights that could not be realized in a sterile office environment. Adopting this method as my own not only helps me to see and understand my clients more accurately but allows me to advocate for them with greater conviction and power. The client's tone of voice, body language, interaction with myself and others is different, often more straightforward at home than at the office and, by the same token, I am more observant about these things than when I am doing a formal consultation. This case was about a family, a family whose integrity I was defending in court, and it was important for me to see how Robin and Russo lived, how they treated one another, and how they provided for their children.

Robin had described herself as a lioness, protecting her cubs. Russo, under no illusion about the long odds we faced, said that, come what may, she wanted her children to know that she and Robin had fought to keep them together, that they hadn't given in, hadn't given up. Of course, as their lawyer, I already understood and sympathized with the mothers and was determined to argue for their rights to the best of my ability. But walking through their apartment, seeing Ry and Cade's bedrooms, the books on their shelves, the pictures on the wall, notes and drawings on the refrigerator, provided illumination of a more visceral sort. They were, in Russo's words, a family worth fighting for.

But there was a second, equally important reason for my being there. It was almost a certainty that Ry's Law Guardian, Bonnie Rabin, would be making a home visit. At this time I really knew very little about her, other than that our first encounter had not been pleasant, and while I couldn't guess what her biases might be or where her sympathies might lie, I did know that her observations, and any official report she filed with Judge Kaufmann, would play a critically important role in our case. Robin and Russo were surprised by the thorough—even ruthless—way I examined each area of their apartment, opening drawers, checking closets. I probably looked under the kitchen sink. And I found photographs similar to the ones the women had brought to my office: Ry, smiling into the camera, her arms around Tom's neck; Tom playing a game with Ry and Cade; Tom with Russo and Robin, relaxing on some summer beach. I took them down from the walls, pulled them off living room tables, and I told the women to put them away, keep them out of sight. In a back closet I found a tan raincoat which Tom had left behind on one of his visits. *Get rid of it*, I told Russo. It was essential that we shape, to the best of our ability, what Bonnie would see and what she would report back to the Court.

This is standard procedure when preparing a case, but I know that some people outside the process consider this "dirty pool"—the kind of unprincipled games that lawyers play, tampering with or undermining "reality." Gaming the truth. To begin with, Robin and Russo's apartment was *not* evidence—we were tampering with nothing prohibited by the court or by the law. Had I not done it, I would have been failing my clients. I had no responsibility to facilitate Tom's case and we needed every advantage we could legally secure; unless everything was perfect, unless everything broke our way, we were going to lose.

But on a deeper level we deal with these questions all the time, in court and out. Russo and Robin felt one way about Tom before he filed the lawsuit. They felt a different way, after. Which feeling was real? Similarly with Tom—he dealt with the women in a certain manner before he met Milton; and in an entirely different manner, afterwards. Was one Tom more genuine than the other? As a divorce attorney, everyone I represent once loved the person they now bitterly confront in court. People change. Feelings change. Circumstances change. So do apartments. When Bonnie, as a court appointed attorney, visited Robin and Russo's home, and she did—"We held our breath," said Russo—it didn't look exactly like the home I had visited. Five years previous, it had looked different, still; and two years hence, it would have changed, once again. That's just the way of things.

An apartment as a stage; a client as a performer. The saying is, "You dress in a manner consistent with the relief you are seeking." A mother is dressed a certain way, a businessman a certain way, a physician . . . I've taken earrings out of ears, nose rings out, bought clients new suits or dresses, insisted they get a haircut, cleaned them up even at the last minute, even as we were walking into court. Does that make their appearance false? The more cynical version of the adage comes from George Ade more than 100 years ago: "Get a good make-up and the part plays itself." That's not completely true but only because, along with make-up, a performer needs to know his or her lines. There are two ways to answer a question honestly in court—a way that is helpful to your case and a way that is hurtful. We spend hours developing a script in which the answers, again, all truthful, are helpful. Direct examination, when you are questioning your own client, can be as much a performance as Kabuki theater but that doesn't make it any less real. I tell the client: I don't want a grimace or a moan or an eyeroll or a sigh. No matter what happens you have to show respect: for the court, for the proceedings, and for the judge.

Peter and I believed that when Judge Kaufmann approved our motion and ordered blood tests for Tom, Robin, and Ry he sent a signal of open-mindedness, a sign that he was, at the very least, willing to consider the merits of our case. And that was a big step for us because we'd been worried he'd turn us down on the principle of *estoppel* and deny us the blood tests on the grounds that Ry and Robin's behavior toward Tom over the past four years had basically corroborated his claims. Court is always a crapshoot and much depends on the experience, temperament, intelligence—even the mood of the judge. The more I learned about Judge Kaufmann, the more impressed I became and the more confident that, if we did go to trial, we would receive a fair hearing. But there's no getting around the fact that court is a gamble. And it's a gamble most do not want to take. As Criminal Court bends toward plea bargain, Family Court bends toward settlement. Over the course of my career I'd estimate about 95 percent of my cases are settled out of court.

But not this one.

Years later, long after it was over, one of Tom's lawyers, talking to Ry, was still bewildered by this failure to reach a settlement. Tom had been dead twenty years. Ry, a married woman with a child of her own, was filming a documentary about the case, trying to understand what she and her family had been through—and why—decades before. "We wanted to settle," the lawyer told her. "Almost any agreement you can reach is better than litigating in a courtroom. We never stopped trying."

Bonnie Rabin tried as well. She made a series of good faith phone calls to both sides, looking for, but never finding, that elusive sweet spot where we might all come together.

"There is always, in every case," my colleague, Peter Bienstock, said, "that moment when the lawyers contemplate compromise" and agreement seems not only possible but likely. He would anticipate that moment and prepare for it. But it never came.

I never believed that a settlement was possible. The intermittent contact and talks with Tom's lawyers never achieved the status of meaningful negotiations. Robin, Russo, and I agreed that we could not compromise under the shadow of Tom's lawsuit. That was the key. You could play around with this or that, try to figure out ways to work out a more relaxed schedule of visits—there were possibilities out there but it all meant nothing unless Tom withdrew his suit and abandoned any claims to paternity. If that happened, if Tom acknowledged that Robin and Russo were Ry's parents, with all the rights, responsibilities and obligations of parenthood, then the women would consider steps the three of them might take to *begin* to restore the trust that had previously existed. That was our position and it never changed.

Tom's position was more difficult to understand. He told friends that he loved Ry and wanted to spend time with her—but he'd spent plenty of time with her before the suit and he was always free to express his affection. His friend and law partner, Nanci Clarence, said Tom was afraid he was going to be erased from Ry's life. The end result was that he filed suit and erased himself. Clarence, Chris Arguedas, and his attorneys—all of them later claimed to have told him that it was a mistake to go to court but it is difficult to understand why not one of them was able to talk him out of this disastrous, self-destructive decision. Even if he won, he would lose because his stated goal was to be with Ry and, as he and his team should have anticipated, the court battle destroyed their relationship forever. They never again had any meaningful contact.

But if Tom maintained that he acted out of love, I began to wonder, even as the case unfolded: love for whom? And I've come to believe that Milton Estes, Tom's partner, bears a heavy responsibility for what happened. He had taken a personal dislike to Russo and, beyond that, began to resent her position in the household. Russo had no biological connection to Ry; Tom did, and it angered Milton to watch Tom defer to her wishes, respect her decisions, and treat her as if she actually was Ry's mother. He took umbrage on Tom's behalf and it became apparent that he was actively undermining the parental authority of Robin and Russo, interfering in matters large and small, while at the same time insisting that Tom take a more proactive role as Ry's *real* parent. When Robin and Russo complained, Tom took Milton's part, and I think many of Tom's subsequent actions were aimed at asserting the prerogatives that Milton, over time, convinced him were naturally his.

Whatever Tom's motives, his behavior changed over the course of the proceedings. He seemed to become angrier, not only toward Robin and Russo, but toward Peter and myself. And given that he was determined to *force* Ry to spend time with him, even to the extent of having law enforcement remove her from her home, I suspect that the anger, in some measure, extended to Ry, as well. As noted, he and his legal team prohibited Russo from attending the daily court sessions. She was scheduled to be a witness so they were within their rights to do so but there was no mystery about what Russo would testify and it was hard to imagine how her presence in the courtroom would, in any conceivable way, harm Tom's case. The decision seemed remarkably petty and, given Russo's emotional attachments, verging on the cruel.

As Tom's behavior changed, his position hardened. He was asked: if you are successful in gaining parental rights for Ry, might you then petition the court for custody? As Robin and Russo feared, he indicated this was a possibility.

"It depends," he said.

* * *

The bloodwork and DNA test results came back, confirming without question, that Tom was Ry's biological father. Judge Kauffmann set a trial date for March 1992.

II

Nothing is harder than trying a case. It wears you down physically, intellectually, and emotionally. Steel v. Young, Docket No. P3884-91 was filed in court in August 1991. The trial began seven months later and final arguments were heard in October

1992. There were, in total, twenty-six days of testimony. Judge Kaufmann issued his ruling in April 1993. Family Court is among the busiest courts in New York City; the judges have cases stacked one atop another, waiting to be argued, waiting to be considered. That period, August 1991 through April 1993, is considered pretty fast work in Family Court. A tidy and speedy resolution.

It felt anything *but* that to my client and her family, who had to endure the great emotional violence and collateral damage Tom had brought upon them; anxiety and tension that seemed to ratchet up as the months went by. Ry, now ten years old, was very much aware that she was at the center of this dispute and, while I don't want to minimize in any way the great psychological burden she was under—there *were* sleepless nights, night terrors, anger and unease, all the emotions you would expect a child to feel in these circumstances—she remained throughout a person of preternatural maturity and determination. I don't think, in my legal experience, I have ever met a child quite like her.

Bonnie Rabin, her Law Guardian, who probably saw more of Ry during this period than anyone other than her mothers or her sister, reached the same conclusion. She met one-on-one with Ry on a number of occasions and knew her to be a child who had strong and considered opinions about what was happening to her and to her family. As Law Guardian, Bonnie didn't represent the "best interests" of Ry—she represented Ry; the difference being that she was charged with making the court aware of what Ry felt, what Ry believed, regardless of "best interests." She would only have been permitted to temper those opinions if she felt Ry either did not understand what she was saying or had been influenced or coerced into saying it. That was clearly never the case, and, as an adult, Ry would remember "this horrible time" and how her ten-year-old self had felt about Bonnie:

"I trusted her."

As did Robin and Russo. As did I.

In August, Judge Kaufmann advised us that he was going to name a neutral court-appointed psychiatrist—what was officially called a Forensic Mental Health Specialist—and he invited both sides to submit the names of possible candidates. This was an extremely important position, as he or she would have wide latitude with the court to conduct interviews with all relevant parties: Robin, Russo, Ry, Cade, and Tom, certainly, but also teachers, work colleagues, friends—anyone who might help him/her understand the case. I submitted the name of Dr. Myles Schneider, a New York City practitioner, specializing in child/adolescent psychiatry, with whom I had previously worked. I'd found him to be a complete professional, unusually sensitive and clearly gifted in working with young people in distress. I couldn't have been happier, or more surprised, when Judge Kaufmann named him to the position. I still don't know how it happened, whether anyone whispered in the judge's ear, but it was, along with the choice of Bonnie as Law Guardian, one of the major breaks we needed if we were to be successful. Court psychiatrist is, by its nature, an intrusive position: someone you don't know is permitted to examine—and make judgments about—the most intimate details of your life. But, understanding all that, I believed that Robin and Russo and their daughters could not have been in better hands.

They had to be because Ry was not the only family member under duress during this period. Whatever Ry had felt about Tom in the years *before* the lawsuit was the way her sister, Cade, had felt. He only saw them when they were together and he was expected to treat Ry and Cade in the same manner. There was deep affection, even love—of a kind—between the girls and Tom. We never denied it, and in any case the pictures and home videos were proof of the type of relationship that he had enjoyed with both girls, equally. But now Tom had filed suit and Cade was very much aware that he wanted Ry, not her; that he was telling the court that his interest and affection had always focused on Ry and never on Cade. This is a difficult thing for anyone, in any type of close relationship, to come to terms with; Cade was twelve years old. Tom and his legal team believed that in order to make his claim to Ry legitimate, they had to delegitimize his relationship with Cade. Or make her disappear altogether: at one point during the trial they presented into evidence a photograph of Ry, laughing with Tom as she sat on his knee—more proof, they claimed, of his unique and close relationship with her. But Robin remembered and told me about the original photograph: Cade was sitting on Tom's *other* knee and the three were laughing together. They'd simply cropped her out because her presence, and Tom's relationship with her, wasn't convenient. For Cade, the "vanishing" and the trial didn't mean that she now had had a different relationship with Tom, it meant that Tom believed they'd never had any meaningful relationship at all. It was, she felt, a "terrible betrayal."

And there was one additional betrayal, equally terrible in its way, that had to be endured. I had expressed to Robin and Russo my misgivings about Chris Arguedas, and my general view that anyone who claims to be neutral during a court case like this is actually supporting the other side. But Russo and Chris had a longstanding relationship. She considered Chris a close friend, and they stayed in constant touch. During a phone conversation shortly before the trial began, Russo suggested to Chris that she might be able to help resolve matters before we went to court: *You know, you could exert moral influence with Tom if you wanted to.*

And Chris replied: *I don't want to.*

Robin, who was with Russo and heard part of the conversation, understood immediately what this meant.

"Hang up the phone," she told Russo. "Just hang it up."

Robin's memory of that moment remained fresh.

"She wasn't our friend. She was on Tom's side. I told Russo: You cannot talk to this woman anymore. Don't give her any information. We're in litigation. Just shut the fuck up."

"She was an important friend," Russo said. "But it was over."

Over, but not finished. Russo and Chris never spoke again, but they did see each other once more. It happened at the Family Court Building, in the hallway outside our courtroom, when Chris arrived to testify on Tom's behalf.

* * *

She was a powerful witness, speaking in low, measured tones that sounded like the Voice of Reason. Russo and Robin had encouraged Ry's relationship with Tom, she explained, and it was apparent to her that Ry thought of Tom as her father and loved him as a father. At one point she described their relationship as the strongest father-daughter connection she had ever seen, and she minimized the importance of the boundaries the women had established. But beneath the, *just the facts, ma'am* demeanor, I thought there lurked a monstrous ego: Chris the puppet master, who had brought all these people together and now was determined to protect her creation.

As performance, it was masterful. But then Chris had always been a masterful performer. She let it be known that she hadn't wanted to testify at all but that there had been no choice: she'd been subpoenaed. This was nonsense, a familiar dance between lawyers and witnesses who want to feign reluctance to be in court, but in this case it was almost comically untrue. The subpoena had been issued in New York State. Chris was a resident of California, where it had no legal weight and could not be enforced. She testified because she wanted to. She testified because she was Tom's friend. She testified to protect her vision of what she called "this new and different kind of family," a vision at odds with and, she believed, superior to the lived reality of Russo, Robin and their daughters.

It was also at odds with Tom's testimony. There was, implicit in what Chris said on the stand, and explicit in what she said off it, a belief that this new type of family might consist of say . . . three parents. Or perhaps four. This was a circumstance for which New York State law made no provision—though we worried for a time that Judge Kaufmann might find the idea intriguing. Tom, in his testimony, stayed well clear of it. He wasn't interested, at least in court, in any "Brave New Family." He presented himself as a divorced dad, a staunch advocate of that most traditional of families—man, woman, child—baffled and angered that he was perversely (and that word is chosen advisedly, as will be seen) being denied access to his natural daughter.

The core of our case, its central coherence, was based on the stable, financially secure family, with two loving parents and two devoted sisters, that Russo and Robin had created. We built a case around this, aimed at empowering the judge to rule in our favor, shaping our arguments in order to make it as easy as possible for him to keep this beautiful, thriving family intact. Tom's "every girl needs her father" argument took the bare bones, central coherence of *his* case, biology is destiny, and dressed it up with a family of its own—to my mind an *imaginary* family. He did this by claiming rights he did not have, imputing feelings to Ry she did not feel, describing familial situations that either did not occur or did not occur as described. And just as Ry had a real sister, Cade, Tom's legal team presented to the court, and put on the witness stand, an imaginary brother: Jacobs Estes, Milton's son.

He testified about the closeness he felt to Ry. He considered Tom to be his father and Ry to be Tom's daughter. He believed Ry to be his sister, an integral part of his family. Jacob was fifteen years old, an intelligent and mature adolescent, and I remain bewildered as to why Tom's legal team put him on the stand and left him so defenseless.

When I am preparing a client for cross-examination, we have something called The Witness Torture School. We spend hours subjecting the client to the most difficult questions—often unpleasant or outlandish—anything that they may face, no matter how remote the likelihood. The point is so that when they are on the stand, being subjected to cross examination by an unsympathetic attorney, they won't be surprised or, at the very least, that the surprises are kept to a minimum. They are *prepared.* Jacob seemed unprepared for even the simplest, most obvious questions, so much so that I had to be careful in my cross, recognizing his youth and not wanting to risk losing the sympathy of the judge.

He believed Ry to be his sister?

Yes.

Did he ever send her a birthday card?

No.

Did he know the date of her birthday?

No.

Had he ever written her a letter?

No

Spoken to her on the telephone?

No.

I only asked him one non yes-or-no-question and that was at the end.

How many times in his life had he even seen Ry?

He wasn't sure, but I was. I had the papers in front of me, and the calendar never lies.

Three times.

* * *

From the moment the results of the DNA tests became known, Tom began demanding that the court permit a meeting between himself and Ry. We opposed his repeated requests, Robin and Russo telling me that Ry made it clear to them that she did not want to see Tom. He had become, in a very personal way, the focus of her anxieties and fears. She began to refer to him as "The Evil One" and had nightmares about him coming to the apartment and forcibly taking her away from her mothers and sister. Tom certainly knew of her antipathy but never understood it, in any meaningful way, in relation to his own behavior. In terms of Ry, Tom had happy, increasingly wistful memories of their past and grand, optimistic plans for their future but the meaning of the present eluded him. The memories and plans no doubt comforted Tom; a simple "I'm sorry," might have provided some comfort to Ry but it was not forthcoming, then or later. He was always professing his love for Ry, trying to make her understand why he had acted as he had, but he never displayed any empathy for what he was putting her through. In this, he was not unlike the type of spouse (usually a man) I encountered in my matrimonial law practice, who had done some grievous harm to his wife but thought that if the two of them just sat down and talked it over she would come to see that it was all for her own good. He could *convince* her that it was all for her own good. Tom was not unlike that spouse, as well, in that the constant proclamations of love, sincere as they might have been, also carried within them an element of rage.

On March 11th Dr. Schneider informed the court that he wished to see Ry and Tom in what he called a "joint interview" and Judge Kaufmann set a date for that meeting for March 15th, a Sunday, when the Family Court building would be empty and an office adjacent to the courtroom would be available. Robin and Russo were furious at the prospect of Ry meeting with Tom but I told them that, as it was a court order, there was no choice but to comply. Ry was also extremely upset, even frightened, about having to see Tom and Robin did her best to comfort her. She told Ry, "You are your own person. You're strong and I know you can handle whatever happens."

Both women accompanied Ry to the courthouse on that Sunday, where Bonnie was waiting. Before turning her over to the Law Guardian, the mothers hugged their daughter, and then stayed behind while Bonnie accompanied her client to what Ry later called "a shitty little office." Bonnie remained outside and Ry went in, where she found Dr. Schneider, sitting at a table, waiting for her. She took a seat and a short time later, from a second door at the other end of the room, Tom walked in.

Ry said she refused to look at Tom. He began by telling her that he wanted to take her to California and wanted to see more of her. He hoped she remembered all the good times that they had together. He called her sweetie. Ry said, "My name's not sweetie." There was silence for a moment and then she said to Tom, "Bug off." She stood up and bolted from the room. The "joint interview" had lasted about a minute.

On Tuesday, March 17, when court resumed, Tom's legal team addressed the court, asking for a second meeting, claiming Ry's actions had been "*very*

disquieting" and that she had been brainwashed into "*bolting out of the room and leaving . . . virtually the moment Mr. Steel entered the room and said hello . . .*"

"*Since the court ordered the interview it appears quite apparent that the child was counseled that she could countermand the court's order and leave. . . . The child was not upset or weepy but was just angry. Surely this fiasco could not have been orchestrated by a ten year old . . . what took place on Sunday March 15 appears to be another manifestation of strange, unseemly and inappropriate conduct in this proceeding.*"

In every case where a child speaks up and one side doesn't like it, there are accusations of brainwashing or coercion, and because Tom completely discounted the effect his own actions had on Ry, he believed he'd been set up, that Robin and Russo had ambushed him. Judge Kaufmann took Tom's request under advisement, presumably conferred with Dr. Schneider, the third person in the room during the joint interview, and nothing ever came of it. The court never ordered a second meeting. But Tom and his legal team never stopped trying to find an alternate reason for Ry's refusal to see him, for her "strange, unseemly and inappropriate" behavior, and it was probably fitting that, after offering the court an imaginary family and an imaginary brother, they finally settled on an imaginary psychological condition.

It was called Lesbian Fusion, and there was not then—at the time of our trial—and there is not now a shred of accepted scientific evidence that it exists.[13] It is now generally understood as one of the uglier anti-gay canards of the 1980s and 1990s rather than as a psychological disorder—the social science corollary to the Heather Has Two Mommies political panic that erupted over the supposed demise of the traditional family. Proponents of Lesbian Fusion examined the intimacy and emotional dependence found in couples, where the partners are said to form a new, single identity. In heterosexual couples this intimacy was generally seen as positive: You complete me. You are my better half. But applied to lesbian couples the condition was invariably pathologized into something dark and destructive—not only to themselves and to society at large but to their children. This was the gist of the testimony from the psychiatrist that Tom's legal team offered as an expert witness.

Women, he explained, had a greater capacity for intimacy than men, and two women together were much closer to each other, in a variety of damaging ways, than a corresponding heterosexual couple. The women become "fused," and refused to let anyone else close to them And the unhealthy way in which they lived their lives and related to outsiders was passed on to their children, who replicated the socially perverse habits they had observed and been taught. In essence, he was explaining Ry's behavior as the result of two injurious factors: she was being raised by lesbians and, because her father was being kept from her, she was growing up as illegitimate.

It can be very difficult to accurately assess the "weather" in a courtroom—to tell if a particular witness or a particular argument is finding favor with the court. And it is easy to fool yourself into believing that a grimace or a sigh from the bench means more than it does. But I do know that everyone on our side in the courtroom listening to that testimony thought that Tom had made a terrible mistake in putting this witness on the stand, and I believed I could see signs that Judge Kaufmann felt the same. Beyond the broadly negative characterization of lesbian relationships, and the specific depiction of intimacy between same sex couples as inherently harmful to children, it seemed a bizarre, almost self-destructive argument coming from a gay man. Many observers in the lesbian and gay communities saw it as an inexplicable attack on Robin and Russo and on the concept of same sex parenting. But Robin and Russo weren't what the trial was about; Ry was. I've always thought that what Tom did reflected desperation on his part to put into the official record—the court transcript—that the aberrant behavior of Robin and Russo was the source of Ry's animosity toward him. And, most insidiously, that their behavior constituted a continuing threat to Ry's psychological well-being. And that Tom was, as he always insisted, blameless.

* * *

The case that we presented to the court didn't depend on psycho-sexual theories or fake siblings or allegations of brainwashing and coercion. It was stripped down, judge-friendly, and, as crafted, elegant in its simplicity. It rested on two easily understood premises. The first and most important was the living reality of the Russo-Young Family: the loving relationship between mothers and daughters, between sisters Ry and Cade. This was the spine of our case, the subtext of all our arguments: encouraging Judge Kaufmann to use his discretion and ensure that this family remained whole. The second point concerned the original agreement between Robin, Russo and Tom. Both women offered powerful and cogent explanations, during direct examination, of their arrangement with Tom, the fact that the terms were made explicit, understood and agreed to by all. Had Tom not agreed, they would not have chosen him as a donor and it was unacceptable, harmful to Ry, that he was unilaterally changing those terms at this late date. A deal is a deal.

We were also able during the course of the trial to refute or, at the least, reframe some of the key arguments made by Tom's legal team:

- Ry and Tom: We argued that Tom had consistently exaggerated the amount of time he spent with Ry—for instance, during business trips to New York, where he might see her for an hour or so but claim to be with her for a longer period, during which time he was actually working or Ry was in school. We also said that Tom fundamentally mischaracterized the time he *did* spend with Ry, emphasizing that just about every minute he was with her, he was also with Cade and Robin and Russo. By leaving them out of

the picture (at least once, literally), Tom offered a skewed picture of his relationship with Ry.

- Photos/videos, Father's Day cards: The personal photographs and videos that were entered into evidence did show a warm, at times, intimate pre-lawsuit relationship between Tom and Ry. And between Tom and Cade. And between Tom and Robin and Russo. We never argued that they didn't but did argue they were not evidence of any particular closeness between Tom and Ry and certainly not of a parental relationship. Ry had sent Father's Day cards to Tom, but she had also sent identical Father's Day cards to Jack Kolb, Cade's sperm donor. They didn't prove that Ry thought either man was her father. They proved that a girl in grade school is likely to go along with her peers when the teacher suggests making homemade cards for Father's Day.
- Father Tom: If this case turned on biology, if blood was the key factor, Tom would win. But Tom was not arguing that he had a biological connection to Ry—all parties stipulated to this once the blood test results were in. What Tom was arguing was that this biological connection made him Ry's father, and this we vigorously opposed. A sperm donor is not a father, we argued. A father is involved in a child's life. A father is a person who provides financial and other support. A father is a decision maker who daily offers encouragement and love. Tom was not a father and he was never supposed to be a father. It was the furthest thing from what the mothers had wanted and from the role that he had agreed to play in Ry's life.

Final arguments were heard before Judge Kaufmann in October 1992. The court was then adjourned and we waited for his opinion.

* * *

There was no Internet, no place for the court to simultaneously "post" a decision once it had been reached. There were no cell phones so, of course, no cell phone alerts. We just waited. Tom went home to California. Ry and Cade went to school. Russo went back to work and Robin continued to manage their home and the other apartments in the building that they owned. And still we waited. Months passed and there was no news and, as we were not permitted to call the court, no way of finding out if we were any closer to a decision. Now that we're all wired this seems impossibly far away, a foreign country, but it was all that we knew. Our file was sitting on Judge Kaufmann's desk and there was nothing we could do to hurry the process along. This was a *consequential* case, everyone involved in it knew that, and the judge was giving it the care and deliberation that was its due.

On Tuesday, April 13, 1993, I received Judge Kaufmann's decision in the afternoon mail. There had been no prior indication it was coming:[14]

Thomas S. apparently believes that Ry, as his biological child, must feel fatherly affection for him. He is incorrect, I think. Ry has been brought up to view Robin Y. and Sandra R. as equal mothers raising two children and to view Thomas S. as an important man in her family's life. In her family, there has been no father. Robin Y. and Sandra R. are deeply committed to this concept of their family, and Ry, who has been raised by them, must also be committed to the concept at this point in her life . . .

Dr. Schneider recommended that there be no declaration of paternity and no court-ordered visitation.

Ry, Dr. Schneider said, considers Sandra R. and Robin Y. to be her parents and Cade to be her full sister. She understands the underlying biological relationships, but they are not the reality of her life. The reality of her life is having two mothers, Robin Y. and Sandra R., working together to raise her and her sister. Ry does not now and has never viewed Thomas S. as a functional third parent . . .

Ry, Dr. Schneider said, views Robin Y. and Sandra R. as having a relationship with each other that should be given respect . . . Ry's own view of her family is that of a warm, loving, supportive environment.

Ry, he said, views this court proceeding as an attack on and threat to her positive image of herself and her family. Her sense of family security is threatened. She has expressed fear of ongoing court involvement and worries about a confusing and threatening period in her family's life. She fears that Thomas S. might seek custody of her . . .

Ry does not want to visit Thomas S. Even the prospect of a visit with him causes Ry much anxiety, and Dr. Schneider believes that she would only visit with him if she were dragged to him kicking and screaming. Therapeutic intervention, he said, would not change her attitude. Any forced visitation would cause her increased anxiety, and would also do nothing to repair her relationship with Thomas S.

Dr. Schneider does not believe that Ry has been "brainwashed" into expressing her views. Of course, he recognizes, as I do, that her views have been shaped by the views of Robin Y. and Sandra R . . .

. . . Ry views this proceeding as a threat to her sense of family security. For her, a declaration of paternity would be a statement that her family is other than what she knows it to be and needs it to be.

To Ry, Thomas S. is an outsider attacking her family, refusing to give it respect, and seeking to force her to spend time with him and his biological relatives, who are all complete strangers to her, for his own selfish reasons.

A declaration of paternity naming Thomas S. as Ry's father, under these circumstances, at this late time in her life, would not be in her best interests. Even were there an adjudication of paternity, I would deny Thomas S.'s application for visitation (see, Family Ct Act § 549 *[a]).*

Accordingly, the proceeding is dismissed.

I tried calling my client, Robin, but I couldn't reach her. It turned out with her daughters, bringing them home from school. Russo was at her Legal Services and picked up the phone on the first ring. Twenty months ea she had called my office, telling me her family faced an emergency and that s needed my help. Now I was returning her call.

"We won," I said.

III

Tom believed that Judge Kaufmann had ignored key facts and misinterpreted the law. The decision, he said, was "without precedent" in the entire United States, and he appealed his case to the Appellate Division, the second highest court in the state of New York. Five justices would hear the case: four men and one woman. It was a "hot" bench—meaning the justices, fully familiar with the submitted briefs, would question the advocates during oral arguments. Tom had decided to argue his own case—he was both the appellant *and* advocate. The five judges sat at a raised bench and the lawyers, myself, Peter, Bonnie and Tom, sat virtually elbow to elbow at a small counsel's table below them and took turns sharing a single microphone. There's a photograph of three of us, me, Peter and Tom, in court waiting to be questioned by the judges, as close together as if we'd been packed into a telephone booth. We didn't exchange a single personal word.

On November 17, 1994, by a 3–2 margin, the court reversed the earlier decision and ruled in Tom's favor:[15]

This appeal presents the narrow issue of whether a sperm donor who is known to his child as her father and who, despite residing in California, has had considerable contact with her at the instance of her mother, is entitled to an order of filiation . . . We hold that he is.

. . . the effect of Family Court's order is to cut off the parental rights of a man who is conceded by all concerned—the child, her mother and the court—to be the biological father. The legal question that confronts us is not, as Family Court framed it, whether an established family unit is to be broken up. Rather the question is whether the rights of a biological parent are to be terminated.

For the majority, Justices Eugene Nardelli, Israel Rubin, and Milton Williams, this was all about blood: Tom had won his case, proven that he was Ry's father, the moment the DNA tests established that biological connection. They explicitly rejected Judge Kaufmann's suggestion that further court action might result in "*severe traumatic consequences*" for Ry and had harsh words for Robin and Russo for "*the apparent manipulation of an innocent child's affections and the obvious damage wreaked upon the once harmonious relationship with her father . . .*"

ier Ry will come to regret the poisoning of her formerly amicable relationship r father is beyond the meager ken of a court of law and must be consigned to nscience of whoever must abide the consequences. It remains to be seen whether tioner's is the only parent-child relationship to be damaged by this dispute.

In dissent, Justices Betty Weinberg Ellerin and Ernst Rosenberger said the case was not about cutting off parental rights but rather about creating such rights where none existed. Biology alone did not confer parenthood, wrote Justice Ellerin:

while the child has always known that petitioner is her biological progenitor, it had consistently been demonstrated by petitioner himself that this factor did not confer upon him any authority or power over her life. To now grant him the standing to claim the very considerable authority and power held by a parent, against her wishes, would change her life in drastic ways Furthermore, and perhaps most important, a declaration of paternity in this case would be counter to this child's interests because it clearly would be only the first step in ongoing litigation which will inevitably cause severe traumatic consequences to the child and her family.

The Appellate Court, in determining that Tom was Ry's father and thus entitled to an order of filiation, had given him standing to litigate questions of visitation and custody and sent the case back to Family Court where he could immediately pursue those matters. In essence, we faced the same dilemma that we had at the beginning of the case three years earlier: how to slow things down, how to prevent the court from ordering Robin, under penalty of contempt, to produce Ry and permit Tom to take her to California. We knew that we were going to appeal but that would take time. What we needed was an immediate stay of the Appellate Court's decision, freezing matters as they presently stood, until the entire matter could be argued before the State's highest court, the Court of Appeals, sitting in Albany. Stays are rarely given so it was a longshot, but it was our only option.

By this time Bonnie and I understood that the best interests of our respective clients, Robin and Ry, mother and daughter, were identical and we worked closely in common pursuit of those interests. In consultation with each other we prepared new briefs for submission to the Court of Appeals and then we took the train together to Albany. We had to find a Court of Appeals judge willing to issue a stay and stop the enforcement of the horrific decision by the Appellate Division. We presented our papers to the Chief Clerk of the Court and he looked them over and said to us: "Your chances of getting a stay are slim to none." Then he told us that it would be a long wait, to find a place to make ourselves comfortable, and he took our papers upstairs to the Judge's Chambers.

Bonnie and I waited for several hours in the Law Library on the first floor and then a young woman found us "You should come with me," she said. "The judge wants to see you." The judge was Vito Titone, appointed to the court in 1985 and gaining a reputation as one of its more liberal members. In 1989 Judge Titone had authored the majority decision in the case of Braschi v. Stahl Assocs. Co., which

a tactic, as a way to frighten their spouse and coerce her to accept a more stringent financial settlement. The husband would give up his spurious claim; the wife would get less money and the children. A tactic and, for a time, a very successful one.

But that was then. When I began practice, most of my cases dealt with single earner households—typically the man worked, the woman kept house. Now I was beginning to see many two earner households, with both spouses working outside the home and both equally ambitious about their careers. Similarly, when I started out, custody usually was awarded to the woman, very occasionally the man, but almost never was there a joint custody agreement in New York. That was now becoming commonplace. We were, increasingly, not dealing with 1950s dads, *Mad Men* fathers, but with men who genuinely saw themselves as caregivers and wanted outcomes in court or through negotiations that reflected this reality. And we were also dealing with women, dedicated to their careers, as determined as their husbands to succeed, who did not necessarily want full custody—successful women who wanted to be free to pursue their goals outside the home. I'll never forget the shock I felt when a client of mine turned *down* the offer of a full summer with her young son, in exchange for four weeks on, four weeks off. She had a career to attend to and she wanted the joint custody provisions of her agreement to be enforced. Custody had been such a touchstone—a social and *moral* touchstone—for my generation of women that, although I understood and sympathized and advocated for my client, it seemed to me, nonetheless, that some type of social Rubicon had been crossed.

So while many of these men were coming to my office seeking representation as a tactic, there were others who came to me because they wanted the best attorney possible in this new and changing environment. Reform had put women and men on a more equal legal footing before the court, and these male clients believed that if they were no longer elevated, if they no longer had a structural legal advantage, they should, at the least, not be penalized either—and I agreed with them. I was selective, I did the proper vetting and, to the best of my ability, I tried to determine if they were genuine in what they were asking of me. And if they were, and if I believed I could help them, I agreed to represent them—even in cases where they were seeking full custody. This caused some controversy in feminist circles at the time, and it still shadows my reputation, but I believed that I was working in the best interests not only of my client but of the child or children in question.

If this was a history book, there would be many sources and many voices offering testimony and somewhere within that dialectic, the truth would emerge. But this is not a history, it's a memoir and so the only voice is mine. I wrote in the first chapter of how suspicious I am of anyone who says: *This is the way it is. This the story, the only story:*

So, while only a single voice and a single perception, I'll have to create my own dialectic in the hope that a kind of truth will become clear.

I remember when I was just beginning my career, watching an opposing lawyer in court and thinking: I wouldn't do that. That's not a method I would employ. But now I know that isn't true. Under the same circumstances and with the same client I probably would do what that lawyer had done. I have *done what that lawyer did. And more. And recognizing this, and accepting it is also part of becoming Harriet Cohen.*

This can be a cold business. A very cold business. Not only for the client but for the attorney as well. You have to feel your way along sometimes and try to change a stark bleak wintery picture into something marginally better. And you have to balance the various demands that are made upon you. You want to do the right thing by your client but sometimes your client doesn't want to do the right thing. And you are making decisions in the real world, not in some imaginary happy place.

I did vet my male clients, and I did screen them very carefully but I don't want to paint myself as some do-gooder who tries to help everyone in the world. The truth of the matter is that I have represented heavies, men and women who are restrictive rather than generous, men and women who approach cruelty in their assessment of the world and their understanding of their place in the world—and in the courtroom. I used to think I'd only represent men like my husband or my father or my brother, but actually I represent all types of husbands and all types of fathers and all types of brothers. And wives and mothers and sisters.

I once represented a female client involved in a multi-million dollar divorce. It was a complicated case, but we had finally worked out a settlement that was extremely generous to her. At the last minute she balked, refusing to sign unless she was given an additional $400,000. The number was plucked more or less out of the air, she wasn't owed it and I tried to convince her why it would be in her best interest to drop the ask and sign the agreement. The generous agreement. She refused. We were preparing to go to court when the other side decided they'd had enough and wrote her a check for the full amount. My client was in the wrong. She was unreasonable. And a reasonable person would not have gotten the four hundred thousand.

There isn't a law firm in the country that can afford to represent only A-1 clients. Sir Galahad and Joan of Arc don't walk through the door every day, and when they do, the system—grinding, wearing, irrational at times—is just as likely to twist them as anybody else.

Laura, embroiled in an increasingly bitter battle over a prenuptial agreement involving monies neither she nor her fiancé really cared about, wondered: *Am I being turned into a gold digger?*

* * *

If the system is imperfect, so are the lawyers and so are the clients. I have represented men and women with anger issues: if they are willing to see a therapist I'll continue to represent them. It is a similar situation if a client has a problem with alcohol or other drugs. It is a gritty, at times unfair world and the people who come to me, many of them, *in extremis*, are trying to deal with failure, the end of a relationship they once believed to be the most important to them in the world; within those realistic parameters I am trying to help them. Genuinely. Unironically. Most of the clients who go through this with me thank me at the end, regardless of the specific outcome of the case. Of course, there are others who just go their own way. And you're left to wonder: Did I do the right thing?

At the present time, more than half my clients are men.

A Summer Romance

I was in the middle of several important cases, including "*Nuclear Family*" and the Laurence Fishburne settlement negotiations, when I was informed that Dan and Howard had decided to go their separate ways and that the firm, Solin & Breindel, was dissolving. There was the usual period of activity and uncertainty during which vigorous efforts were made to collect the outstanding accounts receivable, pay the firm's debts, and distribute the remaining assets among the partners. My major concern was always my clients—and that the care and counsel I was providing them continue uninterrupted. I had assembled a very talented team of lawyers in my matrimonial department, and an impressive and growing client roster, and I was hoping that wherever we ended up most of this team would remain together.

I received many offers and among the most interesting was one from a lawyer based in Chicago named Herb Beigel of the firm of Beigel & Sandler Ltd. Not long before, they had opened an office in New York City with a tiny matrimonial department nominally headed by Lewis Sandler. "Nominal" was not a word one associated with Herb Beigel. He was the power in Beigel & Sandler and he thought big, spoke big and promised big. Herb had prosecuted mob guys as an assistant US Attorney in Chicago and then opened his own firm, specializing in class action lawsuits. He'd represent hundreds, sometimes more than a thousand, so-called "limited partners" who believed they had been unfairly done out of their investments. It was a controversial type of lawyering where the cases involved plenty of litigation but were usually settled out of court and monies divided among the many plaintiffs, *after* expenses and fees were awarded to the law firm. The *New York Times* examined these class action lawsuits and credited Beigel & Sandler with revolutionizing the process. That pleased Herb. He was less pleased with the title of the article: *Millions For Us, Pennies For You*, which featured the plaintiffs from a number of law firms, not only Beigel & Sandler, who complained about the pennies-on- the-dollar settlements they received while their attorneys walked away with fortunes.[17] Herb vigorously defended his conduct to the *New York Times.*

The fees were earned, the expenses were justified, the small payouts were "better than what would come out of a case that goes to court, where many judges have no sympathy for those they view as having gambled on an investment and lost."[18]

"We like to think that we have done a good job in some very difficult cases," Herb told the *Times*.

* * *

He had a rogue's affability and a public charm that, when turned full force upon you, were hard to resist; forty years later I still remember just how much fun it was to be around him. Herb wanted to become a player in the matrimonial field and, being Herb, thought the fastest way to achieve credibility was to purchase it. When he learned that I was on the market he began a pursuit that felt at times like a business deal and at times like a kind of public wooing: intense and personal. I look back on the two years I spent at Beigel & Sandler as a summer romance: a heady time during which I was, in a sense, swept away by the force of Herb's amazing personality. I've never regretted the interlude but am thankful that, as intoxicating as it was, I always managed to keep at least one wary eye open for autumn's approach, so that when the time came I was able to negotiate the inevitable end of the affair with discipline and dispatch.

We were still deep into negotiations and I hadn't made the final decision to sign on with Herb when he flew me out to Chicago so I would, in his words, "get a better idea of how I operate." How he operated was out of the top floors of a magnificent building on South Wacker Drive, sixty-five stories above the street, boasting 360-degree views of Lake Michigan, Millennium Park, Grant Park, and the Chicago River. To the northwest the building was surrounded by a sea of grass, the largest green area in the Chicago Loop. He walked me through a magnificent law library—the internet was just coming in but we still used libraries, still turned the pages of books—how romantic a memory!—and then through huge conference rooms and an elegant reception area. He threw a cocktail party for me with all his partners and associates, each of whom expressed their hope that I would be joining the firm.

Herb then flew me back to New York City—he flew so often on American Airlines he'd been awarded a lifetime pass, like George Clooney in the movie *Up in the* Air—to show me his offices at 750 Lexington Avenue. This was a twenty-eight story building, six years old, that overlooked Central Park, the East River and the 59th Street Bridge which, lit up at night, was of surpassing almost ethereal beauty. The building was topped by a conical shaped crown cobalt blue glass cylinder, buttressed by more glass and granite wings that was also lit up at night. It looked like a satellite with its solar arrays unfurled. This was where Beigel & Sandler had their offices. Herb's personal office, on the top floor, was in the round, with a cascade of windows and views that took one's breath away. I was still taking it all in when he said to me: "This is going to be your office,"

"Herb," I said, "I can't take your office." And in my head I was thinking of those days back at the Nizer firm, bouncing from office to office, pushing a shopping cart.

I told him it would be impossible to share the space with him.

"We're not going to share," he said. "When I come to New York I'm going to sit right there"—and he pointed to a secretarial station with a large desk just outside the office.

"All I need is a desk and a telephone."

And, indeed, that is exactly where he sat when he came to New York, after I said *Yes* and joined his firm. I can see him now, leaning forward at that desk, wearing a headset, a long list of telephone numbers in front of him, self-contained, content. He'd sit for hours, making call after call, working his way through those numbers, drumming up clients for yet another class action lawsuit.

One wary eye . . .

I accepted Herb's very generous offer and became a partner at Beigel & Sandler. My entire Solin & Breindel team came with me and Herb made one of my associates. Patricia Hennessey, a partner, as well. Instantly, Beigel & Sandler was a major force in the matrimonial field, with a client base heavily focused on celebrities.

I thought that was what Herb wanted, but it seemed, at times, that what Herb was interested in were celebrities who, in this case, happened to be attached to my matrimonial department. He was a fanboy and what he *really* wanted, when it came down to it, was to have lunch with Laurence Fishburne, an actor he admired with, to put it lightly, an unusual intensity. When I told Laurence about this, he laughed and said to me, "Let's do it." And we did. The three of us had a leisurely lunch at Herb's favorite Italian restaurant on East 61st Street right off Lexington Avenue. It was, he solemnly told us, Anthony Quinn's favorite restaurant. I don't remember much of what was said that afternoon but I do remember how happy Herb was. And how gracefully and with what good humor wonderful Laurence Fishburne handled himself.

* * *

When the relationship between Dan Solin and Howard Breindel came to an end, I was hoping to be awarded custody of David Kaufman, my numbers man. We worked so well together and our professional relationship was dynamic, in the sense that we were never satisfied with what we'd done but continued to explore ways to improve the product, to marry old fashioned arithmetic to new technologies in ways that informed and enlarged our efforts. His unique insight into the use of spreadsheets, coupled with the knowledge and ease with which we could manipulate the numbers, helped revolutionize the way I understood the cases with which I was dealing. Numbers don't tell a story, they tell any number of stories, some of them true, some of them false. I added my experience and insight into the mix and it became clear to me *which* story to tell; which allowed us to build a case that a judge could easily digest, that would bolster the arguments we were making and encourage a judge to weigh them, sympathetically, in the balance.

Alas, in the wake of the Solin & Breindel dissolution, David Kaufman had other commitments and was no longer available to me. So I began the search for a new "David" and found him while working at Beigel & Sandler. His name was Henry Guberman, a young forensic accountant with great gifts and a sympathetic intelligence who understood precisely what I was trying to do and who worked with me as we refined even further the process I had begun with David Kaufman. With Henry's assistance, the intake, my first meeting in the office with a new client, became the central part of my practice ,and it became legendary within the field. I called Henry "my secret weapon." When a client came to me for the intake, they brought all of the financial documents and information at hand and in their heads, from every drawer in their home or office and every wrinkle in their brain. Henry was always present and the client would sit with us for hours while we examined the documents and financial papers they had brought, extracting the relevant numbers and working them into a spreadsheet from which a concise and comprehensive picture would emerge in those days in pencil. We would do this a number of times and, depending on which numbers we emphasized, different pictures would become clear. And when the intake was concluded and the client left my office, they would have three spreadsheet scenarios—blueprints, I called them—of the path forward: the best scenario, the worst scenario, and the most likely scenario. Arthur used to say that as a doctor, he had to work with whatever information he had at hand, not necessarily complete information, and reach a diagnosis based on the facts as he understood them at the time. But not only the facts. His intuition, based on years of practice, hundreds of patients, all the cases he had seen and the outcomes he had witnessed, also played a part. As it did for me. These scenarios were based on the best information and numbers available at that time and, over the years, they've proved to be extraordinarily accurate. More times than I can count, the opposing side ends up citing the numbers we used, the scenarios—or part of the scenarios—we created, as elements in the case that *they* present to the court. That is how important and how seductive these spreadsheets are: arguments disguised as "just the numbers" filings that, in fact, bent toward our interpretation of the case and all based on and made possible by our fluency with and understanding of the *practical* nature of the figures involved. And the judges love these spreadsheets, because they are concise, easy to read and understand and solidly based on the numbers and the facts that are before them in court.

* * *

My association with Henry was probably the most satisfying professional relationship I've ever had. Our styles meshed, our personalities meshed. We both loved figures; we both recognized that *value* was a plastic concept—the same house is worth one amount if you are a seller; a different, lower amount if you are a buyer—and that the numbers themselves composed a language with which we were perfectly fluent He was an integral part of my practice, sitting opposite me at my desk every time I met a new client and instinctively knowing when to speak, when to keep quiet, when to let our numbers do the talking. We'd move the figures across and down the page and have them assume different levels of meaning and importance according to the needs and expectations of our client, the exigencies of the emerging case and the applicable law. And the case emerged because the spreadsheets, by simplifying and demystifying, permitted the outlines of a likely settlement to become clear. It was exhilarating. No one else could do it. They all tried when they saw what I was doing, but no one has ever been able to duplicate our product.

Of course, one reason we were able to move those figures with such ease and purpose, one reason we could produce so many possible scenarios so rapidly, was that we had the technology at hand to do so. The first proto-spreadsheet I ever saw was done with pencil and paper. Corrections, additions based on new information, any changes at all, required hours and hours of work—erasures, white-out, often starting over again with newly sharpened pencils and fresh colored pens, and a new sheet of paper. We worked like monks laboring over some illuminated manuscript. I remembered Herb walking me through his extraordinary law library on the top floor of 311 S. Wacker Drive—a library of which he was so proud, telling me it was the equal of any in the city; and that he'd had it assembled in the two years since the building's completion in 1990. And neither of us realizing that we were looking at a blacksmith's shop the day the Model-T was introduced; the day the *Kitty Hawk* first took flight.

When I began work at 750 Lexington Ave, I found on my desk a bulky IBM desktop computer. It consisted of a keyboard, a microprocessor and a small, curved, green display screen—similar to those small, old fashioned TV's of the 1950s; lots of cabinet, little screen—a very distant ancestor to the large flatscreen monitors in use today. When you turned it on it needed several minutes to warm up or "boot up" like the radios of my youth, Philco or Dumont, sitting in the living room waiting for The *Jack Benny Show* or *The Breakfast Club.* The electric hum coming from the computer sounded like an airplane preparing for takeoff. And then the screen flashed on and you were looking at the future. Or the future was looking at you.

There were identical computers on the desks of everyone at the firm—partners, associates, secretaries. My secretary, Violet, experienced and diligent, stayed with me after work, talking me through the system, answering questions, supervising my first efforts. I don't think I, or anyone else in the office, truly understood the full implications of this revolution—any more than the first people to use the printing press could understand how it would remake the world; and certainly the idea that this type of computerized system would keep a floundering legal system alive and operating during a great pandemic was inconceivable—Herb's great law library on your phone, carried about in your pocket—but it was clear to me, from the very beginning, that *something* was changing and it wasn't long before Henry was bringing a laptop with him to his meetings with me and he and I were entering formulas onto excel spreadsheets that we then computed, revised and corrected not with a pencil and eraser but with the touch of a finger. We never looked back.

But I did look forward.

Henry and I worked together for over twenty-five years, and when he began to speak of retirement, and saw the look on my face, he told me that a partner in his accounting firm would be a perfect replacement. So I took Henry's partner to dinner and it became apparent to me, within the first twenty minutes or so, that it wouldn't be a good fit. He was smart and he knew his numbers but that was all he knew and I needed something more. Henry was working not only with figures but with people, with my clients, and he never put a foot wrong. Sometimes with associates you settle for 98 percent and accept the fact that for two percent of the time you're going to cringe. I couldn't have that with my forensic accountant, especially during the intake when the client is at their most vulnerable and I am, in a sense, being tested. I told Henry that I didn't want someone who worked *with* him; I wanted someone who had been trained *by* him and who could *be* him.

The logical choice was James, Henry's son, who had just finished his higher education and had joined his father's firm. I'd occasionally meet with a client in Henry's office, and when I did I'd tell Henry that I wanted James to be present during the meeting. I can't say I had a premonition, but it always seemed likely to me that James and I would be working together some day—but not today. He was still not ready to work with me without supervision—that's where Henry's continued training would come—and I wasn't willing to find a temporary hire to cover the gap while I waited for James. The solution seemed simple to me, not so simple to Henry.

"You can't retire yet, I told him. "Not until we both think James is ready to come aboard." It wasn't that I had been spoiled working with Henry—or *just* that I had been spoiled working with Henry. I'd worked with other accountants over the years—sometimes a client would bring in their own—and none of them got it. Not one of them understood the functionality—and the beauty, because there was an aesthetic edge to our product—of what we were working to accomplish.

I told Henry, bluntly, that while I hoped the Guberman connection would continue, if he did retire and I had to find a replacement, that would be that. Our professional relationship would be over.

There were economic factors in play—as my reputation grew and my practice increased, Henry was one of the beneficiaries—but I don't believe these were determinative. What I was hoping, what I was counting on, was that Henry was as proud of what we had done together as I was, and that he'd never, willingly, let it fall into the hands of someone else.

Henry agreed to postpone his retirement and continue training his son to meet my requirements.

I began working with James Guberman in 2019. We are working together, still.

Marti

The agreement I reached with Henry and James was about maintaining the unique nature of my firm and the services that we offered our clients—the factors that helped define the work we were able to do. But in 1993 I hired my oldest daughter, Martha, as an associate, and that proved an even more consequential decision because, while it was impossible to see at the time, it touched on the future of our firm, not only through 2026 but beyond.

Marti had graduated from the law school of Yeshiva University, The Cardozo School of Law, five years after I graduated from Brooklyn Law School. She was working for Shea & Gould, a prestigious law firm not unlike Phillips Nizer Benjamin Krim & Ballon, but by the early 1990s Shea & Gould was in the midst of a dissolution and Marti needed somewhere to land. She was the mother of two young boys, four year old Ezra and one year old Gabe. She wanted to reduce her workload and spend more time with her family but not step off the track completely. Then, as now, part time positions for young mothers were difficult to find.

Marti knew that we were shorthanded and suggested that she come to work for me as a part-time associate. We could certainly use the help, and I wanted her with me but I also felt it was a delicate situation, not without risks, and a decision I could not make alone. I said I would speak to Herb in Chicago and to my partners in New York and ask them what they thought about bringing my daughter into the firm. They were positive, understanding the possible complications but insisting that the decision was mine to make. And for that I will be forever grateful to them.

Marti and I spoke candidly about all that was involved, all the implications. We loved each other, obviously, but this was a different kind of relationship. We had never worked together, never had to develop that kind of professional dependency, that trust that is so essential to a healthy working environment. What if it didn't work out? What if one of us were unhappy? We talked about every potential problem, every concern. We even went over what she should call me. All her life I'd been "Mom" or "Momma," but that was hardly appropriate for a professional relationship. So I became "Harriet" in the office and Momma in the world.

Marti has spoken of the pride she felt at this time watching me at work.

My oldest.

The one thing I never worried about was whether the work would be excellent. Marti was a hardworking, conscientious attorney with a spark of brilliance within her, a gifted writer, and I knew—and she knew—that she could handle anything that was thrown her way. And that's how it worked out, from day one. Marti was thrown into the deep end immediately. She quickly figured out the ins and outs of the office culture, and I don't think there was any real learning curve. She was just there, essential, an integral part of the firm; and it wasn't long before we—my partners and I—were asking her to work full time. We needed her. It turned out so well for all of us—for myself, for the firm, for Marti, but I hope my grandsons understand and forgive the demands I made on their mom.

There have always been so many father-son law firms—even firms celebrated in popular culture like the 1960s television series *The Defenders* and *Harrigan and Son*—but we were one of the first, if not the first, mother-daughter law firm. We have been working together for over thirty years: part time associate, associate and partner. And now, inevitably as time passes, Marti has taken on more responsibility and power within the firm. She has become the rainmaker and, increasingly, the decision maker.

And after all these years when she was my partner, it turns out, finally, that I am hers.

The Great Escape

The work of the matrimonial department was interesting, fulfilling, and profitable. We were, in addition, a congenial group; many of us had been together since Solin & Breindel and the newcomers, like Marti, fit in perfectly. It was a wonderful environment in which to do one's best work. Herb flew in on a fairly regular basis and, as he had said he would, set up shop at the secretarial workspace outside my office, where he'd spend the day, morning to evening, on the telephone, drumming up business, the life of the office flowing around him, effectively and efficiently. He never interfered.

Herb's wife, Nancy, a former American Airlines flight attendant, was a charismatic, charming woman who gave as good as she got and was completely uncowed by Herb's large personality. They had a home in Chicago, an apartment in New York City, a summer place on Cape Cod, and I believe, another home in Florida. Arthur and I were several times invited to their place on Cape Cod—a huge spread, with a beautiful garden bisected by a bubbling brook and a bridge that you had to walk over to get from one side to the other: Herb's fantasy of an English gentleman's fantasy of a summer retreat. There was always lots of food and drink and Herb and Nancy were always the life of the party—generous hosts, looking out for you and making sure that you were enjoying yourself.

They didn't seem to have a care in the world and we always had a marvelous time. That's how I would characterize the two years I spent at Beigel & Sandler: A marvelous time.

And then one day in March of 1994 there was no Beigel & Sandler. There was only Beigel. Sandler was locked out of the New York office, and his name was taken off the door. It wasn't long before he had filed suit against everything Beigel connected and Beigel had filed countersuits against everything Sandler connected. It was all about money, of course, and although the details differed depending upon who was suing who, suffice it to say that when you boiled it all down there just wasn't enough of it. Bridges over brooks, bubbling or otherwise it turned out, don't grow on trees, and overnight the firm dissolved. Herb gave an interview to the *Chicago Tribune* in which he downplayed any problems, said his new firm would be expanding and that the payroll would be met but "under new arrangements." Meanwhile, as the *Tribune* put it; "He flatly denied stiffing creditors"—which, I believed, might be newspaperese for "And now I'll tell *you* one."[19] Autumn was here. It was time to get out of Dodge.

But where would we go?

There had been lucrative offers over the years from firms looking to absorb my matrimonial department and access my client list, but I was finished with the big firm experience. There was always someone looking over your shoulder, someone asking you to explain yourself and your operation. A matrimonial practice deals with individuals, not corporations, so the client pays the retainer and then, depending on how complicated the case is and how long it takes to resolve, they may have trouble keeping up with the bills. Eventually it is resolved, one way or another, but on a monthly or yearly basis matrimonial firms always have a lot of receivables due—a lot of payments owed. The money comes to you in a herky-jerky fashion. That's just the nature of the practice. But the comptrollers in the big firms don't like that and are constantly after you to collect. They want you running around chasing the dollars that are going to come to you anyway, eventually, and it is always a hassle and you only get a percentage of what comes in. And at those firms you feel like you are sitting in someone else's lap—someone who pays the rent and the utilities and the salaries of your employees. It can foster a sense of dependency, an apathy that is not conducive to good lawyering. It's like the lotus eaters of Greek mythology—let someone else handle the practicalities while you dream on.

I remembered what my father had told me all those years ago about being your own boss and having your own business. It was a daunting thought but a practical one. We were all owed money from the Beigel & Sandler dissolution, but we'd never see it and it was better to write it off than to fruitlessly try and run it down; better to make a sharp break than try to hold on to lost illusions. The marvelous times were over. It was time to put aside childish things.

I spoke to Pat Hennessey and Peter Bienstock, both of whom had come over with me from Solin and Breindel and were partners in the firm. The three of us agreed that we'd roll the dice and strike out on our own. Marti agreed to stay with us as an associate, so there were four of us. We knew of good office space and services that would be available when we made the jump and believed that speed was of the essence. We thought it best to proceed with an Entebbe-type raid, in and out, given the exigencies of the situation and the fact that our clients depended on us to give them uninterrupted legal services. It was better to ask forgiveness than permission. It was very much a gamble but we talked it out and thought it out. There was nothing left to do but act.

We began on a Friday evening, after business hours, returning to the office and packing our clients' Redwelds—the classic reddish-brown expanding/accordion-type legal folders that contain case files, attorney notes, court orders, memoranda, all the paper legal paraphernalia associated with each individual case or client. There were hundreds of them and it took us all weekend, until late Sunday night. We'd pack up as many Redwelds as we could carry, then load the elevator, take them downstairs, put them in a car and drive them over to my home—the apartment Arthur and I lived in on the East Side. The new office space wouldn't be accessible until Monday morning. It was nerve wracking and physically exhausting—at the time it seemed like something out of James Bond but looking back it may have been closer to the Keystone Cops—Pat, Peter, Marti, Arthur and I moving surreptitiously though an empty building, where no one was paying any attention to us, and stacking up these thick folders in the back seat, driving off, and then carrying them up to my apartment, unpacking and stacking them up in the foyer, the living room, dining room, kitchen, bedroom—any flat surface would do. Back and forth all weekend. It was very much a "Leave the gun. Take the cannoli" type situation: all we took were the Redwelds.[20] Everything else was left behind. And all throughout that weekend we were all also calling clients, assuring them there would be no interruption in our services. Giving them a new phone number and introducing them to the new firm: Cohen Hennessey Bienstock LLP.

Open for business.

On Monday morning, I called Herb. I told him that I knew he had a lot of worries, but he didn't have to worry about me. We had taken all our files and moved on. I remember I said, "Good luck to you." I didn't mention the ongoing legal dispute with Sandler, and I didn't ask for any explanation.

"That's good," he said. "That's fine." He sounded relieved that we had taken matters into our own hands. Maybe it had forestalled action he'd preferred not to have had to take. Herb liked me and I liked him. In any case he didn't sound surprised and he wasn't angry.

I said that whatever monies were owed us by our clients we would be keeping. *That's all fine*, he said.

We were probably on the phone for less than two minutes.

Afterwards I sat back in my living room at 300 E. 56th street, Apartment 27M, the home I shared with my husband. Redwelds to the left of me, Redwelds to the right . . .

Cohen Hennessey Bienstock.

We probably should have added Feinberg to the name, as it was Arthur's apartment as well.

When I'd imagined having my own firm, my own name upon the door, it hadn't been *quite* this. But it would do. It was a beginning.

PART III

A NEW WORLD

Nothing is straightforward unless you are unintelligent, an unthinking or shallow person. You know, you say: oh, this is great. But if you are smart, you peel the onion a little bit and you see there is a lot going on underneath, a lot going on that implicates other values. Things are seldom what they seem.

9 THE NAMES ON THE DOOR

The Firms: An Autobiography in Office Space

I

We were all worried that we wouldn't survive, that we had founded a firm that wouldn't be able to make any money. There was this exhilaration, this "band of brothers" feeling when we were planning the move, when we took the Redwelds and brought them to my apartment, but then came the inevitable letdown. What now? The task before us just seemed daunting.

That first week we brought all the Redwelds down from my apartment to our new rented space on Third Avenue and East 37th Street. We picked out our offices and set up secretarial stations. There was a small kitchen, large conference rooms, a file room, and reception area. I had a large corner office with a commanding view up Third Avenue. It was a cozy arrangement, we had no second thoughts but we worried, Pat and Peter and Marti and I, whether we'd be able to make it. I had to match up our receipts and our outstanding bills and hope we would come out ahead each month. It felt great not having a managing partner constantly haranguing me about receivables; now, as the senior partner and the firm manager, I could harangue myself about making the nut each month. It felt, for a time, that it was touch and go.

But our clients came with us; new clients came aboard. The celebrity pipeline from Franklin Garbus had long since been shut down, but celebrities found us, nonetheless, drawn to us by word of mouth and the results we achieved and the tact with which we handled their cases. I represented Alison Stern, Howard Stern's first wife, during their divorce, and if I was surprised at the intelligence, focus, openness, and modesty he displayed during those talks—so unlike his "public" persona—he seemed impressed at the professionalism and focus and discretion I brought to the table. It was, all things considered, one of the more successful and pleasant negotiations I've been involved in, and afterwards he mentioned on his radio show that "Alison's lawyer" was one of the few attorneys he respected.

We were busier than we had been, and we worked within a mutually supportive atmosphere of trust and friendship. We all liked each other. I had a large couch in my office, and just about every afternoon, the partners and associates who were not in court would come to my office and we'd share a lunch of sandwiches and coffee and soda, discuss our cases, talk about the latest doings inside court and out. When I had imagined what it might be like running my own firm, this was how I had imagined it. Although, even in my dreams, I hadn't dared believe it might be so satisfying.

My book had just been published, and our office was directly across Third Ave from Court TV. The O. J. Simpson trial began just after the New Year in January 1995 and I became one of the regular commentators, whether because I offered such particular insight or because they could call me at a moment's notice and, if I were not in court or with a client, I could just slip out to their studio across the street, get in the chair for hair and makeup, and be on camera within fifteen minutes. Whatever the reason, it worked out for both of us, and it all sparked more interest in both my firm and me. There were appearances on *Nightline* and other news shows as well, speaking engagements, book signings, lectures, debates—every public appearance bringing more clients to the firm.

The firm's reception area was on the 29th floor and had large windows with an unobstructed view down Third Avenue to the World Trade Center at the southern tip of Manhattan. On Tuesday, September 11, 2001, a beautiful sunny, cloudless morning, I stood at those windows and watched the twin towers burn. There were large visible gashes on the upper facades of both buildings, and I saw billows of black smoke pouring out, the smoke rising, thick and dirty, into the clear, intense blue sky. None of us, thankfully, were due downtown in court that morning, so we watched together. Someone had turned on a radio or television that played quietly in the background, and we knew what was happening. Shortly before ten o'clock, the South Tower, WTC 2, imploded, sending a combination of smoke, ash, debris, and atomized bodies shooting across lower Manhattan and rising to cover the sky. About thirty minutes later the North Tower collapsed. We stayed by the windows, in silence, watching the apocalypse unfold before us.

Somewhere, in all that smoke and debris, was Chuck Zion, Nancy's childhood friend, and James Reilly, who called his parents, Virginia and Bill, as the North Tower burned and assured them that he was fine. That was the last they heard of him.

In the days and weeks that followed, you smelled the ash and smoke and debris, felt it in your nose and in the back of your throat, acrid and heavy, the air itself marked by their passing.

II

We remained at 605 Third Avenue for eight years, until 2002, when we decided to end our tenancy and find a place of our own. We were a thriving, growing firm, and I found a beautiful space at 11 West 42nd Street, just off 5th Avenue, 19th floor. Once again, I was across from the Public Library within hailing distance of my old friends, Patience and Fortitude, but this time across from Bryant Park which had been transformed into glorious gardens with summer concerts, a merry-go-round and activity, day and night. The move brought home to me certain truths, evoked certain memories: Mr. Nizer and all those lessons on the *business* of law—a refusal to see any contradiction between arguing and winning landmark legal cases and appearing on "What's My Line?"

Welcome Mystery Challenger, and will you sign in please?

As eminent and successful as he was, Mr. Nizer never stopped hustling and I haven't either—a relentless and consuming advocacy; an understanding of the responsibility I have assumed to my clients, but also to my partners and my employees. I know the intensity I bring to my work—on both the advocacy and the business side—has evoked criticism at times, from friends as well as critics. I want to be the best lawyer possible, but I am also a businesswoman who has to meet a payroll and protect my employees. And like Mr. Nizer, I see no contradiction in these roles and refuse to assume that one is more important than the other.

III

We signed the lease at 11 West 42nd Street as *Cohen Hennessey Bienstock LLP* in 2002; when we left, eight years later, we were *Cohen Hennessey Bienstock Rabin LLP*. I had brought Bonnie Rabin—whom I'd met while working on "The Case of a Lifetime"—into the firm as an associate and then made her a partner. In 2011 we moved to the 28th floor of 7 Times Square, my office eyeball to eyeball with the top of the tower from which they dropped the New Year's Eve Ball. By then we were *Cohen Rabin Stine Schumann*. Marti (Stine) had long since been a partner, but it was here that she became a named partner. In 2014 we moved to 11 Times Square, 10th Floor, and remained there until 2020. The next year, we opened our new firm *Cohen Stine Kapoor*. My office looks down into the heart of midtown Manhattan, past some *Blade Runner*-ish billboards that seem to look toward the future. As does, I believe, *Cohen Stine Kapoor*.

* * *

Cohen Rabin Stine Schumann parted ways after ten years. We have all remained friends. Covid and the changing times had brought out different philosophies among the partners that forced on me a clarity for which I was grateful. My vision for the future and Marti's were aligned.

And out of that clarity was born our new firm.

10 KADDISH

I am with my brother, Alvin, who is seven years old, and we're walking along the boardwalk in Asbury Park. It's a hot summer morning in the summer of 1945, and I can feel the sun on my back, feel Alvin's hand in mine, as we pass the Ferris wheel and carousel, the Skee Ball concession, and miniature golf course.

And I'm also with my mother at the kitchen table of our home at 70 Davis Street in Providence, Rhode Island. I'm younger than Alvin was that day on the boardwalk. From the radio comes Don McNeill's "Call to Breakfast":[1]

Good morning Breakfast Clubbers
Good morning to ya
We woke up bright and early
Just to howdy-do ya

Marion stands up and takes my hand, and we parade around the kitchen table while the song plays on.

And now I'm walking with Arthur along the beach in the Rockaways. It's our first date. I have a bad upper respiratory infection and pleurisy and can't suppress my coughing. Arthur says, "You know, I don't believe in the germ theory." I think: "He's going to kiss me."

And now I'm listening as my grandson, Benjamin Ziegelbaum, the middle son of my daughter Amy, speaks at Arthur's funeral service. He's seventeen years old, a beautiful young man, a writer, a poet, a visionary. He loved Arthur deeply. Hundreds gather that day to pay tribute to Arthur, and they listen as Ben describes, "the man I am proud to call my grandfather . . . the single most influential man in my life."

And now, a mere five months later, I am lying on a bed with my weeping daughter, Amy, holding her, feeling her body spasm and shake, trying to silently comfort her. We're in the bedroom of her home on Old Colony Lane in Great Neck, and below us, on the first floor, I can hear low murmurings as family and friends begin to gather. The door to the bedroom opens, and David, Arthur's son, comes in. He was at work when he learned but left immediately and now he is here. "I'm so sorry," he says.

I'm sitting at a table at the Lotos Club in New York City, while friends and family speak in my honor, celebrating my 90th birthday. Alvin, who has stage four lung cancer, has made the trip from Toronto with his wife, my sister-in-law, Ruby, and he speaks about what I have meant to him, what we have meant to each other.

"A lot of people here have known Harriet for a long time," Alvin says, "but I am sure I have known her the longest—more than 84 years. My earliest memories are of walking home from school with her in Providence and complaining to her that the hill was too steep, of going with her to meetings of the Chopin Juvenile Club, of looking up at the high-water mark from the hurricane of '38 and being the annoying baby brother schlepped along to the movies to see 'Lassie Come Home.'"

Alvin is a physician, an esteemed gastroenterologist, and understands the nature and prognosis of his illness. He concludes his speech with the hope that we can all meet again, in five year's time, to celebrate my 95th.

* * *

In *Death Comes for the Archbishop*, Willa Cather wrote:

He sat in the middle of his own consciousness; none of his former states of mind were lost or outgrown. They were all within reach of his hand, and all comprehensible.[2]

Comprehensible yes, but reconcilable? No simple matter in a world that seems increasingly, inevitably, marked by absence, and so many of those who remain seem wraithlike, pale ghosts in comparison to those who have vanished.

Morris

Morris was born to lead one kind of life but ended up living quite another. I imagine the space between these two lives came to define him: empty space that, over the years, filled with dreams and memories, ghostly half-forgotten faces and voices, spirits, dybbuks, recollections of ritual and righteousness, and visions of great brutality and violence.

He was born Moshe Nejman on September 15, 1905, in the town of Pechera, on the southern Bug River, about 170 miles south of Kyiv. There was a small but thriving Jewish community in Pechera, numbered in the 1900 census at just under 1,000 people. In 1908, when Moshe was three years old, male members of the community, joyously singing and dancing, carried him off on their shoulders to the Cheder, the Jewish primary school, where he would begin his education. It was the introduction to a way of life that stretched back, virtually unchanged, for centuries. This was the life that Morris was supposed to live, a life centered on worship and study and work. This was his inheritance.

After the Bolshevik revolution of 1917, when Moshe was twelve, Ukraine became a charnel house.[3] Red armies battled White armies, and both fought a third army of Ukrainian Nationalists led by the warlord Simon Petliura. A fourth army made up of thieves, deserters, criminals, and freebooters—the riffraff of postwar Eastern Europe—was also involved in the fighting, which went on for five years, until 1921. None of these armies was particularly proficient; they mauled each other, retreated, advanced, retreated again. Their great talent was killing Jews: between 1917 and 1921 it is estimated that between 100,000 and 200,000 Jews were murdered in Ukraine in a series of actions collectively given the title the Petliura Pogroms. It was the largest mass slaughter of Jews in European history prior to the Holocaust.

There was a pogrom in Pechera in 1918. Most of the Jews who survived fled to the Jewish cemetery high on a ridge overlooking the Bug River, but Moshe never made it there. He hid in a basement, occasionally raising his head to peer through a broken window. He told me he saw Cossacks cut off his grandfather Avroom's side curls, his *payos*, and then murder him. He saw his older sister Annie, who was sixteen, raped. He watched as homes were looted and set on fire.

This pogrom was neither more nor less violent than any of the others during the period, but in the backwash Moshe and other surviving family members became part of the final surge of Jewish immigration from Europe that had swelled the Jewish population of the United States from 400,000 in 1890 to 3.4 million in 1920. That was the year Moshe ended up in Pawtucket, Rhode Island, working for his Uncle Shloima. That was where he became Morris Newman.

Annie, Morris's sister, also emigrated to the United States at this time. She was considered to be "damaged goods" because she had been raped, so she was married off to a "lesser" man, a man the family considered beneath them. This was also part of the Nejman family inheritance.

During World War Two, Morris's hometown, Pechera, was occupied by Romanian troops and was the site of the Pechora concentration camp.[4] Jews from the surrounding villages were sent to Pechera, where they died of starvation and disease, primarily typhus. Those who didn't die fast enough were sent east to slave labor camps in the Nazi zone of occupation, where just about all of them were murdered. Pechera itself was a relatively small cog in the German killing machine, but it did its part. About 11,000 Jews went through the camp during the war, of which an estimated 9,500 died.

By 1945 virtually everyone Morris had known in Ukraine had either emigrated or been murdered. There was no one left. Even the landscape of his youth had more or less vanished. Pechera was reduced to about a dozen homes, almost all of them empty, and a Russian Orthodox church. And a Jewish cemetery, locked behind rusted gates, pillaged, overgrown, and abandoned.

* * *

My father was a committed Jew but not an observant one. Moshe, in Pechera, had been a student, learning the lessons of observance, ritual, and piety that were expected to last him a lifetime. But Morris, in Pawtucket, Providence, and New York City, was a businessman who worked six days a week and was unable to obey the most fundamental of the Commandments: *Remember the Sabbath day to keep it holy.* He always felt, he told me, the shadowy pull of righteousness and despaired that he could not honor it. I think of my father's hesitancies, his silences and physical clumsiness, his inability to express the great emotion and love he felt inside him, and I believe that all his life he suffered from PTSD. Yet I know that he valued his life, not for what he had lost, what was taken from him, but for what he had been given and what he had earned. A veteran of the twentieth century.

He loved this country. He was a great patriot.

Morris was a heavy smoker, Lucky Strike cigarettes—there was always a pack at hand, a Lucky between his fingers. Eventually, the habit broke him and his body began to shut down. He suffered a stroke, and Arthur and I drove him to Arthur's hospital. Morris was hospitalized for about a week, and one afternoon a physician came in and told me that they had to perform a series of tests on him. If Arthur had been there, I'm sure he would have stopped it, but Arthur was now in Wyoming, at a meeting of the American College of Physicians, and I was intimidated by the white coats. I accompanied my father as they wheeled him into an elevator and then down down down into the very bowels of the hospital, where the scan, or whatever it was, was located. They took him inside, and I waited in the basement corridor, lit by fluorescent light, cool and alone in an ominous silence. And suddenly from inside the room there was a harrowing scream—my father's scream, loud and echoing down the empty hallway. I don't know what—if anything—they did to him, but I still feel, to the very moment you are reading this, such a deep shame that I did not prevent it, that I did not protect him.

He died a day or two later, on September 15, 1985, his eightieth birthday.

Marion

It was Arthur who first recognized what was happening. Every day Marion would drive from her Rockaway home to North Shore University Hospital to sit with Morris during his final illness. The effort clearly exhausted her—it seemed at times an act of will. My daughter Susie and her husband Bruce were both residents at the hospital, and one evening Marion was so tired that, rather than drive back home, she slept overnight up the hill, in the Residents' housing that had been provided for them. She lost her keys at one point, searched high and low for them, but they couldn't be found. They were later returned to her—the key ring had ended up wrapped in Morris' bedsheets in the hospital laundry. I didn't think much of it. Who doesn't occasionally lose things?

Arthur kept quiet watch and began to notice small changes in behavior and verbal skills. Lapses in memory. She went shopping at the supermarket and forgot where she'd parked her car. It might happen to anyone. But Arthur told me that he believed Marion was in the early stages of Alzheimer's or some other form of dementia and it was time to consider options of treatment—there weren't many—and care.

I had a hard time accepting this. My mother wasn't an old woman—she was in her mid-seventies, youthful looking, vigorous, very energetic, seemingly capable of living on her own. All my life Marion had been the center of my emotional being—the person I confided in, the person whose advice I sought; the beating heart of my family's life and soul. I wasn't prepared to lose her, but now, unmistakably, she began to lose herself. She would wander away from her home—just down the block from me in the Rockaways—and the police would bring her back. She didn't know why she had wandered off—didn't know where she'd been or where she was going. It was like she was sinking, slowly, inevitably, no pain, no awareness; sinking into final incomprehension and silence.

We hired round-the-clock caregivers, some of whom were wonderful but others of whom were scam artists, who frightened Marion and took advantage of her helplessness. The disease itself added to her agitation and fear—as if, in some small remaining part of herself, she was aware of what was being taken from her. I looked for some way to calm her, to bring her, if only momentarily, some peace.

* * *

This is a story my mother would tell when I was a child and which became part of our family legend:

My mother was born in the town of Zyrardow, just west of Warsaw, in what was then part of the Russian Empire. In the winter of 1915 when she was four years old, her father, Hersch Wulf Zeitman, took seriously ill and had to be hospitalized. The family hired a wagon and driver and set out for the Jewish Hospital in Warsaw, about 27 miles away. Evening was falling and a storm was moving in, and in the dark and difficult conditions, the wagon hit a ditch and rolled over. There were cuts and bruises, but no serious injuries except for Sam, one of Marion's five older brothers, who'd been sitting up front with the driver and who suffered a badly broken leg. There they were in the dark, in a swirling rain and snow storm, sitting along the side of the ditch while the driver tried to collect and calm the frightened horses, and Sam moaned in pain and Molka comforted her dying husband. And out of the night along the road came a group of uniformed Cossacks patrolling, on their magnificent horses, the routes into the capital city. They were fully armed: rifles, pistols, and the traditional, much-feared *shashka*—a combination long knife and saber, with a slightly curved blade whose tip is sharpened on both sides. When the Cossacks charge the crowds at the beginning of *Doctor Zhivago*, they wield the *shashka* to slash and kill.

My mother told me that the Cossacks determined what had happened, and then several of them took Sam and Hersch Wulf to Warsaw. The remaining Cossacks took the rest of the family, Marion, Molka, another brother, Phillip, and a sister, Helen, to a nearby encampment and provided food and shelter for the night. The next morning the storm had passed and the Cossacks brought the family to the Jewish Hospital, where they found that Samuel's leg had been set and he was resting comfortably. He had not been told that his father, Hersch Wulf, had died overnight.

This story sounds unbelievable—just add a pack of starving, snarling wolves chasing the wagon on the road into Warsaw and you have a Russian folktale. But apparently it is all true. Hersch Wulf did die in the Jewish Hospital. Sam did suffer a broken leg. As for the rest of it: my mother was probably the only Jewish woman in the world who had a genuine fondness, even affection, for Cossacks; and those feelings extended to her hometown of Zyrardow and her neighbors, Jewish and non-Jewish alike. Years later, in Brooklyn, she was the lone Jew in a group of women who met weekly to play bridge. They were all comfortable with one another—indeed Mation said they all loved one another—at least as much as a group of cut-throat bridge players *can* love one another.

* * *

Every day there seemed to be less of her. She seemed to be moving backwards in time. I bathed her, washed her hair, and combed it dry. Tried to soothe her nameless fears. I had once been her child, and now she was mine, and I thought I might provide comfort by bringing back to her some of the happy scenes of her childhood. If I had shown Morris pictures of Pechera, he would probably have risen from his sickbed, risen even from the grave itself, to rain down curses on the place and its inhabitants. But Marion had nothing but warm feelings for Zyrardow and the people she had known as a child, and while there were no films of Zyrardow, there were a series of Yiddish films that had been made in Poland in the mid to late 1930s. They were the work of a producer/director named Joseph Green, who brought prominent Yiddish actors from America back to Poland to film a series of melodramas and musical comedies, including *Yiddle with His Fiddle, Mamele (Little Mother), A Letter to Mother, The Jester.*[5] All were filmed in Polish towns and villages between the years 1935–1938.

I bought cassettes of the films, and my mother and I would watch them sitting together on a couch in my den. They soothed her, at least from moment to moment, and she took pleasure watching them over and over, hearing the language of her youth, the language she first spoke, Yiddish, and seeing reborn before her the world of her childhood—the streets and street signs, the shops, the schools and places of worship. Her favorite was *Mamele,* filmed in Lodz and starring Molly Picon as a young woman who has to assume responsibility for her family after the unexpected death of her mother. There is much drama, many misunderstandings, but it all ends happily when the young woman marries her sweetheart from across the courtyard.

I know that amid the roiling incomprehensibility of her world, the chaos she instinctively felt inside herself, Marion was brought, at least briefly, to a place of quiet and comfort by these films: a visceral sense of calm and belonging.

* * *

My mother was spared not a single of the indignities the disease visits upon its victims, but I believed, or I made myself believe, that there existed a part of her, perhaps no bigger than a spark, that remained resistant to total erasure. When we could no longer watch the Yiddish movies, I would sing to her. She liked "*Bei Mir Bis du Shein*" (by me you're lovely) which had been a nationwide hit for the Andrew Sisters in 1938, but her favorite was *Honey*, first recorded by Rudy Vallee and his Connecticut Yankees in 1929.[6] I would sing a line and Marion would come in on *Honey,* singing the word—she could no longer speak but miraculously she could sing a single word in perfect melody. I'd sing another line and Marion would come in again, in tune and at exactly the right time . . .

I'm in love with you
Honey
Say you love me too
Honey
No one else will do
Honey
Seems funny but it's
True!

Music was always so important to my mother, so it was appropriate that the last language she spoke was the language of rhythm, melody, and tone, the most universal of languages. And the most beautiful.

My mother died on November 12, 2003.

Arthur

For years afterward I would dream that Arthur had left me, had ended our marriage, and I did not know why. In the dream this uncertainty haunted me, a continuing presentiment of unease and unhappiness because I knew that Arthur was a good man and that meant that whatever had happened, whatever had caused the breach, must have been *my* fault. But I could not remember what it had been. Some details might change but the focus of the dream was always the same and it always ended this way: I see Arthur on the street, and I follow him, silently, as he walks into a building. I'm so happy to see him after all this time, but I want to catch up to him and ask him: *What did I do? Why did you leave?* I am close behind, but I can never quite reach him, and I watch as he enters an elevator. He doesn't see me as I rush up but the doors close in front of me. Over and over, in every dream, the doors close before I can reach him. Before I can ask: *Why?*

* * *

Marion spent her last years at the Extended Care Facility at North Shore University Hospital, a facility that Arthur had founded and of which he was Medical Director. He looked in on her several times a day and though she was no longer aware of it, made sure that she was provided with the best possible care under his loving and watchful eye.

It was an end-of-life experience he was determined to avoid, making it clear to me and to his children, Nancy and David, that when the time came—and it would come—he wanted no extraordinary efforts to keep him alive. Arthur would quote de Gaulle, *Old age is a shipwreck*, and, as a clinician and a dedicated and knowing physician, he was under no illusions about the depredations and humiliations that illness and age can bring to the patient. He measured his own health by his ability to engage with the world. He had a fear of dependency, of being trapped in his body and forced to rely on the care—or the love or the mercy—of others, be they family or strangers.

It wasn't just a matter of leaving a DNR—Do Not Resuscitate—protocol. It was the knowledge that offering the best possible care to a patient often meant, at some point, acknowledging the limits of care. Physicians always want to order one more test—the example of my father comes to mind: diagnosticians want another X-ray, another scan; surgeons want to cut; and everyone is familiar with the notion that the cure can be worse than the disease. And if so, then what? Of course the decisions are rarely clear cut but Arthur believed in providing the patient with a series of possible outcomes; and sometimes the choice might be to forgo the difficult problematic operation, the long and painful—both physically and psychologically—recovery in exchange for just living your life, on your own terms, for as long as possible, be that six months, a year, or more. Being a person instead of a patient.

It was the choice he made for himself. We lived a full and happy life: vacations, cruises, movies, theater, a circle of loving family and friends who were so important to us. Arthur was a loving and ardent husband, a wonderful companion—witty, funny, fully engaged with life; his mind as sharp as ever. Physically he began to run down as heart disease claimed more of him. He was determined to avoid hospitalization for as long as possible, and I was his co-conspirator, choosing to believe that as long as he wasn't in the hospital, he wasn't really sick—and I could remain in denial that he was coming to the end of his life.

There came a time when he couldn't walk half a city block without stopping to catch his breath, when he couldn't make it from the bedroom to the bathroom without huffing and puffing, and when getting up from a chair was a struggle that he often lost. He entered the hospital the day before Thanksgiving 2005, and his heart surgery was scheduled for the morning after the holiday. David and Nancy visited him on Thanksgiving morning. Arthur asked David to walk with him and, arm in arm, they made a slow circuit of the hospital floor, talking of this and that, nothing too serious. Arthur thought the operation might give him, at best, another year or so. He did tell David to make sure everyone knew that, if they were with him post operation, he might say some foolish or ugly things as he came back into consciousness. That's what often happened when people came out of anesthesia, he said, he'd seen it often, and he wanted to make sure that no one would take it seriously, that no one would be hurt or offended.

How typical of Arthur that at a moment of great personal stress, he would seek to ease the concern of others. As it turned out the warning was unnecessary as, to all intents and purposes, he never came out of the anesthesia.

* * *

Arthur wanted me to spend the night before the operation with him. It was Thanksgiving evening. The entire family celebrated the holiday at our home in the Rockaways, and toward the end of the meal I left to drive to the hospital, carrying with me their messages of love. David and Nancy were to join me the next morning and we would sit together during the operation and then see Arthur in the recovery room in the ICU. That was the plan.

Arthur and I spent that last night together in the narrow hospital bed. I didn't think they would allow it, but being a top officer at the hospital had its benefits. In the early morning he got up and I helped him to shower. He was such a beautiful man. They came for him shortly afterward—it was scheduled to be the first operation of the day. His chest was shaved, and he was put on a gurney. I remember thinking that they handled him too roughly, almost carelessly, but, following Arthur's lead, I said nothing. I still don't understand it. It was like they were angry with him. He was lying on the gurney, and I held his hand as they wheeled him down the corridor. When they reached the double doors to the operating theater, they stopped, and I leaned down and we kissed. I told him I loved him and would see him later. They pushed him through, and I watched as the doors swung shut in front of me and I was alone in the corridor.

* * *

There was our grief—the family's grief—at Arthur's passing, but there was also a public grief that at times seemed to subsume our private sorrow. Hundreds of people attended the funeral service, overflowing the auditorium and requiring the opening of several listening rooms. There was family, of course, and work colleagues and friends, but there was also Jeanne and Arthur's old friends from years ago in Great Neck, when Arthur was a young physician trying to establish his practice, not all that long out of the Army, with a young wife and two young children.

Another world.

And from that world came patients or the sons and daughters of patients, who had been treated by Arthur half a century before, and who had never forgotten the exceptional care and the kindness they and their loved ones had experienced.

There were old colleagues from the Columbia College of Physicians and Surgeons, Arthur's beloved P&S; from the early days at North Shore, when it was still a small community hospital and not the University behemoth it has become; students taught by Arthur long ago who were now the respected and established elders in their fields. It seemed as if almost every person who had ever met Arthur felt indebted to him in some way and wanted to express to me and to his children, however briefly, their memory of his calm and knowledgeable manner, his diagnostic skill, the human touch that he brought to all such encounters and what that had meant to them during periods of uncertainty and distress.

There were so many beautiful eulogies, but among the most beautiful was the tribute of my grandson Benjamin Ziegelbaum, seventeen years old. He described Arthur as "the single most influential man in my life, the greatest man I have ever known. The model on which I hope to base my life."

Ben wrote a poem "In memory of my beloved grandfather." This is an excerpt:[7]

I once knew a man with the gift of the sun
Who brought light into every room
Warmth into every heart
And burned selflessly
Making sure I was never in the dark.

Ben

Benjamin Ziegelbaum died on April 23, 2006. He was in a car with his father, Michael Ziegelbaum, and they were driving to a Vassar College orientation for incoming freshmen when he suffered a fatal cardiac arrhythmia. Michael, a medical doctor and surgeon, was unable to revive him. Ben was seventeen years old.

There was always a special bond between Ben and Arthur. We all saw it, and I like to think that to some small extent I was a part of it. Arthur loved Ben's wit, his humor, his intelligence and exuberant creativity, his spirit, and he sympathized with whatever difficulties Ben was experiencing. We took Ben on vacation to Puerto Rico once because, as Ben put it, Arthur "was worried I was unhappy at home." That unhappiness was centered around a sometimes volatile relationship with his father—a relationship that, because of Ben's sudden death, never had the time to resolve itself, however that would have turned out.

Ben once described his "General Interests" as "Finding New Ways to be Offensive yet Mildly Lovable," and, like many teenagers, he succeeded admirably. He loved his older brother Matthew and his younger brother Jonathan, who suffered from a number of serious developmental difficulties and who was often unpredictable and full of rage, prone to acting out. Ben once described his mission in life as "bringing peace to the upstairs hallway." Jonathan, Jonny, later transitioned, becoming "Alice" thereby finding some small measure of tranquility. Of his mother, my daughter Amy, who loved and protected all her sons, Ben wrote:

Mom, you're brave, and I don't think there is a single person who knows you who doesn't know that. Other than Grandpa and maybe Grandma you are my biggest advocate . . . Not once did I feel that I could not go to you with something . . . you always understood and I've never really given you credit for that. I don't think I've ever told you how much I appreciate your ability to see things from my point of view. Thank you for helping me turn into who I am. I love you.

When Arthur died at North Shore University Hospital, Ben spent time, alone, in the hospital room, at the bedside, with Arthur's body. He never spoke about it and, while I am not inclined to metaphysical thinking, in the light of what subsequently happened I do believe there was some kind of communion, some dialogue between souls. I like to think so, anyway. In a booklet of Ben's writings, published shortly after his death, Amy wrote:

For the past 17 years, I woke up every day with a nagging sense of dread, a vague sense of worry that something was going to happen to one of my children. I dismissed it and shook off that heavy feelings every day, figuring that every mother worried about her children. I was not an overprotective mom. When I heard of Ben's death it finally made sense to me—I had known that something was going to happen, I just hadn't been able to put my finger on it. I no longer wake up with that sense of dread. I am grieving and in agony, but that edgy feeling of doom is gone. I cannot explain it.

Isaac Bashevis Singer was once asked if Jews believe in reincarnation. He answered something along the lines of only in the sense that God has prepared such trouble for you, including sorrow, that it is impossible to fit into one life.

If Ben were alive today, at the moment I am writing this, he would be thirty-eight years old.

How many lives will it take to accept this, to come to terms with this loss, to fill the hole in our hearts made by his passing?

Alvin

We spoke at least once a week, every Sunday morning, alternating calls but not standing on ceremony—sometimes I'd call twice in a row, sometimes Alvin. On a Sunday in the spring of 2022, Alvin, my beautiful younger brother, said he had something important to tell me: he'd been diagnosed with stage four lung cancer and was considering treatment options. He'd consulted with some doctors in

Toronto, he'd consult with some in New York and then he'd make up his mind. As he wrote in an essay in February 2022, *before* his diagnosis: "It's not that I am afraid of death, I'm afraid of dying because modern high-tech medicine can make the leaving of this world really ugly." And he quoted a Jewish aphorism: *Do not shorten life and do not prolong death.*

Alvin Newman was born on June 8, 1938, my half birthday. I was 5 ½ years old and always felt it was the best present I'd ever been given. How I'd longed to be a big sister! And he was a perfect younger brother, and the perfect companion to the "Little Mother" persona I'd assumed—or had assumed for me—within the family. I often brought him along with me when I was dating Phil because Phil's family had a car and my family didn't. So Phil would drive up in the car to spend an afternoon with me, and there would be Alvin—I wanted him to enjoy being out and about. And he'd climb in the back seat and marvel at it all and chatter away, and Phil would turn around and glare at him and then glare at me.

"Can't that kid ever shut up?"

But I didn't want that kid to shut up. I loved whatever he was saying. Loved seeing him so happy and excited. And I kept bringing him along.

All my life it felt like Alvin and I were in the same movie, as if we shared a life. He was my oldest friend. My dearest friend.

When I was a sophomore at Barnard, I'd commute to class, leaving each morning and returning each evening to our home deep in Brooklyn. One time a friend, Bonnie Bonoff, asked me to stay with her for two weeks at the Majestic, their posh Central Park West apartment building, while her parents were away on vacation. We were both seventeen years old. I stayed with her, and one day a letter was delivered to me. The Bonoff address was written in Marion's handwriting, but inside the envelope were letters from my young sisters, Molli and Sandee, and from my 12 ½-year-old brother, Alvin. Here is what he wrote:

> Dear Harri,
>
> As you probably know I miss you very much. Things have gotten boring since you left. I miss the "noise" that you create and the "riots" that we start. Our house is getting dull and uninteresting. In short, I miss you so come on home.
>
> *Sincerely yours,*
> *Alvin (the one and only).*

Two and a half years later, fifteen-year-old Alvin was off to college himself, the University of Chicago. Then into the Army, where he served with distinction as a medical officer, a Captain, with US forces in Thailand. When he was discharged, he returned, briefly, to Brooklyn where he met Ruby Klappholz—who had been a classmate of our sister Sandee in elementary school. Six weeks later, they were engaged. Alvin and Ruby married on January 25, 1970, and had three children: Rabba Amy S. Newman, Prof. Michael Z. Newman, and Kurt Newman, PHD.

Alvin and Ruby moved to Toronto to raise their family. Alvin became a nationally known gastroenterologist. He lectured frequently, literally wrote the book on irritable bowel syndrome, and was a proud member of the American College of Gastroenterology.

* * *

After consultations Alvin decided not to seek treatment for his lung cancer. There was extensive scarring of the lungs (pulmonary fibrosis), and he did not believe treatment would help in any significant way. What treatment would do, he believed, was make him very sick, very soon, and he did not want to spend whatever time he had left as a patient. Moreover, he knew, as a physician, how difficult it was to withdraw treatment once it had begun, and he did not want to leave that hard decision to his family. There were other personal reasons as well, reasons that merged with his lifelong experience as a physician. He wrote:

For many years I was a gastroenterology consultant at a chronic care hospital and I was frequently asked to insert a gastric feeding tube through the abdominal wall into a terminally ill or profoundly cognitively-impaired patient's stomach. Technically, this was a simple endoscopic procedure that I could accomplish in six or seven minutes. I often tried to talk families out of this procedure as it provides nothing beneficial aside from calories to the terminal or near-terminal patient. I was never successful in convincing the families to forego the procedure. Once that tube was inserted it was never removed. I was convinced I was prolonging death. I should have refused.

In the end he had about fifteen months. He got to see his grandson, Leo, Michael and Elana's son, play Tevye in *Fiddler on the Roof*; attend operas with Kurt and his life partner Stephanie Pope; continue with pleasure his hobby of woodworking—the last thing he made was a bimah, a raised platform from which the Torah is read, for his daughter Rabba Amy Newman. He didn't get to see his grandson Ezra's Bar Mitzvah, although I like to think that maybe he did. He loved his five precious grandchildren. He came to New York and spoke at my ninetieth birthday celebration, concluding with the wish that we'd all meet again in five years' time to celebrate my ninety-fifth. And then adding a line from the song *I'll Be Home for Christmas:*

If only in my dreams . . .[8]

While he was still strong enough, he traveled and visited with his children and his grandchildren. He said goodbye to his sisters. And then he returned to Toronto.

Alvin was hospitalized, feeling very weak but not in pain. Even in the last days he was himself: alert, witty, intelligent, aware. I watched him consult with his physicians about his care and they asked, as a courtesy, if they could speak freely in front of me. Alvin said: "She's been listening for 85 years. Why stop now?"

Alvin had written:

all of my contemporaries wish the same exit. We want to drop dead with no warning or fuss and may God curse any fool who attempts to resuscitate us I fervently hope I can continue living a fun and comfortable life interacting with my loved ones and enjoying a good meal, a good book, a good puzzle and a good joke. But when those things are no longer possible, I really do want to go gentle into that good night . . .

Alvin. The one and only.

O God, Filled with mercy,
Please care for Alvin's soul
Under your sheltering wings of peace.

11 INTO THE WORLD

Cohen Stine Kapoor

Our firm emerged into the post-pandemic world and, in many ways, was shaped by the exigencies of that world. But it is one thing to recognize that change is coming and quite another to remain adroit and agile enough not only to avoid being crushed by those changes but to survive and prosper: any number of bankrupt crypto "billionaires" can attest to that hard truth. Cohen Stine Kapoor is probably the last firm that will bear my name and the firm that will continue under my daughter Marti's leadership after I'm gone. We had to get it right the first time. There would be no do-overs.

There are three equity partners: myself, Marti, and Ankit Kapoor, and we each represent a different generation of lawyering that, combined together, adds up to what I think is an almost unprecedented depth and variety of experience. Ankit, the youngest, came to this country from India as a nine-year-old. He became a New York City police officer; a uniformed patrolman walking the beat during the day, he went to my alma mater, Brooklyn Law School, at night, and after graduation joined the New York City Corporation Counsel, which is the city's law department. It was in this capacity that he impressed Supreme Court Justice Lisa Sokoloff. She didn't know if I was hiring, but she knew Ankit was a star in the making and she knew I would recognize this.

We met in my office and I was impressed with his moxie, his style, intelligence, and maturity. He had no matrimonial law experience, but he had experience that I respected: he'd worked as a police officer, was hyper-observant, and knew how to read people. As a lawyer for the City, Ankit had taken depositions, negotiated settlements, argued in court, and handled trials. He was fearless, and I knew I could train him to be an excellent matrimonial lawyer. My final question was: *What do you want?*

I want my name on the door, he said.

I offered him a job on the spot.

And then came Covid, and the world as we knew it faded away. Marti and I realized that the time had come to form a new firm, and we asked Ankit to join us as an equity partner. *Cohen Rabin Stine Schumann* was dissolved on December 31, 2020, and *Cohen Stine Kapoor* was born on January 1, 2021. Two other associates complete the roster, and among the five of us, we are probably handling about 100 clients at a time. The brilliant, indefatigable Nicole Margulis was born to be a lawyer. It's no exaggeration to say that Amy Cohen, my Number Two daughter, really runs the firm, making sure each of us knows where we're going and when; solving problems almost before they arise. Anne Marie Gargiulo, our file person and managing clerk, handles our internal filing and e-filing of our court papers in litigated cases. Our receptionist Jodi DeVito is also our all-around assistant. The firm could not function without our controller, Daniela Gorynski, or our IT man, Nick Rosselli. And the summer of 2025 brought us my grandniece, Sam Mezrich, a Barnard junior and a classics major like me, as our talented intern.

Eight plus people in all. And a ninth, my forensic accountant, James R. Guberman, who is not *in* the firm—he has his own business—but is *of* the firm. We have been working together for seven years, ever since his father retired. All the complex accounting methods that the big firms are now learning—Henry and I pioneered decades ago and handed down to James. We speak the language of numbers, and yes, it can be more daunting now, and the figures we deal with are exponentially larger, but even the largest number, no matter how outrageously big, will find its place on James' spreadsheet along with its more modest brothers and sisters, becoming just one part of a larger story that we present to the judge and promote to the advantage of our client.

* * *

Cohen Stine Kapoor is a close-knit and mutually supportive group. We have to be. At a large firm, rivalries, even enmities, can, at times, spark a creative competition that is beneficial to the overall operation, but at a small firm like ours, this kind of tension would be destructive and impossible to contain. We are a family law firm, but I like to think, *a law firm of family* as well and whether people will get along together is a top priority when it comes to hiring. There are other priorities, of course, but the group dynamic is the most important. We root for each other, celebrate together when we win an important case, and lament together when we don't. There are no secretaries—a huge change from my earlier firms. We are all skilled at word processing and on the computer, skilled video conferencers, at sharing our documents with our clients, our experts, our adversaries, and the courts, and skilled with AI. We are small but tough and knowledgeable, and we are up close and personal with our clients—there is no layer of employees that separates us. We are available 24/7.

None of this happened by accident. When Covid shut down the city, closed the court system, and prevented us from using our office, my first professional reaction was to learn to use Zoom. Everything was closed, and there was no guarantee when it would re-open—those of us who lived in New York City woke up and went to sleep with the sound of ambulances racing through the streets and saw morgues being established in parking lots and in Central Park. And while it was happening, my work and the work of my firm had to go on because our clients needed us, and the depredations of the heart continued even if there were, at the moment, no legal means to address them. Covid, in fact, brought us a host of new clients, anxious to consult with us about their legal options in a rapidly shrinking world. One of those was Tom Brady—who'd won six Super Bowls with the New England Patriots and would soon win a seventh with his new team, the Tampa Bay Buccaneers.

In the end the lockdown protocols proved impossible to bend and so many of my clients had to put their hopes in abeyance until the pandemic played itself out. It was a hard lesson to accept. But in this uncertain time the one thing of which I was sure was that when the world *did* resume operating, it would be a different world than the one we had known; and it would be a crime visited upon myself and my clients not to prepare to confront it.

And the world did open up and we were prepared, or as prepared as anyone could be to deal with a kind of hybrid world, part old, part new. Court opened, but we could now file and serve our motions electronically. And while we attend some trials and oral arguments in person down on Centre Street in New York City and elsewhere, other court sessions continue to be teleconferenced, including out-of-town cases which we can now handle once we're moved into the case *pro hac vice*—by which a lawyer is permitted, for one particular case only, to practice law in a venue in which they are not licensed. It's very much a patchwork of legal procedures, some good, some not so good, and every change seems to ripple outward, provoking even more change. For instance, before the pandemic Anne Marie Gargiulo worked at a desk outside my office. During the pandemic, when our office was closed, Anne Marie and her wife moved to Georgia, and afterwards, during the recovery, she asked if she might be allowed to continue working for us from her Georgia home. I was skeptical but agreed to give it a try, which we did. Our electronic court filing and calendars are now handled from a thousand miles away. There is a dedicated button on my phone, and when I press it, Anne Marie answers immediately and asks what I need. Her voice always comes through loud and clear.

As if she's working from a desk just outside my office.

As It Is

I

I was always in a hurry, a hurry to grow up, to become educated, to get married, and have children. But most of all I was in a hurry to pursue my career as an attorney. There just never seemed to be enough time, and I approached the work with a take-no-prisoners philosophy that was, at first, mandated by circumstance but which, sometimes—too often—bled into my personal life as well: my interactions with people, friends, and relatives as well as strangers. There was sometimes a relentless intensity to my approach—whether in a professional encounter in court or in questioning a loved one at a family dinner. I could interrogate a grandchild about a seventh-grade report card with an intensity that suggested they were hiding marital assets.

It was Arthur who slowed me down, who showed me, by example, a different path: the possibility of marrying professional excellence with personal equanimity. The kindness that was so central to his personality came from a place of great strength, as did the rigor with which he understood and carried out his responsibilities as a physician. For Arthur, these qualities, kindness and capability, reinforced each other, making each of them stronger, rather than, as with so many people, working at cross purposes. He provided a role model worth emulating, and although our temperaments were different, I try to keep his example in mind. I've never reached his level of calm and composure—I don't know anyone who has—but it was and it is, even at ninety-three years, very much a work in progress.

II

Perhaps the quantum physicists are right and each moment contains within it a hundred, a thousand, an infinite number of other moments; other possibilities, other futures. I wonder sometimes what my life would have been like had I not chosen to run an insurgent campaign for the presidency of the Women's Bar Association of the State of New York. An easier path, I'm sure of it: being on the winning side usually is. And perhaps, somewhere, there is a version of me that is living that life, enjoying the friendships that were truncated, the opportunities that were denied, the rewards that, implicitly, were being offered. Or I might be living, still, in the Dreaming Suburb, never having awakened from its somnolent embrace, like so many of the women I knew. An unloved wife sliding toward despair and anonymity.

Or I might be walking, forever, along the Asbury Park Boardwalk, coins in my pocket, holding the hand of my beloved brother Alvin.

It's difficult enough trying to figure out the life I *am* leading, rather than imagining all the others I am not. Even now, events I thought I understood, memories safely put to bed, come back to haunt me, suggesting new meaning, new understanding, or new mysteries. I dream often of Mary Tucker Thorpe, the principal of the Henry Barnard School. She was a godlike figure to five-year-old me, but she was something else as well, mysterious and feminine.

In the dream, she is holding my hand as we walk down the center of the first floor corridor, her thick braid swaying slightly from side to side with each step, all the other boys and girls watching us. I've always assumed the small figure is me, because in the dream it *feels* like me, but now that I have learned something about Mary Tucker Thorpe, I wonder. Could it be that she is holding her own hand, the hand of the child she was before she assumed this new identity—four-year-old Mary Dahood, brought to this strange new world from Syria and facing an uncertain future? And now I am one of the children watching them, seeing one of the great mysteries of my life pass before me, slowly stately beautiful enigmatic. The child and the woman walking down the hallway together in fear and anticipation.

III

From the moment I entered law school I was determined that no one was going to outwork or outprepare me. My concept of hard work hasn't changed—if anything, it has become more rigorous—but my understanding of "preparation" has evolved over the years. When I began to practice, it involved reading documents, research, and mastering all the material before me, and it still involves all that, albeit most often on a screen rather than on paper. But there is emotional preparation, as well, and this can only be learned through experience. You have to teach yourself to listen to your client, to understand what they are telling you and what they are trying to tell you—often not the same thing—as well as what they might be concealing, out of guilt or embarrassment or simple carelessness. You have to understand your client's mood and relate to them on that level. You have to gauge the temperature of the courtroom, the attitude and prejudices of the judge, and adjust your case accordingly. And you have to be prepared to give bad news to your client and to understand and accept the implications of that news on your efforts to help them. But as complete as your understanding of the case and all its inferences may be, as hard as you work and as diligently as you prepare, success is never guaranteed and coming to terms with "failure," with the limitations of the law and the case and your own abilities, is an important part of any professional's continuing education.

One of Arthur's favorite short stories was *The Miracle of the Fifteen Murderers*, by Ben Hecht.[1] It's about fifteen eminent physicians who meet four times a year "*to confess to some murder any of them may have committed since the last meeting . . . We are concerned only with those cases in which the doctor, by a wrong diagnosis or by a demonstrably wrong medication or operative procedure has killed off a patient who, without the aforesaid doctor's attention, would have continued to live and prosper.*"

"*Murder by stupidity.*"

The Miracle of the Fifteen Murderers was published in *Collier's Magazine* in January 1943 when Arthur was in medical school—the Columbia University College of Physicians and Surgeons. It was pulp, but in the time of *Doctor Kildare* and *Doctor Gillespie*, *Doctor Christian* and others, it attempted, in ways other more serious literature did not, to examine the limitations of a physician's abilities within the often shambolic conditions that exist in a busy hospital. Arthur had grown up reading and being inspired by *Microbe Hunters* and *Arrowsmith*—the romance of medicine, the physician as idealist. The physician as hero. Hecht was writing about the practitioner as a human being, subject to all the human frailties: a flawed professional. And his writing illuminated part of that life, the hidden part, hidden from outsiders, from the non-initiated, that Arthur was experiencing. Misdiagnosis, wrong prescription, exhaustion, inability to understand what a patient is saying—simply being distracted at a crucial moment—all the snares and pitfalls to which human beings are subjected; the factors that come into play and express, Arthur believed, an essential part of the truth of what it means to be a physician.

In his short story Ben Hecht described two main reasons for medical failure. The first is "*the eternal charlatanism of the patient, who is full of fake diseases and phantom agonies. The second is the basic incompetence of the human mind, medical or otherwise, to observe without prejudice, acquire information without becoming too smug to use it intelligently, and most of all to apply its wisdom without vanity.*"

For an attorney it's not "fake diseases and phantom agonies" but rather the omission—conscious or otherwise—on the part of the client to convey pertinent information, often information that might help their case. Every lawyer is familiar with the "doorknob conversation"—a client, fully debriefed by counsel, will pause at the doorway before leaving and say something like "Oh, by the way . . ." or "I'm sure this isn't important but . . ." and offer some fact or describe some circumstance that alters or throws out all prior assurances and assumptions the lawyer may have formed—information that may vitiate much of what has been said previously. The result is that the case the attorney believed they had disappears, and a new, fundamentally different case takes its place. Coupled with this may be an inability on the lawyer's part to regroup and understand exactly what it is the client is now telling them, or trying to tell them, and a consequent failure to recognize certain existential facts that are right before them and apply those facts in the best interests of the client. To paraphrase Orwell: sometimes the hardest thing to see is what's right in front of your nose.[2] This failure may often be traced to exhaustion or inattention or laziness, and I work hard, very hard, to institute procedures within my office to keep those problems to a minimum.

It is a bit harder, of course, to find workarounds to what Hecht called "the basic incompetence of the human mind." And it can be difficult, as well, particularly for an experienced attorney who has achieved some success, to train oneself to apply "wisdom without vanity"—that is, to see the client before you as an individual and not just a collection of anxieties, concerns, and grievances, all of which you have seen and dealt with, over the years, in countless other clients on countless other occasions. It takes an effort to see each case, each client as *new*, to use the experience you have gained as a stimulant, bringing the case before you into sharper and more accurate focus, rather than, through repetition, as a soporific.

Of course, it is certainly more difficult to identify when a lawyer fails than when a physician does, and as death is (usually) not our adversary, the results we achieve can be hard to measure. A lawyer may "win" in matrimonial court and then lose on appeal, and there are cases whose outcome flips back and forth, through court after court until finality is achieved. Or appears to be achieved, because there are those cases, long decided, that spring back to life, zombie-like, and you find yourself back in court litigating (supposedly) long settled questions of child support, spousal support, or other matters. Moreover, the uncertainties of divorce court—the judge's mood, an obstinate client, a wily opponent—can sometimes make it difficult to distinguish between success and failure. I have worked along lines of excellence, never missing a beat, and ended up reaching a settlement with opposing counsel that leaves both of our clients equally unhappy. That can count as a success. I have also negotiated a spectacular settlement that left my client with much more than could reasonably have been expected. But she refused to settle. If her wealthy ex had agreed to this much, surely he could be pressured to cough up even more. My client wouldn't accept "yes" for an answer, and I had to petition the court to be relieved of her representation because she wouldn't listen to my advice. She found a new attorney, and I later learned that her maintenance package had been dramatically reduced.

The lure of *more* has a very strong appeal, in court and out, and not everyone can resist it.

Hecht's key point, cocooned within the melodrama of his story, was that the public's understanding of the medical profession, an understanding that the profession itself promotes, fails to adequately comprehend the complexity and often compromised reality physicians face in their work, day in and day out. This is a fact that all professionals, whatever field they are in, have to come to terms with: there is the truth that they present to the public and the truth as they understand it among themselves. Lawyers understand that a case can often look very different from the inside rather than the outside. I had a client, battered physically, economically, and emotionally by her brutal husband, who, in consultation with me, decided to battle him in what we both knew would be a bitter and prolonged fight. But the battle itself was meaningful. My client finally stood up to her bully of a husband, was no longer his victim, and, just as important, no longer saw herself as a victim. The outcome was not everything she or I would have wanted, but my client, who became my friend, never regretted the decision she made to end the abuse because that decision, made in full consciousness of the emotional cost and the vagaries of litigation, was in and of itself a victory.

"You never remember your successes," Arthur would say. "They all seem to blend together. But the failures stay with you forever. You can never forget them."

And I have been involved in cases that carry a full measure of regret, most of them involving children. One, in particular, concerned my client, a woman with two young children, involved in a bitter custody battle with her husband. She said she wanted to take her children to Italy for a visit with her family. Her husband strenuously objected, insisting she would never bring them back. My client assured me she understood her responsibilities, and I used my own credibility with the court to help convince a skeptical judge to grant permission for the trip. As the husband had warned, she didn't return.

I regret that my client betrayed my confidence in her and, by the same token, I regret that I was not more alive to the degree to which fear and apprehension had convinced her that the system was rigged against her and that she had to take the law into her own hands. This was not true—but despite my best efforts, and the efforts of the court, the dark forces within her could not be appeased. With apologies to Mr. Nizer, it was one of those times I wasn't hardheaded enough. I wanted those two children to see their grandparents and I wanted to trust my client when I should have wanted my client to trust *me* and trust my assurance that the system was not out to get her. As for the trip to Italy—I should have said "No."

Whatever hard lesson this case taught me, in whatever ways it made me a better lawyer, the lesson for my client was harder and deeper. Federal Marshals, under the Hague Convention, went to Italy and returned the two children to the United States. The husband was granted full custody. Their mother, who faced criminal charges, remained in Italy. To my knowledge, she never saw her children again.

IV

I was alone in the office, working late on a Friday evening when I received a settlement offer on a case I'd been negotiating for over a year. After a long and frustrating back and forth it now appeared that we had finally reached agreement on the difficult question of marital assets. If we'd been in California, a community property state, the case would just about have been over: we'd split the pot 50/50, as state law mandated, and each side could go their own way. But in New York, under equity, what it meant was, potentially, more arguments, more delay, perhaps for months, perhaps for years as we negotiated exactly *how* the assets would be divided. What in California marked the end of the conversation, in New York marked just the beginning. It's why divorce in my state is often protracted, complex, and expensive.

The great regret of my professional life is that we had to settle for equity—fair—not equal, when divorce law reform was passed back in 1980. It was a choice of half a loaf or none—a 50/50 division of marital assets was never going to pass the overwhelmingly male legislature, and, after years of effort, we felt that we had to have *something* to show for it. The bill that emerged was more than something but less than what I'd hoped. Those of us working for passage were correct that some form of reform had to be enacted, but the critics were right that the measure, by giving judges the discretion to determine what "fair," meant, retreated from our stated goals and put too much faith in a judiciary that was, by historic standards, noticeably unenthusiastic about the empowerment of women. And so "fairness" itself seems to flicker on and off depending on the mood of the judge, who, in divorce court, is given extraordinary discretion. But the problem goes deeper than the peccadilloes of the individual judge. It is systemic, built into the structure of the reform law itself.

And the result? Exactly how much equity, how much fairness you can expect in court has been compared to "The Chancellor's Foot," which, of course, varies in length from chancellor to chancellor or from judge to judge. The reference comes from a famous essay written by seventeenth-century legal scholar John Selden.

One Chancellor has a long foot, another a short foot, a third an indifferent foot: 'tis the same thing in a Chancellor's conscience. [3]

Selden concludes—and I think most New York State divorce lawyers would agree:

Equity is a roguish thing.[4]

What I've always believed is one of my great accomplishments—passage of divorce law reform—is inexorably twinned with a great conundrum: would equal have been better?

When I went to work for Julia Perles all those years ago at the Nizer firm, she told me, "We're going to change the world."

And we did.

And as reformers so often learn, the world changed us, as well.

V

I've written of that difficult time in the mid-1970s when I was just out of law school and had met Arthur and was trying, at age forty-one, to begin my career. You can see movies from that period, or read novels or histories, and learn about second-wave feminism and the changes wrought in individual lives and families and in society at large. I lived it, and so did my daughters, and everything you read in a novel, or watch on the screen, or are taught in school—we went through it and, collectively, we experienced it all. We were spared nothing.

At one point Marti had moved out of the house and down the street to live with Marion and Morris. The emotions within our home were just too charged, and she needed a place of calm and quiet to continue her studies. Amy withdrew from me completely—lived her own life, made her own mistakes, carried on, protected herself from the maelstrom as best she could. Susie was at home helping to care for Patti. Though she was accepted by Barnard College I would not let her go, forced her to attend Brooklyn College, because I could not do without her help. It caused a deep resentment, a wound that has taken a lifetime of healing.

And there was another resentment as well: the consuming love I felt for Arthur meant my daughters were no longer my first and only consideration. Nothing was ever said; it didn't have to be. They knew it.

If you had taken a photograph of the five of us then, me, Marti, Amy, Susie, and Patti, you might wonder what became of this family.

Well, two of my daughters, Marti (my partner at law) and Amy (our office manager) work with me at Cohen Stine Kapoor (each of them is also a musician—Marti a trained singer and Amy a professional flutist). Susie graduated *summa cum laude* and *Phi Beta Kappa* from Brooklyn College and then obtained her MD degree from Cornell Medical School. She and her husband, Dr. Bruce Hirsch, are both beloved doctors affiliated with Northwell (formerly North Shore University) Hospital, Arthur's hospital. Patti, another gifted flutist, graduated from Brooklyn Law School and lives and is a prominent trial lawyer in Madison, Wisconsin, where her practice focuses on defending physicians from malpractice litigation. All four of my daughters are married to lovely and accomplished men.

Whatever individual routes we have taken from that moment in the 1970s, we have arrived together, at this moment, a close family—daughters and husbands, sisters, nieces and nephews, grandchildren and great grandchildren, with all the strengths and faults of common humanity but yet joined together in love and understanding and acceptance.

VI

One morning in February 2023, I stepped out of bed and stepped onto a needle, a sewing needle that had embedded itself in the carpet. How it got there I do not know, but I stepped on it with such force that it snapped, and three-quarters of the steel shaft was driven into my foot, right above my pinky toe. I knew exactly what it was—I could see a quarter of the needle, white thread through the eye, in the carpet—and the pain, the shock, was so intense I almost fainted. I went to a podiatrist that morning who told me to soak the foot—he said it was like a wood splinter that would likely work its way out within the week. I was scared, but this was the diagnosis I wanted to hear. I had a busy day ahead of me, and I felt that if I didn't have to go to the hospital, it couldn't be that serious.

Within a week the foot was swollen, the pain was intense, and I couldn't walk on it. I consulted a surgeon who told me I was in a dangerous situation and had to have the needle out as soon as possible. The operation was scheduled for the next day, at four in the afternoon, and I was told not to eat or drink because I'd be given anesthesia.

My doctor was superb, but it was a difficult time. My blood pressure surged to dangerous levels before the operation and afterwards, when I was in the recovery area, it spiked above 200. They were having trouble getting a line into my arm because my veins were so small, having had no fluids for about twenty hours. I could hear the nurses arguing among themselves as they kept sticking me, trying to find a vein. I was still feeling the effects of the anesthesia and told them to leave me alone—a belligerency born of fear. I knew something was very wrong. Amy, who was with me, leaned down to tell me: *"Mom you have to let them do their job. They're trying to help you."*

The head nurse came into the room and said to Amy, "Tell your Mom I'm going to put the line in. I'm going to do it on my first try and I'm not going to hurt her."

And he did, and my blood pressure was brought down and the crisis passed.

I was lying on the gurney, feeling each beat of my heart, wondering if I would survive . . . and I know at such a time you are supposed to be thinking lofty thoughts or weighing the pluses and minuses of a life well lived or walking toward the light with the serenity of the righteous. But I didn't feel any of those things. What I felt was anger—almost rage. *This is how the story ends? Because of a sewing needle?* I know death is no friend and no respecter of dignity, and there are 1,000 ignominious ways to die, a thousand banana peels to slip on, a thousand tragedies in the making. But the will, the drive, the hard-headedness that has served me throughout my life—for good and for ill—the sheer orneriness of my personality, rebelled against this possible fate and helped me to survive.

A sewing needle? Not likely.

VII

My mother opens the front door onto a scene of devastation and woe. There is mud two inches deep on the sidewalk and, on Davis Street itself, rivers of even deeper mud, along with huge old downed trees and power lines, and fields of waste and debris. The storm surge has receded leaving behind this grim reminder of the Hurricane's power and promiscuous destruction. It is a sunny Monday morning in September 1938 and I am five and a half years old. My mother has heard that school will be open, but because the phone lines are still down, we can't be sure. Marion asks me if I want to go to school, the Henry Barnard School. It is more than a mile and a half away and, as there is no trolley service down Smith Street Hill, and no bus service, it means that we'll have to walk through the blasted wreckage of the city.

I say, "I want to go to school," and I feel the front door close behind me.

My mother takes my hand and I step out into the world.

NOTES

Introduction

1 Matt Sedensky, Too old to work? Some Americans on the job late in life bristle at calls for Biden to step aside, *Associated Press*, July 19, 2024.

2 Rob Edelman, *Tommy Henrich*, https://sabr.org/bioproj/person/tommy-henrich/.

Chapter 1

1 W. S. Gilbert and Arthur Sullivan, *H.M.S. Pinafore* (1878).

2 Background on Abraham "Kid Twist" Reles, https://themobmuseum.org/blog/eighty-two-years-ago-this-month-murder-inc-s-abe-reles-took-a-mysterious-fall.

3 Burton B. Turkus and Sid Feder, *Murder, Inc.* (New York, Farrar Straus and Young, 1951), p. 435.

4 Yisrael Gutman, *The Jews of Warsaw* (Bloomington, Indiana, Indiana University Press, 1982). Jeffrey Veidlinger, *In the Midst of Civilized Europe* (New York, Metropolitan Books, 2021). Rosaline Schwartz and Susan Milamed, *From Alexandrovsk to Zyrardow, A Guide to YIVO's Landsmanshaftn Archive* (New York, YIVO Institute for Jewish Research, 1986). Virtual Shtetl (https://sztetl.org.pl/en/towns/z/372-zyrardow/99-history/138352-history-of-community). Photo of abandoned factory Zyrardow: https://stock.adobe.com/search?k=%C5%BCyrard%C3%B3w&asset_id=384998715.

5 Edgar Guest, *It Couldn't Be Done* (Detroit, Breakfast Table Chat, 1914), p. 148. *Public Domain.*

6 Rita Bicho: Rhode Island College of Music, Theater, and Dance: Music Student Handbook: The Rita V. Bicho Memorial Scholarship consists of equal monetary value from the following four categories: (1) A Keyboard Player, (2) A Brass, Wind, or Percussion Player, (3) Vocalists, (4) A String Player (including Harp and Guitar). What's News @ Rhode Island College (pdf), May 11, 1979.

7 American Experience, *The Hurricane of '38*, PBS, first broadcast November 17, 1993.

8 *Mary Tucker Thorp*, Wikipedia, last modified February 16, 2024, https://en.wikipedia.org/wiki/Mary_Tucker_Thorp. Rhode Island College Mary Tucker Thorp Award.

9 Elliott Thorpe, 91, Army Attache Who Warned of Japanese Attack, *New York Times*, June 29, 1989.

10 James Agee, *A Death in the Family* (New York, McDowell, Obolensky, 1957), p.3.

Chapter 2

1 Hula Hoops: https://high.org/collection/nuns-hula-hooping/

2 Pop Culture Violence: https://houseofgeekery.com/2019/07/31/classic-scene-the-grapefruit.
https://isitfunnyoroffensive.com/honeymooners/.

Chapter 3

1 Martin P. Durkin and Frieda S. Miller, *Status of Women in the United States 1953* (Washington, D.C., Women's Bureau Bulletin 249, 1953), https://fraser.stlouisfed.org/files/docs/publications/women/b0249_dolwb_1953.pdf.

2 "Macher" in Yiddish means a "big shot" or an important and influential person.

3 "*Happy families are all alike; every unhappy family is unhappy in its own way.*" Leo Tolstoy, *Anna Karenina* (New York, Random House, 1939).

4 *All Gone*, music and lyrics by John Dankworth, 1963, https://www.youtube.com/watch?v=VK1C9ZTlDqk.

5 James Tiptree Jr. [Alice Bradley Sheldon], *The Women Men Don't See* (The Magazine of Fantasy & Science Fiction, 1973).

Chapter 4

1 Alumna of the year: Brooklyn Law School Holds Annual Alumni Luncheon, *New York Law Journal*, February 10, 2020, https://www.law.com/newyorklawjournal/2020/02/10/brooklyn-law-school-holds-annual-alumni-luncheon.

2 Ruth Bader Ginsburg, *Litigating for Gender Equality in the 1970s* (Speech at Wilson Center, May 21, 2002), https://www.wilsoncenter.org/event/presentation-litigating-for-gender-equality-the-1970s.

3 *Kruzel v. Podell*, 67 Wis. 2d 138 (Supreme Court of Wisconsin, 1975).

4 Ginsburg, *Litigating for Gender Equality in the 1970s*.

5 *Frontiero v. Richardson*, 411 U.S. 677, 684 (1973).

6 Randall Jarrell, *A Sad Heart at the Supermarket* (New York, Atheneum, 1962), p.20.

7 Pauline Kael, Last Tango in Paris, *The New Yorker*, October 28, 1972.

8 Background on prenuptial agreements: Harriet Newman Cohen and Ralph Gardner, Jr., *The Divorce Book* (New York, Avon, 1994). New York State Bar: https://nysba.org

/NYSBA/Coursebooks/Summer%202016%20LPM%20Coursebooks/Bridging%20 the%20Gap%20August%016/3a.%20Baiamonte%20-%20Sample%20Prenuptial%20 Agreement.pdf?srsltid=AfmBOorzFBuBSQJvIiEHtut2o4ts1qkoclo-OccOkE0zhVF kYHw1KXgv.

New York City Bar: https://www.nycbar.org/get-legal-help/article/family-law/marital-agreements/prenuptial-agreements.

9 Lenore J. Weitzman, *The Divorce Revolution* (New York, The Free Press, 1985). Meaghan E. Howard, Modern Reformation: An Overview of New York's Domestic Relations Law Overhaul, *Touro Law Review*, Volume 29, Number 2, October 2013.

10 Kin Hubbard, *Short Furrows* (Indianapolis, Bobbs-Merrill Co., 1911), p.42.

11 Ernest Rutherford, *The Oxford Essential Quotations Dictionary, American Edition* (New York, Berkley Books, 9780425163870, Anna's Archive, 1998), p.380.

12 Winston Churchill, as recorded in the Alanbrooke Diaries, December 9, 1941. See Arthur Bryant, ed., *The Turn of the Tide, 1939–1943* (New York, Doubleday, 1957), p.231.

13 John Banville, The Eighth by Stephen Johnson Review—Mahler and Sexual Creativity, *The Guardian*, May 16, 2020.

Chapter 5

1 *Meet Dr. Christian*. Wikipedia, last modified December 12, 2024. https://en.wikipedia.org/wiki/Meet_Dr._Christian.

2 *Forbes Quotes, Thoughts on the Business of Life*. https://www.forbes.com/quotes/6145/.

3 Jennifer Drake, *Third Wave Agenda* (Minneapolis, University of Minnesota Press, 1997), p.2.

4 William Glaberson, Howard M. Squadron, 75, Influential Lawyer, Dies, *New York Times*, December 28, 2001.

5 Deirdre Carmody, Murdoch Wins Magazine Fight, *New York Times*, January 8, 1977. J. Edward Moreno, What Rupert Murdoch Owns, and How He Built His Media Empire, *New York Times*, July 25, 2024. Thomas Kiernan, *Citizen Murdoch* (New York, Dodd, Mead & Company, 1986). Jonathan Mahler and Jim Rutenberg, How Rupert Murdoch's Empire of Influence Remade the World, *New York Times Magazine*, April 3, 2019.

6 Murdoch Voices Anxiety Over Divided New York City, *New York Times*, May 13, 1977.

7 Phillip Knightley, *The First Casualty: From the Crimea to Vietnam: The War Correspondent as Hero, Propagandist, and Myth Maker* (New York, Harcourt Brace Jovanovich, 1975), pp. 209–212.

8 Death in Spain, *Life Magazine*, July 12, 1937, pp.19–25.

9 W. H. Auden, *Another Time* (London, Faber and Faber, 1940), p.112.

10 Amanda Vaill, Did Robert Capa Fake "Falling Soldier"? *Foreign Policy*, April 22, 2014.

11 Richard B. Woodward, Elliott Erwitt, Whose Photos Are Famous, and Often Funny, Dies at 95, *New York Times*, November 30, 2023. https://www.magnumphotos.com/photographer/elliott-erwitt/. https://www.elliotterwitt.com/.

12 Tom Seymour, *The Art Newspaper*, July 20, 2021.

13 Mena Davidson, Transgender Legal Battles: A Timeline, *Jstor Daily*, May 12, 2022. Associated Press, Key Dates for Transgender Rights in the US, *Associated Press*, February 23, 2017. Hugh Ryan, How Dressing in Drag Was Labeled a Crime in the 20th Century, *history.com*. June 25, 2029, https://www.history.com/news/stonewall-riots-lgbtq-drag-three-article-rule.

14 News Desk, Arresting Dress: A Timeline of Anti-cross-dressing Laws in the United States, *PBS News*, May 31, 2015.

15 Perles background: Eric Pace, Julia Perles, Groundbreaker in Divorce Law, Is Dead at 84, *New York Times*, July 3, 1998.

Chapter 6

1 Di Long, *Divorce in New York State from 1850s to 1920s* (Athens, Georgia, University of Georgia, 2013). Brooke Grossman, The Evolution of Equitable Distribution in New York, *NYU Annual Survey of American Law*, Volume 62, Issue 3 (New York, New York University, 2007). Illyan Woo, The Long History of Difficult Divorces, *Wall Street Journal*, August 13, 2010. Stephanie Coontz, The Origins of Modern Divorce, *Family Process Journal*, February 2007.

2 Wife must take husband's surname: *Kruzel v. Podell*, 67 Wis. 2d 138 (Supreme Court of Wisconsin, 1975).

3 David Margolick, Till Debt Do Us Part, *New York Times*, December 15, 1991.

4 Louis Nizer, *My Life In Court* (Garden City, New York, Doubleday, 1961), p.153.

5 Louis Nizer, *My Life In Court* (Garden City, New York, Doubleday, 1961), p.154.

6 Lenore J. Weitzman, *The Divorce Revolution* (New York, The Free Press, 1985). Meredith A. Nelson, California Family Law Act, *University of Michigan Journal of Law Reform*, Volume 3, p.425, 1970, https://repository.law.umich.edu/mjlr/vol3/iss2/8. Pat Morrison, California Settled the No-fault Divorce Question Decades Ago. Why is it Back in the News?, *Los Angeles Times*, May 24, 2024. Sharon Johnson, No-Fault Divorce: 10 Years Later, Some Virtues, Some Flaws, *New York Times*, March 30, 1979.

7 Reagan Signs First Major Divorce Reform, *Desert Sun*, Volume 43, Number 29, September 6, 1969.

8 W. Bradford Wilcox, The Evolution of Divorce, *National Affairs*, Fall 2009.

9 Donna S. Hershkowitz and Drew R. Liebert, *The Direction of Divorce Reform in California: From Fault to No-Fault . . . And Back Again?* A report prepared for the Assembly Judiciary Committee, California State Legislature. 1997.

10 Meaghan E. Howard, Modern Reformation: An Overview of New York's Domestic Relations Law Overhaul, *Touro Law Review*, Volume 29, Number 2, October 2013.

From the Legislature to the Court of Appeals: New York's Conversion Divorce Under Domestic Relations Law Section 170, *Fordham Law Review*, Volume 38, Issue 4, 1970.

11 Lauren Guidice, New York and Divorce: Finding Fault in a No-Fault System, *Journal of Law and Policy, Brooklyn Law School*, Volume 19, Issue 2, 2011.

12 J. Herbie DiFonzo and Ruth G. Stern, Addicted to Fault: Why Divorce Reform Has Lagged in New York, *Pace Law Review*, 2007.

13 Georgia Dullea, Women's and Bar Groups Fault Divorce Law, *New York Times*, August 5, 1985.

14 Louis Nizer, *My Life In Court* (Garden City, New York, Doubleday, 1961). Louis Nizer, *The Jury Returns* (Garden City, New York, Doubleday, 1966). Louis Nizer, *Between You and Me* (New York, Beechhurst Press, 1948). Eric Pace, Louis Nizer, Lawyer to the Famous, Dies at 92, *New York Times*, November 11, 1994. Jeremy Gerard, John Henry Faulk Is Eulogized In a Gathering at Public Theater, *New York Times*, July 11, 1990. Men in the News, *New York Times*, January 21, 1971. Quentin Reynolds Wins Libel Action; Court Awards $175,001 in Suit Against Pegler and Two Hearst Concerns, *New York Times*, June 29, 1954.

15 Eric Pace, Louis Nizer, Lawyer to the Famous, Dies at 92, *New York Times*, November 11, 1994.

16 Martin Gottlieb, New York Court Disbars Roy Cohn on Charges of Unethical Conduct, *New York Times*, June 24, 1986.

17 Samuel Allis, Fresh Crusades of a Cold Warrior, *Washington Post*, August 30, 1979.

18 Lewis Robbins, Post Prandial Notes, *New York Times*, July 11, 1948.

19 Louis Nizer, *Reflections without Mirrors* (Garden City, New York, Doubleday & Company, Inc., 1978), p.368.

20 Louis Nizer, *My Life In Court* (Garden City, New York, Doubleday, 1961), pp. 167–68.

21 *The Scribner Encyclopedia of American Lives*, Volume 4, Kenneth T. Jackson, editor-in-chief, (New York, Charles Scribner's Sons, An Imprint of the Gale Group, 2001), p. 390, https://www.encyclopedia.com/humanities/encylopedias-almanacs-transcripts-and-maps/nizer-louis-0.

22 Ronald Smothers, Divorce Reforms Gaining in Albany, *New York Times*, May 20, 1976.

23 Ronald Smothers, Fiscal "Equity" in Divorce Dies in Albany, *New York Times*, June 3, 1976.

24 Pranay Gupte, Legislators Get Opposing Opinions On Proposed Divorce Law Change, *New York Times*, February 5, 1977.

25 Lawrence Van Gelder, Albany Moves Toward Divorce-Law Change, *New York Times*, March 12, 1979.

26 Ari L. Goldman, Bill Establishing "Equitable" Divorce Settlements Is Stalled in Albany, *New York Times*, March 9, 1980.

27 Law of tyrants. Quoting from Bouvier's Law Dictionary, originally published in 1839.

28 Pranay Gupta, Legislators Get Opposing Opinions On Proposed Divorce Law Change, *New York Times*, February 5, 1977.

29 *Orr v. Orr*, 440 U.S. 268 (1979).

30 Ari L. Goldman, Bill Establishing "Equitable" Divorce Settlements Is Stalled in Albany, *New York Times*, March 9, 1980.

Chapter 7

1 Emily Jane Goodman, With New Law, Divorce Fees Soar, *New York Times*, January 18, 1983.

2 Angel Castillo, Divorce Costs Rise Under New Law, *New York Times*, February 2, 1981.

3 Emily Jane Goodman, With New Law, Divorce Fees Soar, *New York Times*, January 18, 1983.

4 Angel Castillo, Divorce Costs Rise Under New Law, *New York Times*, February 2, 1981.

5 Emily Jane Goodman, With New Law, Divorce Fees Soar, *New York Times*, January 18, 1983.

6 Jan Hoffman, Counsel to the Broken Hearted, *New York Times*, August 16, 1995.

7 James Barron, The New Millionaires: Making It In Tough Times, *New York Times*, August 15, 1993.

8 *Pendente lite* means "while the lawsuit is pending."

9 Arthur Schwartz in conversation with David Feinberg.

10 Ross Macdonald, *The Goodbye Look* (New York, Knopf, 1969), p.1.

11 Mike Tyson, 1987, prior to Tyrell Biggs' fight. "Everybody has a plan until they get punched in the face."

12 *Porgy and Bess*, music by George Gershwin, lyrics by Ira Gershwin, libretto by DuBose Heyward, 1935.

13 1 Corinthians 13:13.

14 Emily Jane Goodman, With New Law, Divorce Fees Soar, *New York Times*, January 18, 1983.

15 Eugene Field, *The Duel (The Gingham Dog and the Calico Cat)*, first published in *Love Songs of Childhood*, (New York, Charles Scribner's Sons, 1895) p. 32. Poem is in the public domain.

16 Aleksey Andreyevich Arakcheyev: Russian general and statesman who served under Catherine the Great and Tsars Paul and Alexander I.

17 *Lasky v. Kempton*, 206 Misc. 962 (New York State Supreme Court, October 18, 1954).

18 Marie Brenner, After the Gold Rush, *Vanity Fair*, September 1990.

19 Sam Roberts, Jay Goldberg, Tenacious Lawyer for Celebrities, Dies at 89, *New York Times*, December 14, 2022.

20 Now divorced, Trumps bicker over gag order, *Associated Press*, May 23, 1991.

21 Now divorced, Trumps bicker over gag order, *Associated Press*, May 23, 1991.

22 Murray Kempton, The Proof That Trump Is a Self-Made Man, *New York Newsday*, June 4, 1989.

23 Jimmy Breslin, Violent Language, Between You and I, *New York Newsday*, May 2, 1989.

24 Jimmy Breslin, Violent Language, Between You and I, *New York Newsday*, May 2, 1989.

25 Jimmy Breslin, *The Gang That Couldn't Shoot Straight* (New York, Viking Press, Inc., 1969), pp. 6–7; *Essential Writings* (New York, Library of America, 2024).

26 Sheela Kennedy and Steven Ruggles, *Breaking Up is Hard to Count: The Rise of Divorce in the United States, 1980–2010*, Demography, April 2014. Donna S. Hershkowitz and Drew R. Liebert, *The Direction of Divorce Reform in California: From Fault to No-fault . . . and Back Again?*, prepared for the Assembly Judiciary Committee, California State Legislature, 1997.

27 W. Bradford Wilcox, The Evolution of Divorce, *National Affairs*, Fall 2009.

28 W. Bradford Wilcox, The Evolution of Divorce, *National Affairs*, Fall 2009.

29 Harriet Newman Cohen and Ralph Gardner, Jr., *The Divorce Book* (New York, Avon, 1994).

30 Jody N. Gerber, *Divorce and Property Rights*, New York City Bar Legal Referral Service, January 2019, https://www.nycbar.org/get-legal-help/article/family-law/property-rights/. Domestic Relations Law § 236, part B, subd 1, para c: marital property is defined as "all property acquired by either or both spouses during the marriage and before the execution of a separation agreement or the commencement of a matrimonial action;" (see also *Majauskas v. Majauskas*, 61 NY2d 481 (New York State Court of Appeals, April 3, 1984).

31 Harriet N. Cohen and Adria S. Hillman, *Analysis of Seventy Select Decisions After Trial Under New York State's Equitable Distribution Law, From January 1981 Through October 1984*, 4–5 (1984).

32 Harriet N. Cohen and Adria S. Hillman, Report to Task Force, Diagnosis Confirmed: EDL Is Ailing, *Fordham Urban Law Journal*, Volume 15, Issue 1, Article 4 (1986). The authors pointed out that only 70 EDL decisions had been reported between July 1980 and October 15, 1984. Report of the New York Task Force on Women in the Courts, *Fordham Urban Law Journal*, Volume 15, Issue 1, 1986. Harriet N. Cohen and Adria S. Hillman, Score 2 for Fairness in Divorce Courts, *New York Times*, August 14, 1986. Georgia Dullea, Women's and Bar Groups Fault Divorce Law, *New York Times*, August 5, 1985.

33 Henry Foster, Doris Freed, and Joel Brandes, *Law and the Family, New York: Equitable Distribution* (Rochester, New York, Lawyers Cooperative Publishing Company, 1987). Cited in Report of the New York Task Force on Women in the Courts, *Fordham Urban Law Journal*, Volume 15, Issue 1, 1986.

34 Georgia Dullea, Women's and Bar Groups Fault Divorce Law, *New York Times*, August 5, 1985.

35 Georgia Dullea, Women's and Bar Groups Fault Divorce Law, *New York Times*, August 5, 1985.

36 Harriet N. Cohen and Adria S. Hillman, Score 2 for Fairness in Divorce Courts, *New York Times*, August 14, 1986.

37 *(It Will Have to Do) Until the Real Thing Comes Along*, Words and Music by Mann Holiner, Alberta Nichols, Sammy Cahn, Saul Chaplin, and L.E. Freeman (New York, Chappell & Co., 1936).

38 Harriet N. Cohen and Adria S. Hillman, Score 2 for Fairness in Divorce Courts, *New York Times*, August 14, 1986.

39 Joan Ellenbogen, a Bar Association Founder, *New York Times*, October 29, 2001. Ellen Holtzman, *Tribute to Joan Ellenbogen*, Women's Bar Association of the State of New York, https://www.wbasny.org/past_presidents/joan-l-ellenbogen/.

40 *O'Brien v O'Brien*, 66 N.Y.2d 576 (New York State App. Div. 2d Dept., December 26, 1985). David Margolick, Key Ruling Due on Ex-Wife Seeking a Share of a Medical License's Value, *New York Times*, December 25, 1985.

41 New York Laws/Domestic Relations, Article 13—Provisions Applicable to More Than One Type of Matrimonial Action. Section 237—Counsel Fees and Expenses, https://law.justia.com/codes/new-york/dom/article-13/237/.

42 *Myrna Felder, 1976–1977*, New York Women's Bar Association, https://www.nywba.org/myrna-felder/. Robin Finn, Public Lives; Felder's Partner, and Wife, Keeps Her Own Counsel, *New York Times*, May 25, 2001.

43 Stakes are so low. https://anthonybonato.com/2015/03/16/sayres-law-required-wisdom-for-all-academics/.

Chapter 8

1 Angel Castillo, Divorce Costs Rise Under New Law, *New York Times*, February 2, 1981.

2 Artie Shaw, *I Love You, I Hate You, Drop Dead!* (New York, Fleet Publishing Corporation, 1965).

3 Nadine Brozan, Chronicle, *New York Times*, July 3, 1992.

4 Plutarch, *Lives of the Noble Grecians and Romans*.

5 New York State Domestic Relations Law § 236B(5)(d)(7).

6 Sources/background to *Case of a Lifetime*: Harriet Newman Cohen's notes and memories. *Thomas S. v. Robin Y.*, 157 Misc. 2d 858 (New York County Family Court, April 13, 1993). *Thomas S. v. Robin Y.*, 209 A.D.2d 298 (New York State App. Div. 1st Dept., November 17, 1994). *Nuclear Family*, a three-part documentary directed by Ry Russo-Young, HBO Documentary films, 2021, https://www.hbo.com/nuclear-family. Nancy D. Polikoff, brief submitted by *Amicus Curiae of the National Center for Lesbian Rights; Lambda Legal Defense and Education Fund; Gay and Lesbian Advocates and Defenders; Center Kids; and Gay and Lesbian Parents Coalition International in Support of Respondent-Appellee (Robin Y.)* (New York County Family Court, Docket No. P3884/91). *Culture Closeup: Ry Russo-Young + Gabriela Herman*, HBO, https://www.hbo.com/nuclear-family. Carlyle C. Douglass, *Lesbian Child-*

Custody Case Redefine Family Law, New York Times, July 8, 1990. Dennis Hevesi, Judge Rejects Sperm Donor's Claim for Custody, *New York Times*, April 16, 1993. David W. Dunlap, Sperm Donor Is Awarded Standing as Girl's Father, *New York Times*, November 19, 1994. Amy Clyde, Beyond Stonewall: Gay Struggles, 25 Years On, *New Yorker*, June 12, 1994. Kevin J. Hellmann, Policy Review: Introduction to Thomas S. and Robin Y., *Journal of Law and Policy*, Volume 3, Issue 2, 1995. https://www.vulture.com/article/ry-russo-young-nuclear-family-interview.html. https://www.salon.com/2021/09/26/nuclear-family-hbo-lesbian-family-sperm-donor/. https://www.vanityfair.com/hollywood/2021/09/09/lesbian-family-court-doc-nuclear-family-is-disappointingly-conventional. https://www.latimes.com/entertainment-arts/tv/story/2021-10-10/nuclear-family-hbo-ry-russo-young-documentary-tom-steel. https://www.hollywoodreporter.com/tv/tv-features/ry-russo-young-hbo-nuclear-family-1235017727/. https://www.nytimes.com/1998/08/09/nyregion/thomas-steel-a-lawyer-known-for-civil-rights-cases-was-48.html.

7 Oliver Herford (1863–1935). "*She has a whim of iron.*"

8 Lyle Denniston, Gay marriage and Baker v. Nelson, *SCOTUS Blog*, July 4, 2012, https://www.scotusblog.com/2012/07/gay-marriage-and-baker-v-nelson/. *Baker v. Nelson*, 191 N.W.2d 185 (Supreme Court of Minnesota, October 15, 1971).

9 Leslea Newman, *Heather Has Two Mommies* (New York, Alyson Books, 1990).

10 Richard Vigilante, Heather's Mommies vs. Heather's Parents, *New York Times*, December 12, 1992.

11 Elon Green, Leslea Newman: So What Was That Like? *The New Yorker*, April 24, 2014.

12 Todd S. Purdom, President Would Sign Legislation Striking at Homosexual Marriages, *New York Times*, May 23, 1996. Alison Mitchell, Clinton Signs Bill Denying Gay Couples U.S. Benefits, *New York Times*, September 21, 1996.

13 Jo-Ann Krestan and Claudia S. Bepko, The Problem of Fusion in the Lesbian Relationship, *Family Process*, September 1980. David Frost and Michele Eliason, Challenging the Assumption of Fusion in Female Same-Sex Relationships, *Psychology of Women Quarterly*, March 2013. Laura Gold, A Critical Analysis of Fusion in Lesbian Relationships, *Canadian Social Work Review*, 2003.

14 *Thomas S. v. Robin Y.*, 157 Misc. 2d 858 (New York County Family Court, April 13, 1993).

15 *Thomas S. v. Robin Y.*, 209 A.D.2d 298 (New York State App. Div., 1st Dept., November 17, 1994).

16 Karl Marx and Friedrich Engels, *The Communist Manifesto* (London, 1848).

17 Kurt Eichenwald, Millions for Us, Pennies for You, *The New York Times*, December 19, 1993.

18 Ronald A. Schy, Lawyers, Class Actions and Fees, *New York Times*, January 2, 1994.

19 Change, Criticism Not Bugging Beigel, *Chicago Tribune*, March 22, 1994.

20 Francis Ford Coppola, Mario Puzo, *The Godfather* (Paramount Pictures, 1972).

Chapter 10

1 Don McNeill, *Good Morning, Breakfast Clubbers*, The Breakfast Club, ABC Radio.

2 Willa Cather, *Death Comes for the Archbishop* (New York, Knopf, 1927), p. 293.

3 Veidlinger, *In the Midst of Civilized Europe,* (New York, Metropolitan Books, 2021).

4 *Pechora concentration camp*, Wikipedia, last modified December 18, 2024, https://en.wikipedia.org/wiki/Pechora concentration camp.

5 Ralph Blumenthal, J*oseph Green, 96, Creator of Yiddish Film's Heyday (dies),* New York Times, June 22, 1996. Loren King, *Celebrating the National Center for Jewish Films*, Boston Globe, April 26, 2014.

6 *Honey*. Music by Richard A. Whiting, lyrics by Haven Gillespie and Seymour Simons (1928).

7 Benjamin Ziegelbaum, *When the Sun Sets In the Morning* (New York, privately printed, 2007).

8 *I'll Be Home for Christmas*, lyrics by Kim Gannon and Buck Ram, composed by Walter Kent (Gannon and Kent Music Company and Piedmont Music Co., 1943).

Chapter 11

1 Ben Hecht, Miracle of the Fifteen Murderers, *Collier's Weekly*, January 16, 1943, p.11. James L. Franklin, *Ben Hecht, and the "Miracle of the Fifteen Murderers."* Hektoen International, Summer 2022.

2 George Orwell, In Front of Your Nose, *The Tribune*, March 22, 1946.

3 John Selden, *Table Talk: being The Discourses of John Seldon Esq; or His Sence Of Various Matters of Weight and High Consequence Relating Especially to Religion and State*, (London, 1696).

4 John Selden, *Table Talk: being The Discourses of John Seldon Esq; or His Sence Of Various Matters of Weight and High Consequence Relating Especially to Religion and State,* (London, 1696).

ACKNOWLEDGMENTS

In the Jewish tradition, the naming of names, the living and the dead, is not only a matter of memory and respect but a way to approach the ineffable, to glimpse the divine. And so, I offer these names, the loved ones for whom I originally began writing this memoir and whom I have kept before me as I told my story, which is also our story.

My daughters

Marti Stine and her husband Eric Goldberg

Amy Z. Cohen and her husband Bruce Wasserman (thank you to Amy for her extraordinary work in design, format, and style)

Susie and her husband Bruce Hirsch

Patti and her husband Andrew Putney

My grandchildren

Ezra Stine and his partner Anastasia Golovanova

Gabe Stine and his wife Ana

Matt Ziegelbaum and his wife Elizabeth Caudle

Ben Ziegelbaum (deceased)

Alice Ziegelbaum

Eric Hirsch and his wife Lauren Hock

Zach Hirsch

Jake Hirsch

Oliver Epstein (thank you, Oliver, for your technical help with the manuscript)

Natalie Epstein

My great-grandchildren

Abigail Ivory Ziegelbaum

Arthur Benjamin Ziegelbaum

Anna Madeline Hirsch

Joseph Samuel Hirsch

Baby boy Stine on the way

* * *

My siblings

Alvin Newman (deceased) and his wife Ruby

Molli and her husband Reuben Mezrich

Sandee Newman and her husband Jack Kerry

My nieces and nephews

Michael Newman and his wife Elana Levine

Kurt Newman and his partner Stephanie Pope (Kurt worked on an early version of this memoir and his intelligence and insight can be felt on many pages)

Amy Newman and her husband David Preiss

Jonathan Mezrich and his wife Lisa Dickstein

Ben Mezrich and his wife Tonya

Josh Mezrich and his wife Gretchen Schwarze

My grandnieces and grandnephews

Leo and Noah Newman

Ezra, Jesse, and Dani Preiss

Tyler Mezrich

Asher and Arya Mezrich

Sam and Kate Mezrich

* * *

My stepchildren

Nancy Feinberg and her husband James Rheingrover (deceased)

David Feinberg and his wife Madelaine Gill (thank you is not enough for David without whom this book could not have gotten out of my head)

My step grandchildren

Sarah and her wife Daniela Stellino

Jenny and her husband Ed Edson

Andrew Rheingrover and his wife Kira

Gillian Linden and Forth Bagley

My step great-grandchildren

Charlotte and William Edson

Addie and James Rheingrover

Larkin and Sam Bagley

Vincenzo Stellino

And, of course, my revered parents

* * *

Thank you also to Federal Judge I. Leo Glasser for his lifelong friendship; to former president of the Lotos Club, J. Roger Friedman, for his hospitality and advice; to Jack Sussek, current president of the Lotos Club, my partner in crime as we co-roast our fellow members on Founders' Days at the Lotos Club; to Laura Ann Rosenbury and David Meyer, my fearless presidents, respectively, of Barnard College and Brooklyn Law School; to Anita Arnell, my ward, for what she has taught me; to the "Lotus Divas," Dr. Wilma Bulkin Siegel, Dr. Roberta Goldring Coles, Dr. Isabel Pavao Horvath, Dr. Judy Seinfeld, Nancy Hall-Duncan, and Laury P. Franks; to Beowulf Sheehan, photographer extraordinaire, for an artist's intuition. And to Nicole Margulis, without whose technical skills and loving encouragement, my manuscript could not have been put together.

* * *

And finally, not a person but a place.

Shortly after Arthur died, I was asked to give a talk at the Lotos Club in New York City. The club, founded in 1870 by a group of writers, artists, and critics, and soon joined by Mark Twain, is located in a Gilded Age mansion just off Fifth Avenue. My talk, "Divorce in Literature," was well-received, and I was given a year of privileges. During the year, I came to know the club, its officers, and members. I was encouraged to apply for membership, and now, the Lotos Club, along with family, work, and friends, has become a center of my life.

I was chair of the Music Committee, elected to the Board of Directors, the Admissions Committee, and awarded the Medal of Merit—a great honor bestowed upon me by then president, Michael Yon. And I have been able to meet and be befriended by people like Ron Carter, the great bassist, legendary journalists, Carl Bernstein and Lance Morrow, novelist, Tom Wolfe, former president of Georgetown University, Leo J. O'Donovan S.J., and many others. The brilliant historian Elizabeth D. Samet lectured on the genius of Ulysses S. Grant and offered insight into West Point's valorization of confederate officers during the Jim Crow era and beyond—another controversy—like abortion and women's rights—long believed settled that has sprung to life, zombie-like, in twenty-first-century America. Elizabeth generously offered me a personally guided tour of West Point, but, unfortunately, the Covid lockdown derailed that plan.

People often describe Lotos as a second home, a feeling I share—but even deeper. I have felt since first walking through the doors all those years—all those decades ago!—that I was coming home.

* * *

DF: Gillian Linden for a crucial early read. Nancy Rheingrover for constant support. Ross Klavan for a lifetime's friendship. And Madelaine Gill for countless readings, fearless criticism, and wise suggestions. And for always and everything.

ABOUT THE AUTHOR

Harriet Newman Cohen is one of the nation's most respected matrimonial and family law attorneys, a recognized advocate for divorce law reform and the rights of women and children. A founding partner of Cohen Stine Kapoor LLP, she is a *cum laude* graduate of Barnard College, Bryn Mawr (MA Latin), and Brooklyn Law School, where she was an editor of the *Law Review*. Ms. Cohen publishes regularly in the *New York Law Journal* and comments on legal issues on television and radio, online and in the print media, as well as to bench and bar. She is on the Board of Directors of the Lotos Club and of the Stecher and Horowitz Foundation, which established and oversaw the biennial New York International Piano Competition, a prestigious event that for decades attracted talented young pianists from around the globe and that has now transitioned to collaborating with the Music Teachers National Association to give major gifts and awards to prodigiously talented young pianists. Ms. Cohen is the author of *The Divorce Book for Men and Women: A Step-by-Step Guide to Gaining Your Freedom without Losing Everything Else.*

* * *

David Feinberg, a graduate of Columbia University, is an award-winning journalist and editor.

www.ingramcontent.com/pod-product-compliance
Ingram Content Group UK Ltd.
Pitfield, Milton Keynes, MK11 3LW, UK
UKHW051551280426
470444UK00010BA/38

9 798765 164679